LIVING OFF THE STATE
A CRITICAL GUIDE TO UK ROYAL FINANCE

SECOND EDITION

JON TEMPLE

Copyright © Jon Temple 2012

The right of Jon Temple to be identified as Author of this Work has been asserted in accordance with the UK Copyright, Designs and Patents Act 1988.

Progress Books
2 Thackeray House
Ansdell Street
London W8 5HA
www.progressbooks.co.uk

First Edition: 2008
Second Edition: 2012

All rights reserved. Except for the quotation of short passages for the purpose of criticism and review, no part of this publication may be reproduced, stored in a retrieval system, or transmitted, in any form or by any means, electronic, mechanical, photocopying, recording or otherwise, without the prior permission of the publisher.

ISBN: 978-0-9558311-1-9

A catalogue record for this book is available from the British Library.
Cover design and text layout:
Ben Eldridge ben@bitmap.co.uk

Contents

PREFACE		v
1	INTRODUCTION	1
2	MONEY AND THE MONARCHY	13
3	'NICE LITTLE EARNERS': THE TWO DUCHIES	99
4	WINDSORS' WORLD: LIFE AT THE TAXPAYERS' EXPENSE	155
5	CHARITY AND ROYAL 'BRAND' OWNERSHIP	187
6	THE ROYAL COLLECTION: 'HELD' FOR THE NATION	213
7	LOOKING TO THE FUTURE	229
NOTES		265
BIBLIOGRAPHY AND SOURCES		273
APPENDIX 1: SOVEREIGN GRANT ACT		279
APPENDIX 2: ROYAL WEDDING SECURITY COSTS		283
APPENDIX 3: BANK OF ENGLAND NOMINEES LTD		285
INDEX		287

Preface

PREFACE TO THE SECOND EDITION
In the four years since the first edition of this book appeared, the consequences of the banking crisis which was unfolding at the time are still becoming apparent. The effect of the ongoing problems within the Eurozone – and, equally importantly, those within the international banking system – are, at the time of writing, yet to be fully realised, and their consequences for the UK, Europe and the global economy remain to be seen. Within this fragile and uncertain context, Great Britain set out the flags, rearranged the deckchairs, and organised its tea parties and pageants as part of the Queen's Diamond Jubilee. The recent announcement of the campaign for a referendum on Scottish independence, scheduled to take place in 2014, reminds us that the prospects for the very existence of Her Majesty's 'realm' are uncertain and that the days of the 'United Kingdom' in its present form could soon be numbered. Britain's antiquated constitution still awaits proper modernisation. Our second chamber of the legislature – the House of Lords – still consists of the 'Lords' and 'Ladies' who sit on its red leather benches, appointed by patronage and democratically unaccountable – and some of whom are still the remnants of the old hereditary system. The present coalition government is now preparing to finish what New Labour started in the reform of this curious

and undemocratic institution, and this time we must hope that the work really will be completed. What of a Bill of Rights and a written constitution? Still no progress...

Following a remarkably low-key debate, and similarly low-key media coverage, the Sovereign Grant Act – the UK's new system of financing the British monarchy – recently passed into law, and is due to take effect in 2013. As is traditional in the British system, Parliamentary debate on the monarchy is managed in such a way as to ensure a low profile – and ensuring that it coincides with international tennis during Wimbledon fortnight and other events in the British society summer 'Season' is as effective a means as any. Whilst the Act may improve overall Parliamentary accountability, the actual means of assessing the annual funding level of the monarchy that has been chosen seems retrograde – and is already looking rather generous. Ultimately, only time will tell, for it rests, as ever within the British system, upon the level of determination within Parliament to choose whether or not to pursue a somewhat harder bargain with the monarch and their family.

For the time being, the monarchy seems to enjoy a period of enhanced popularity. However, wider financial repercussions could yet impose stresses upon the UK population which might have serious implications for the future of the Windsor family – the most expensive monarchy in Europe. While the Queen and the Prince of Wales enjoy a combined personal income from state assets – the Duchies of Lancaster and Cornwall respectively – of over £31million a year, it will remain to be seen if this situation, itself less than perfectly understood by the population as a whole, will be tolerated for much longer. This money does not include the £140million plus which it costs to operate the British monarchy as a whole. As I write this, the economic prospects for Spain – poor already – may worsen considerably, and the fate of their monarchy in such stressful times may prove a pointer as to how our monarchy could fare in the future. Already, hitherto unheard-of criticism has surfaced in Spain, toward an institution which has enjoyed widespread popularity in the past.

Last year's royal wedding between Prince William and Catherine Middleton occasioned an extra public holiday. For the first time, we have begun to see considered criticism of the questionable wisdom of calling such impromptu holidays – effectively at the whim of the royal family – at a time of severe economic difficulties. It is notable that these warnings derive not from critics of the monarchy but from economic experts and accountancy firms. As with the Jubilee celebrations, any economic benefit generated directly from such events themselves appears to pale into insignificance compared to the cost of shutting down whole sections of the productive economy, especially when they occur close to other public holidays. Despite monarchist protestations of 'kill-joy' criticism, there are now real concerns about these costs, which can run not into millions, but billions, of pounds and have a discernible impact on the nation's growth figures. Only now are we beginning to understand the true cost of the monarchy. Whilst royal websites may contain far greater financial detail than in the past, still they fail to paint the full picture, lacking a balancing perspective from which it is necessary to view this grandiose institution. A combination of Jubilee celebrations and London's Olympic Games may occasion a summer in which the monarchy can bask, assuming they are safe from any threats to their privileged lifestyle, but no-one could deny that there are – to echo the words of the Bank of England's Governor Sir Mervyn King – 'storm clouds gathering'.

Once again, my thanks to all those who have helped with the preparation of this new edition, in particular Ben Eldridge, John Curnow and Professor Stephen Haseler. There are a lot of facts and figures contained within this book and I must point out that any mistakes contained therein are entirely my own.

This is also a point where sadly one must note the passing in recent years of notable republican campaigners, in particular John Campbell, Claire Rayner, and fellow Common Sense Club member Jon Norton. They helped to campaign for a cause which is much more than it is so often popularly viewed – as simply 'anti-monarchist'. Far more than just that, it is about the way in which our nation needs to reappraise its place and its role in the world – and equally importantly, to embrace constitutional reform and to reconfigure its institutions of state. They have a constitutional dimension but also, equally importantly, cultural and economic ones as well. The monarchy does not sit outside this landscape. Until our institutions change, it will be hard to effect a proper understanding of how our nation – and its place within the world – has altered so fundamentally – and thus how we must adapt. Only then can we move forward with any constructive sense of purpose.

We stand poised upon the brink of an era in which many of the assumptions about the western world's power and prosperity which so many have taken for granted for so long are not just questioned fundamentally – they have in many cases already changed. In such a changing world, the retention of a grandiose imperial styled institution such as the British monarchy becomes ever more inappropriate, and ever more of a delusion than ever before. With the Diamond Jubilee, an attempt may have been made to try to recreate the feel of the post-war celebrations when the present Queen succeeded to the throne, but it could be said that the reign of Elizabeth II merely benchmarks a period of continuing UK decline within a changing world order. Nostalgia-tinted glasses obscure the view of the route ahead. Delusionists may claim that the Queen has steered the nation through the last six decades, but in reality she has been little more than a highly privileged passenger. Indeed, her very existence as grandiose monarch serves to perpetuate an anachronistic view, both within the country and abroad, of our nation's self-image.

There seems, worryingly, little apparent widespread acceptance of the need to reconstruct the nation in a form appropriate for the twenty-first century – it could be argued that in the case of the twentieth century, the UK perhaps 'missed the boat' entirely. Plans for constitutional reforms are endlessly deferred by those who claim that the public are not interested, and more concerned with 'real' issues – employment, the price of fuel, groceries, and so on. Rarely does anyone consider the potential indirect impact that the way we organize our constitution can itself have upon these issues.

We also move inexorably forward to the time of the next succession – always the point of ultimate stress for any dynasty. Will Charles Windsor – probably by then a septuagenarian – decked out in his ersatz medals, an absurd Ruritanian eccentricity, but with a serious propensity to wish to intervene upon contentious constitutional matters – be acceptable as King? Not merely to the people, but also to the political establishment, something that contains echoes of the circumstances surrounding the 1937 abdication crisis. If not, and I believe that it is highly likely this could be the case, will he step down in favour of his son and heir, William? And by then would a monarchy on anything approaching the present scale – and in the face of worsening economic times – be deemed appropriate? Such a 'rearrangement of the deckchairs' might smack of desperation, but to do nothing could appear equally complacent. There will be many during this summer's Jubilee who have felt as they wave their Union flags that the British monarchy is 'unsinkable'. A century ago, the nation said the same of the doomed liner 'Titanic'...

Jon Temple
September 2012

PREFACE TO THE FIRST EDITION
There is certainly no shortage of books on the British monarchy. Yet by far the majority of these tend to concentrate upon the individuals or the institution itself in a personal or cultural context. It is curious that one of the most crucial aspects, namely the financing of this hereditary institution, is rarely addressed in any significant depth. Phillip Hall's 1991 book, *Royal Fortune* is practically the only example, which thus, with the exception of newspaper and periodical contributions, leaves a significant gap. Since 1992, a great many important changes affecting the institution have taken place. It also faces, within perhaps the next few years, the inevitable prospect of a change of monarch. Before this, however, in 2010, Parliament is due to debate the next review of royal finances. All this will take place in a climate which is considerably less deferential than that of even just a decade ago, and as economic prospects worsen.

As one who has spent many years appearing in the media commenting upon the monarchy, it became apparent from an early stage that there was a surprising dearth of effective explanatory material on financial matters. Whilst details are available, they are often unrelated to the broader picture. This encourages a situation in which official sources may make statements which, whilst ostensibly correct, fail completely to put the facts selected in a proper context. This practice encourages misunderstandings and, sadly, a wide degree of ignorance on the part of not only the public in general, but even of many politicians in particular. This is not helped by an unwritten constitution, a persisting deferential culture and the frequent use of Ruritanian language which, for all its quaint historical – and more often pseudo-historical – veneer, does little other than confuse.

Capitalising upon such a situation, the monarchy and the royal family have been able to exploit this situation to their very considerable financial advantage. Not only have they been able to accumulate considerable wealth, but are now beginning to further exploit, in a more commercialised environment, the conveniently blurred boundary between the 'public' and 'private' realms. This is exemplified by the heir to the throne's aggressive use of charity and royal branding for the purpose of both personal promotion and outright commercialism. Yet this is a public institution which is ultimately answerable to Parliament, with a lineage established by statute, but is able to profit handsomely from what are, undeniably, public assets.

A consistent majority of the population still favour the retention of an hereditary monarchy in this country, at least in respect of the present Queen. Many of those supporters, however, still perceive the need for much further reform. They may well be less indulgent towards her successor. It is highly likely that the current popularity of the Queen is in no small way assisted, not only by simple public inertia, but also by widespread misunderstanding relating to the privileged status in which she and her family are maintained by the taxpayer. At the present time, a book such as this, aimed at a wide audience, is long overdue. No proper debate can take place, even if only in relation to simple reforms, if the basic information necessary is either not easily available or properly understood. Official facts and figures are invariably presented from a viewpoint which is still profoundly deferential, disjointed and extremely selective. The use of arcane terminology also makes broader comparisons with other public institutions conveniently difficult.

For a nation such as Britain to have by far the most expensive head of state – and royal family – when compared to its European and other international counterparts, is both curious and absurd. The monarch and heir's excessive official incomes largely avoid the proper processes of Parliamentary accountability. They are remaining manifestations of a former imperial power which has yet to adapt to its changed reality. The present Queen represents a unique 'bridge' between very different eras, and the process of real adjustment has thus yet to take place. The indulgent treatment accorded to both her and her family is archaic and inappropriate in an era where there is growing disquiet over rising wealth inequalities in our society. The institution is reluctant to surrender its privileged status, and widespread ignorance and deference collude to perpetuate this situation.

PREFACE

In my many years of involvement with the constitutional reform and republican movement, I have met, debated with, and worked with so many whose contribution has been fundamental to the writing of this book. From the many members of 'Republic' – some sadly no longer with us – and those of the former Common Sense Club, the opportunity to discuss issues and introduce them to a wider public arena has been a true privilege. Memories are short, it should not be forgotten that little more than a decade and a half ago proper media debate on the British monarchy was all but taboo. Ultimately, however, this book would not have been possible without the support, advice and encouragement of Professor Stephen Haseler, of London Metropolitan University, for so many years Chair of 'Republic'. Together with his wife, Bay, their contribution in respect of the editing and publishing of this book has been invaluable. I would also like to thank Dr Philip Smith and Malcolm Hill for their support, and the assistance of Ben Eldridge, Henning Meyer, Roy Greenslade and Claire Rayner, together with that of my many friends and members of my family. Finally, also, to the surgeons and staff of Moorfields Eye Hospital in London, without which it might not have been possible at all.

Jon Temple
July 2008

1
Introduction

He had bought a large map representing the sea,
Without the least vestige of land:
And the crew were much pleased when they found it to be
A map they could all understand.
The Hunting of the Snark – Lewis Carroll

Many of the British are proud of their country's political and constitutional system. It is, after all, as they are so proud of repeating, the 'mother of Parliaments'. The monarchy is a key element, an hereditary institution which embodies for so many 'a thousand years of history'. Yet the present lineage dates back to an Act of Parliament just over three centuries ago. Before that, it has included a republican period – following a monarch tried and executed for treason – and yet further into the past, successions of dynasties, sometimes brief in duration, populated by what would now be regarded as little more than tribal warlords or Mafia bosses. The much-praised 'continuity' of the institution is in reality a stream of violent incidents, the patching together of tenuous generational links and coup d'etats – and its demise in 1649. The very concept of monarchy is, by definition, anti-democratic, and Britain – itself in its present form a relatively 'young' concept historically – did not see anything which we would regard as having much in common with our present understanding of the term until the late nineteenth century – and women had to wait for their turn to vote until well after the First World War.

By the twentieth century, attempts were made to modernise one of the most anti-democratic aspects of our Parliamentary system – the hereditary peers who made up the legislature's upper chamber, the House of Lords. The first, in 1911, was unsuccessful, and the country had to wait until the very end of the century when the New Labour government attempted again to remove the hereditary element. They were, up to a point, successful, but a hereditary 'rump' remains, having the dubious legitimacy of having been elected from amongst the hereditaries themselves, most of whom were destined to leave the privileged position of helping to make the nation's laws from the basis of birthright alone.

At the time of writing, however, we still await the further reform needed to make the chamber fully – or at least in greater part – democratically elected.

NAVIGATING WITH A BLANK MAP
Britain has so far resisted demands for a Bill of Rights and a written constitution. The lack of the former has in part been met by the Human Rights Act, but as a simple statute it could easily be overturned by a parliamentary majority of just one. Indeed, this Act is still widely condemned by many, and its future, certainly in its present form, is by no means entirely assured. Whilst the notion of an 'unwritten' constitution is not entirely correct, for written statute makes up a large part of the country's constitutional infrastructure, there still remains an embedded resistance to the notion of properly codifying the way in which a twenty-first nation governs itself. Widely perceiving written constitutions and entrenched 'rights' as undesirable 'foreign' concepts, many of the British appear to prefer an evolving and often uncertain system based upon custom and precedent.

By definition, if something is unwritten, then producing concrete evidence at crucial moments can be a little uncertain. An unwritten contract may technically be enforceable in law, but the ability to produce supporting evidence can be the weak link in the chain of proving its legitimacy. Inevitably, by a process reminiscent of the party game of 'Chinese whispers', the British constitution 'evolves'

1 INTRODUCTION

and modifies organically. Whether this is altogether a desirable way to run a nation is by no means certain. It can lead to uncertainty, and may be exploited by the government of the day using its prerogative powers – themselves an element of pre-democratic forms of government inherited from the monarchy itself. Indeed, at the beginning of the twenty-first century, Britain's government felt obliged to finally state what these 'prerogative powers' actually were. They produced a list, but then stated they themselves were unsure if that list was complete. In such an amorphous context, Britain operates, with even the government not knowing what its own powers are. In such a situation, trying to decide if a government is acting 'unconstitutionally' is a rather difficult task.

Within this uncertain territory, the hereditary British monarchy continues to exercise its considerable power. Whilst it may now ultimately be subordinate to Parliament, the notional power embodied in the term 'the Crown in Parliament' conveys a distinct sense of its importance within the system. It may be essentially a 'cipher' for elected power, but that is by no means the entire picture. While many may protest defensively that the monarchy 'have no power', the reality is that they most certainly do. On the basis of birth right, successive monarchs exercise power by hierarchical status, influence, statute, custom, precedent and their place in the cultural landscape. A head of state, whether hereditary or elected, is at the apex of a nation's constitutional and cultural pyramid. Who they are, and the manner in which they are elected, appointed – or born – into their position, and then the way in which they are regarded – and rewarded – says much about a nation's values and how it perceives itself in a broader global context. Within its traditionally secretive and unwritten constitution, Britain entrusts the role of head of state to the eldest offspring of one family, regulates them by custom, precedent and arcane protocols, couched in pseudo-historical Ruritanian language. They are dressed in contrived ornate bejewelled theatrical costume and invented ceremony of comparatively recent provenance. In return for performing this role they are also rewarded most generously, generation upon generation.

THE FIRST MODERN MONARCH, OR THE LAST OLD ONE?

On June 2nd 1953 Queen Elizabeth II was crowned, in an event almost unprecedented in the scale of pomp and pageantry created for the occasion. However, the scale of this extravaganza hid an uncomfortable fact. Britain was no longer the nation it had been just a decade or two before, let alone the previous century. The first 'television era' monarch, Elizabeth had been propelled into her new role by the premature death of her father George VI, and much was made of her youthful image to symbolise the birth of a new period for a nation emerging from the difficult immediate post-war years. As such, she combined the difficult role of symbolising both continuity and change. Gone was the old 'British Empire', and in its place came the new 'Commonwealth'. Britain no longer 'ruled the waves', the world order had changed with power now balanced in a 'Cold War' between the United States and the Soviet Union. The nations of the European mainland were rebuilding and consolidating in a new spirit of unity from which Britain distanced itself. While the nation struggled to adapt to its place in a changing world order, the population was wooed with the 1951 Festival of Britain, intended to herald a 'New Elizabethan' era for a recovering post-war nation. However, for all its 'brilliant colour and bright imagination' it distracted the public from the fact that while our European neighbours were investing in modern public infrastructure[1], Britain, meanwhile, was spending an unprecedented sum on the new royal yacht *Britannia* – and a secret deal meant that the Queen's investments would be tax-exempt for nearly half a century, enabling the monarchy to build up a wealth base estimated at well over £1billion by 2001[2].

Whilst other European nations were using their Marshall Aid dollars to finance infrastructure renewal and industrial investment, the UK instead used the money to prop up a declining imperial role, to strut the world stage as a major power with disproportionately large armed forces. These were stationed around the globe in the remaining outposts of our colonial past which were, one by one, relinquished over the ensuing years. The 1956 Suez crisis underlined the reality of the UK's by then secondary role in the world order. The Coronation might have been a technological milestone – watched by an audience of millions on television – but the public were using the new technology to look backwards – at an image that symbolised the past rather than the future[3]. The changing social landscape of the 1960s was a difficult one for the monarchy. Deference may have been in decline but was by no means dead. There had been rumours of marital problems at Buckingham Palace for years and the Duke of

1 INTRODUCTION

Edinburgh's long absences abroad did not help the hoped-for image of a 'happy family'. Differences, however, seemed to be healed by the births of the Queen's 'second generation', with the birth of Prince Andrew in 1960 and his younger brother, Edward, in 1964. The heir to the throne, Prince Charles, assumed the title of 'Prince of Wales' just a few years later, with his investiture at Caenarfon in 1969. An absurdly concocted theatrical extravaganza of neo-Ruritanian ceremony, the event was staged amid concerns of disruption by Welsh militants. Together with the BBC's early attempt at a 'fly-on-the-wall' television documentary, 'The Royal Family', this was an attempt to re-invent the Windsor dynasty as a modern 'family monarchy'. Reluctant as the Windsor family may have been to take part, television was a medium they could no longer ignore.

A more personable royal style was attempted, a more intimate version of the wartime model. Whether it worked is another matter. Like the nation they represented, the Windsor family had – to borrow Dean Acheson's words – lost an old role but struggled – or more properly resisted any attempts – to re-invent themselves in a new one. Britain still languished outside Europe, torn between the Continent and the United States. The 1970s, a decade of industrial relations and social turmoil, was a period of tension for British democracy. Inflation had delivered a shock to the economy and recession once again loomed. An attempt to restructure the finances of the Royal Family to take account of the changes of the late 1960s had been attempted but moves to modify the institution along the lines of its European counterparts were thwarted, with politicians acceding to the grandiose pretensions of the Palace. North Sea oil revenues boosted the economy in the 1980s, but ironically dealt a death-blow to the UK's struggling manufacturing industry by pushing up the value of the pound, making exports uncompetitive. However, the feel-good factor was accompanied by a steep rise in property prices, council house sales and boosted by easy credit enabled by financial deregulation in the City of London. The economy was changing as the service sector eclipsed the country's declining manufacturing industry. While the Falklands campaign might have asserted a kind of mini-Imperialistic sentiment, it also underlined quite how far the country's military power had shrunk.

There were two royal weddings. Both brash and conspicuous, the extravagant scale of these 'fairy tale'-style events reflected the mood of the period. The monarchy's popularity grew while the miners, a symbol of the country's industrial past, were challenged, confronted and defeated. There may have been a party going on but by no means was the whole country celebrating. The monarchy enjoyed enhanced popularity when the electorate felt good. Wealth and conspicuous consumption were in vogue in this 'loadsamoney' era, and Britain's over-scale monarchy fitted the bill. Unreformed, with financial advantage lavished upon it by the taxpayer for generations, it continued to enjoy its privilege undisturbed. However, by the end of the 1980s, many were beginning to question Britain's unreformed ahd largely unwritten constitution, the lack of a Bill of Rights, with a House of Lords still largely composed of hereditary peers. The 1990s, however, were different. The first Gulf war and world recession signaled a change in mood. The UK house-price boom of the 1980s led, inevitably, to bust, and the financial markets faced a crisis in 1992 on 'Black Wednesday'. The party was over.

THE 'ANNUS HORRIBILIS'
The Queen herself famously described 1992 as her 'annus horribilis'. The breakdown of two of her childrens' marriages, accompanying scandals, and a major fire at Windsor Castle did not make for an easy year. What might in previous times have evinced public sympathy brought only criticism – not easily accepted by an institution used to a long period of indulgence and approval. As the recession took hold, public opinion hardened, turning ultimately to anger at the monarchy. Despite the royal family's 'private' troubles they were not seen to be sharing the harsh economic realities experienced by the rest of the country. Their financial privilege had been overlooked in the period of economic boom and conspicuous consumption but the emphatic refusal of taxpayers to meet the costs of the repair to the Castle marked a clear change of sentiment. Most damaging of all for the Queen had been the revelation that whilst being the richest woman in the country, she was paying virtually no tax.

PRESSURE FOR CHANGE
The following year, further revelations of infidelity by the Prince of Wales heralded a public relations disaster for the monarchy in general and the heir to the throne in particular. The affair raised serious questions about the Prince of Wales's fitness to succeed as both monarch

1 INTRODUCTION

and – in the context of Britain's established Church of England in its constitution – as Supreme Governor of the Church of England. The royal family as a whole were criticised for their lifestyle – hypocritical of family values – whilst at the same time living rather too well at the taxpayer's expense. They had to be seen to atone for their faults, and in a form which would hurt most – financially. The Major government forced a reluctant Palace to agree to a number of concessions which were to take effect in April 1993.

The Queen and the heir to the throne were to pay tax – admittedly only voluntarily – though at the same rates and on the same basis as ordinary citizens – but with the notable exception of inheritance tax. Whilst Parliament would continue notionally to pay 'allowances' – in effect official salary/'expense' annuities (their exact purpose has always been slightly vague as no details of what they are spent on are ever released) – to the other 'working royals', the Queen would now have to reimburse these costs personally. The public mood had changed. In May a prominent conference organised by the constitutional reform group Charter88 and the *Times* newspaper publicly debated the future of the monarchy. In this new atmosphere, where the very principle of the monarchy was now questioned widely in the media, it was clear thath the virtual taboo on discussing such matters had truly been broken. However, as the monarchy's star waned, that of Diana, Princess of Wales, emerged enhanced. Having managed a transition to celebrity beyond her royal status, she began to carve out a new career for herself with a popular style that contrasted sharply with the staid image of the rest of the Windsor family. Prince Charles, meanwhile, sought to develop a means of rehabilitating himself in the eyes of the public. Though over the next few years his attempts to rebuild his image would be overshadowed by his ex-wife, the Prince began a concerted public relations campaign spearheaded by his expanding charitable works.

Meanwhile, Charles' unpopularity even led to rumours that the Palace was considering that it might 'skip a generation' and install William in his place. William was perceived as having inherited his mother's qualities and there was now a distinct sense of the emergence of two 'Courts'; Charles' 'traditionalist' one as an extension of his mother's monarchy, while the second promised a 'new' monarchy, perhaps prepared to adapt and change and more likely to down-size in an image more redolent of its European counterparts.

DEATH OF THE PRINCESS OF WALES: THE MONARCHY AT RISK
1997 was a watershed year. The 'New Labour' government was returned in May with a programme that promised change. Britain's antiquated constitution was clearly an early target. In such a climate, how much longer could an hereditary monarchy – the most elaborate and expensive in Europe, hope to withstand serious scrutiny and reform? After nearly two decades of Conservative rule, there was a hope that the new government would herald a very different era.

Then, just months later, in the early hours of August 31st, came the news that would shock not merely the nation, but the world. Diana, Princess of Wales, was dead – killed in a car crash in Paris. A nation, if not entirely in mourning, came almost to a standstill as if it were. Although by then divorced from the Prince of Wales and pursuing a life apart from the Windsor family, Diana had become a royal celebrity in her own right, and was beginning to embody an alternative and less traditional, more modern style of royalty. The Queen was forced for the first time to make a live broadcast to deflect criticism of her perceived failure to engage with the national mood. With help from the new Blair government, the monarchy was rescued but it would never be the same. The significance of this should not be underestimated. A reluctant monarchy was forced to act in an unaccustomed fashion by a new government which appeared to embrace the very change which the royal family so feared. The tension was heightened by the fact that the person whose death had precipitated this crisis had herself been increasingly identifiable with the government – or at the least, with its style – that was now threatening the monarchy's very future. A decade on, as Alastair Campbell would reveal in his diaries in 2007, it was clear that the Princess was by this time developing a more political dimension to her personal 'campaign'. Freed from the constraints of being a part of the royal family, with the inherent restrictions upon involvement in politically sensitive matters, she was now free to act in a way that her ex-husband, as future head of state, could not do without courting serious constitutional controversy. In meetings with Tony Blair and Campbell before the election, she had hinted that she wished to become involved with New Labour's aims. Whilst free to do so, this was a contentious area in which her popular appeal that so easily eclipsed the Windsor family could be such a threat to their own standing[4].

Although the monarchy emerged from the crisis intact, there was little doubt that it had to adapt to an uneasy truce with the very government that had termed Diana 'the People's Princess'. This was an institution that did not want – nor indeed, probably could not envisage – genuine change, but from now on, more than ever before, it would have to compromise and bargain for the popularity it needed in order to survive. From now on it would have to campaign for its future.

A MONARCHY FOR A PAST ERA

By 2012, the Queen, symbolic of a past Imperial age, remains on the throne. Now well into her eighties, she has noticeably reduced the number of official appointments, many being now performed by assorted junior members of the family as well as her son and heir, Charles. However, it is a job for life, not just for Christmas broadcasts. And despite the Palace's attempts to get 'on trend', with the Queen ostensibly social-networking on Twitter, it appears as little more than a contrivance. In the opinion of *Le Monde*'s London correspondent, Marc Roche, speaking about his book *Elisabeth II: La Derniere Reine*[5], she 'represents a country that has now gone'. Yet the scale and profile of the British monarchy still far exceeds its European counterparts. Honours suffixed 'of the British Empire', 'OBE's,' MBE's, and 'CBE's, themselves dating only from 1917, when the 'Empire' itself was firmly on the wane, are still distributed by the Palace. It remains an Imperial style monarchy whose time has passed yet which still clings resolutely to a life of wealth and privilege propped up by deference. There is little appetite for accountability or reform, although more challenging economic times have now developed the former with the passing of the Sovereign Grant Act. For Stephen Haseler, in his book *The Grand Delusion*, the monarchy reinforces an image of a nation that retains its delusions of grandeur: 'In 2012, in the midst of the gravest economic crisis since the 1930s, with the households of Britain facing widespread financial insecurity, official Britain nonetheless deemed that the people should celebrate not their country or their citizenship, but a Queen who, for all her service, most perfectly represents both the imperial past and super-rich present. That in itself stands testimony to the continuing power of the "grand delusion"'.

Her intended successor seems little different, an adherent to the concepts of 'natural order' – a notion reinforcing the idea of deference and hierarchy. Despite his advocacy of numerous social causes he appears unwilling to acknowledge the irony demonstrated by his own extravagant lifestyle – and the privilege of his position. He is poorly suited to a changed world and a changed nation. He mourned the loss of Hong Kong from a nostalgic Imperial viewpoint and even that of the long-lost American colonies, opining that a royal tour by George III might have been enough to dissuade George Washington, Benjamin Franklin, et al, from declaring their independence. He has been, nevertheless, very happy to accept large donations to his charities from wealthy American meritocrats.

A MODERN MONARCHY?

For an institution as pivotal to the present British constitution as the monarchy, it is strange that it is in most respects so poorly understood. The constitution is essentially unwritten, though statute law defines much of its practice. The remainder is left to custom and precedent. Myths and misunderstandings persist to a point where even within the space of a generation memories become blurred. Relatively recent changes can acquire or be given a false historic provenance which deepens a sense of 'mystique'. This acts on an emotional level, but the institution also wields real constitutional power and cultural influence despite the development of popular democracy. Considerable support still persists for a hereditary institution whose very existence runs counter to the otherwise accepted notions of modern democratic values.

GET RICH, STAY RICH

Within this landscape, the monarchy has been permitted to obtain, retain and augment its financial wealth. In an age in which real power has now migrated to the institution of a democratically elected Parliament, the royal family still retains a privileged position. Deference still exists. It is evident in the behaviour and language surrounding the institution which has been, since the beginning of the 18th century, a creation of Parliament. The British monarchy depends utterly upon Parliament for its present lineage and very existence. Yet much practice would appear scarcely to recognise this fact. The monarchy behaves as if many of the developments of three centuries had never happened. This is still reflected in the present financial treatment of the institution. Anomalies persist, with the institution and its members accorded privilege and exemptions not available to the rest of the population. The failure to use clear language about the monarchy's finance aids misunderstanding and confusion. The use of terms such as 'the Crown', or 'the Crown in Parliament', confuses, suffused as it is by imagery of monarchical regalia and combined with a general ignorance of even the most basic elements of the British constitution. Talk of 'Civil Lists', 'Grants-in-aid' and 'Duchy surpluses' conveys a Ruritanian gloss that conceals the reality of many millions of pounds of taxpayer's money.

Financial accountability of the monarchy is far from rigorous – even with the recent passing into law of the Sovereign Grant Act. The subject is permeated by arcane language, the terminology used neither readily understood nor easily comparable with everyday usage elsewhere. For the most part past practice is accepted and rarely challenged. Change, where it occurs at all, is slow – some of it taking place outside even the democratic forum of Parliament, as was the case with the 1993 Memorandum of Understanding. Deference and secrecy prevail and dubious precedents are accorded an undeserved status. Studies of royal finance are extremely rare. It is fair to say that even the most basic elements of the financial arrangements are often widely misunderstood. Money derives from a variety of sources for a variety of purposes. Cloak it all in strange language, present different financial figures at different times subject to varying interpretation and many – not least the public themselves – will get rather confused and unquestionably accept the version that is presented to them.

Today, the monarch and her heir receive multi-million pound official incomes which are disguised by obscure language as the 'surpluses' of the Duchies of Cornwall and Lancaster. These incomes are subject to little proper scrutiny nor have their scale and function hardly ever been seriously challenged. In August, 2007, for example, the *Guardian* newspaper revealed the pay league 'Boardroom Bonanza' of the country's highest earners. Between £9 and £23million, there were two notable exceptions – the Queen and the heir to the throne. Ranking in the middle of this top earning league – with well above inflation increases – they are unique in that their huge earnings derive from what are public sources – ultimately the taxpayer. Even then, such money is camouflaged to appear not as earnings, but as 'something' somehow different, and thus not attracting comparable criticism[6].

Poorly regulated by an unwritten constitution, beyond the monarch, there are no legally defined roles for members of the royal family. Yet they receive, directly or indirectly considerable amounts of public money – far greater than their royal European counterparts – and occupy prime public properties under exceedingly favourable terms. The heir to the throne may have run a commercial company using the branding and infrastructure which he assumes through his official status but few seem to care. Not only that, he may also promote interests not dissimilar to his own commercial ones whilst speaking officially as the Prince of Wales. The requirements to declare financial interests which apply to Members of Parliament and civil servants do not apply to the royal family. Financial review has been infrequent and our elected MPs are discouraged from debating royal matters, especially money. Welcome to the Windsor's financial world.

2
Money and the Monarchy

The King was in his counting house
Counting out his money...

Even a nursery rhyme can convey strong cultural messages. The relationship between the British people and their monarchy has been characterised by the struggle to control the nation's wealth. The growth of parliamentary democracy and, with it, a move away from absolutist monarchy meant that the power centre had shifted. With that went the power to raise taxes and accordingly to allocate that money. No longer could the monarch raise money and decide, unchallenged, what to do with it. The English Civil War arose largely as a result of attempts by Charles I to levy money without the authorisation of Parliament. The Declaration of Independence of the American colonies resulted from their struggle against the iniquity of 'taxation without representation' by a remote monarchy.

Despite the constraints imposed on a constitutional monarchy operating within a parliamentary system, tensions remain. With their political powers restricted, the monarchy's finances remain as one of the few areas in which they can attempt to assert a degree of self-importance and comparative privilege. The bargaining process to preserve that wealth is heavily influenced by cultural tradition. Even today, deference and secrecy remain as tangible remnants of a more absolutist period.

The concept of inherent right, which attaches to the very notion of monarchy, inevitably brings with it a degree of arrogance which may or may not be mitigated by the good manners of the incumbent and tempered by the attitude of the elected government. This attitude will, in turn, be influenced by the esteem in which the monarchy is held by the nation.

The 19th century British republican movement drew much of its support from the perception that Queen Victoria had grown rich at public expense. The feeling grew that, with her withdrawal from official duties in the years following the death of the Prince Consort, the public was not getting the monarch for whom they were paying so much. The famous *Punch* magazine cartoon of an empty throne and the accompanying 'Where is she?' caption, captured the mood of many in the country. At its height in the 1870s, this was part of a broader social pressure to assert the economic and political status of the working classes. Earlier in the century, the Chartists had sought to advance the political power of their supporters and the emerging trade unions campaigned for the rights of their members in an increasingly industrialised society. The old 'feudal' overtones of a society centred around landowning were fast disappearing. The increasingly wealthier parts of the middle class had migrated up into the aristocratic hierarchy, imitating their landholding aspirations. Queen Victoria's husband, the German Prince Albert, sought to establish the 'Saxe-Coburg-Gotha' dynasty in the mould of the English country landowning class. Hence the acquisition of the Sandringham, Balmoral and Osborne estates.

With the growth of the Empire, the late 19th century 're-invention' of the monarchy added a further layer, that of imperial spectacle and grandeur which the monarchy had hitherto lacked. This was to a large extent an attempt to counter the threats to social order – from trade unionism, general social dissatisfaction inherent in what was a very unequal society and the accompanying emerging political threats to the 'old' order. This gave rise to the 'bread and circuses' approach in the latter stages of Victoria's reign whereby grandiose 'State Openings' of Parliament, Jubilees, and other spectacular events were devised with Ruritanian carriage processions – bewigged attendants dressed in pastiche costume redolent of what was the Victorian era's 'golden age' – an ornate rendition of a vague eighteenth century styled period with the hint of the mock-Baroque. To reinforce this concocted image was added a pantomime mixture of re-hashed royal protocol and figures which, whilst they had some elements of genuine historical precedent, were largely no more than a cast list of some camp theatrical extravaganza.

Thus Britain acquired its overblown image of its 'imperial' monarchy. Whilst the nation's comparative economic decline set in by 1870, the nation strode forward into the twentieth century wrapped in gilt and ermine delusion, behind which the decay gathered pace. The First World War – with the nation bankrupt by 1916 – deflected republican pressures in favour of a more united patriotic focus. Despite this, the tremors of the 1917 Russian revolution in and industrial unrest at home were warnings of dangers to the old order. Anti-German sentiment during the conflict proved difficult for a royal family with a German name closely related to that of the enemy's ruling family. A swift 're-branding' from 'Saxe-Coburg-Gotha' to the quintessentially English-sounding 'Windsor' was enacted in 1917, with 'Battenburg' cousins became 'Mountbattens', 'Tecks' becoming 'Kents', and other relatives changed their unsuitable Teutonic names too. Russian and German royal relations disappeared from the map, and the economic crises that followed in the inter-war period carried risks to the British monarchy, but the Second World War again provided a convenient alternative focus away from reformist or even abolitionist pressures that might have otherwise resulted from the pre-war abdication crisis. The royal family reconfigured itself as a somewhat less grand 'family monarchy' while boosting its popularity in a beleaguered wartime Britain. Post-war euphoria and sympathy for the young Queen following her father's early death meant that criticism was largely absent. The reality of the post-war disappearance of the British Empire was to a great degree softened by the invention of the 'Commonwealth', and this helped to conceal from the nation the changing reality of the world order. The Suez crisis was an embarrassing lesson for a nation which, bankrupted in two world wars, would never again be able to pursue a truly independent foreign policy of its own. Supported by Marshall Aid and destined to make heavy Lend-Lease payments until beyond the end of the century in return for the huge assistance it had received during the war, the nation rebuilt itself.

For the monarchy, this was its 'New Elizabethan' era, and it might now be thought that criticism of the young Queen and other members of the royal family in the 'never had it so good' period – the decade following the Coronation – would have been largely absent. This was not, however, the case. In 1962, at a time often now thought of as a 'golden age' for the present monarch, there was considerable public anger at the news that Lord Snowdon, celebrity society photographer and husband of the Queen's sister, Princess Margaret, had benefited from £85,000 worth of work to his Kensington Palace apartment – a very considerable sum in present day values – all paid for by the tax-payer. This was the greatest public attack on the royal family since unprecedented criticism in 1957 by playwright John Osborne, writer Malcolm Muggeridge and journalist John Grigg[1]. An emerging 'anti-Establishment' movement, encompassing powerful political, social and cultural criticism and satire, exploiting in particular the medium of television began to challenge institutions which had previously felt themselves safe, sheltered by a hitherto more deferential society. Do not forget, too, that the monarch's head only first appeared on some – not all – UK banknotes in 1960, excepting the brief appearance of the King's head on an issue of Treasury bonds during the First World War.

'HONOUR', 'DIGNITY' – AND LOTS OF MONEY
Money is, like it or not, a key indicator of status, and the monarchy still protests its need for a level of wealth that it deems commensurate with that status. The belief that a British head of state requires an 'appropriate' level – a lot – of personal wealth in order to fulfil the role, in keeping with the 'honour and dignity' of the position, persists today. This notion is still implicit in official attitudes and reflects a curious view of a modern society which otherwise likes to think itself committed in its policies to enabling a culture of greater equality of opportunity. One family, through birth alone, regards itself as deserving not just of a constitutional position but of a guarantee of accompanying wealth. The matter of the Queen's wealth is, of course, a matter only for speculation. Whilst, as mentioned above, an amount in excess of £1billion pounds has been suggested in view of her likely investments at the time of her accession – and enhanced over four decades by a secret tax deal – a figure of £320million was suggested by the 2008 *Sunday Times* 'Rich List'. Given the value of Sandringham and Balmoral alone – and a doubtless considerable number of artworks held privately, rather

2 MONEY AND THE MONARCHY

than in the Royal Collection – this figure seems modest indeed. The reality is that in a culture of secrecy, abetted by trusts, nominee companies, and so on, the truth is, and is likely to remain, an elusive commodity. A common failing, too, is that of including items 'held' in the monarch's official capacity, such as assets in the Royal Collection, reflecting an inability – or unwillingness – to distinguish properly between the individual and their public role.

Since the 18th century, the monarchy's official role has been financed by an annual Civil List payment and the 'Grants-in-aid' (to be replaced by a combined equivalent annual Sovereign Grant payment from 2013) which is agreed at the outset of each reign and normally subject to regular forms of review. In addition to this, the monarch and heir to the throne are paid annual incomes deriving from the profits of the Duchies of Lancaster and Cornwall respectively for their personal benefit. The present Queen has been financed in this way, but inflation in the late 1960s and early '70s meant that by then some form of review was becoming necessary, resulting in the Civil List Act of 1972. Henceforth, reviews of royal finances would take place on a ten-yearly basis.

The Civil List payment is intended to cover the costs of performing the role of head of state, and is supplemented by the 'Grants-in-aid' to cover the cost of official air and rail travel and the running costs of the 'Occupied' royal palaces. Other members of the royal family who perform official roles are included within this payment system. The exception to this is the heir to the throne. Some of his expenses are met by his income from the Duchy of Cornwall although the costs of air and rail travel and of running his official residence, Clarence House, are met by Grants-in-aid. Constitutionally, it should be remembered, however, that the heir to the throne's 'role' – and thus the 'tasks' he performs – are undefined. A number of other payments are paid directly by government departments and the Crown Estates. This situation has now been amended by the introduction of the Sovereign Grant Act in 2012, intended to simplify and clarify the financial affairs of the monarchy, details of which will appear later in this chapter.

CHOOSING TO PAY TAX...
Phillip Hall's book: *Royal Fortune*, published in 1992, described in eloquent detail the historic basis of royal finances[2]. For that reason it

is not the intention of this work to explore in too great a detail the situation which pertained in the years prior to that. Traditionally, the monarch and the heir to the throne have been exempt from the requirement to pay tax in the normal way. This situation resulted from the monarch being treated as if they had only official 'public' status, and no separate 'private' role. As it would be illogical for a Crown body to pay tax, in effect, to itself, the monarch and heir have thus claimed – and consistently received – immunity from normal taxation obligations. The heir's claim to exemption is much less credible. After all, they have yet to succeed to the position of monarch.

For reasons of political expediency, monarchs have usually agreed to pay tax. Queen Victoria, for example, paid tax on her income. However, there was never any consistent pattern. It has varied from reign to reign, the assumption being that any arrangement is individual and voluntary between the monarch and the government of the day. Present arrangements still persist in treating them in a manner different from the rest of the population and there still remains a high degree of 'blurring' between their public and private roles to their undoubted benefit. Private agreement with the government, rather than solid legislation, still forms the basis of the monarch's taxation status, with deals sometimes made completely in secret as, for instance, that agreed between Prime Minister Winston Churchill, his Chancellor 'RAB' Butler and the then Princess Elizabeth in 1952 exempting her from tax on her investment income.

...BUT NOT INHERITANCE TAX

Political pressure, however, has caused the monarchy to be gradually more open in its affairs, and the poor public approval ratings of the early 1990s forced a reluctant Palace to agree to concessions which would mean paying tax on a basis broadly equivalent to that of ordinary taxpayers. Whilst there was no statutory obligation to do so, any attempt to turn back the clock would be likely to have had grave implications for their popularity – and indeed their very continuance. The 1993 Memorandum of Understanding – another essentially 'private' deal – formed the basis upon which the present monarch and the heir to the throne pay tax, in almost all respects the same way as anyone else, save for the significant fact that they were permitted exemption from inheritance tax.

2 MONEY AND THE MONARCHY

The exception for inheritance liability was included to protect the passing of wealth between royal generations. A reflection of the curious notion that a head of state needs to be personally wealthy to perform their role, it ensures that wealth is passed on undiminished. This is increasingly perceived as an unfair and anomalous privilege. It derives in part from a persistent failure to create a totally clear divide between the 'public' and 'private' roles of the monarch. Whilst it should be remembered that all the official 'treasures', including the Crown Jewels, the Royal Collection, and so on, are 'held for the nation' by the Sovereign purely in their official capacity, the exact provenance of some of the wealth supposedly possessed as a private individual is still far from adequately defined. Official treasures cannot therefore be sold or given away, but simply passed on from one monarch to the next. Wealth held personally is, however, illogically treated in the same way.

It might have been thought that any future reappraisal of royal finances would meet with a House of Commons that was far less deferential and accommodating than was the case in the past – even as recently as 1992. Though criticism of the monarchy is not new, MPs have become progressively less inhibited in voicing it. Parliament played no part in the 1992 agreement, the new arrangement between the Palace and Number Ten was announced to the House of Commons as a *fait accompli*. This is a reminder of that part of the British constitution that remains beyond democratic accountability, the world of prerogative power.

However, the passage of the Sovereign Grant Bill in 2011 overseen by the coalition government met with little media attention. Though it could be argued that comparatively little in reality – in terms of the basic amount of money and the fact that Parliament remains, as ever, in charge – was changed by this legislation, it also underlines the ability of our system to suppress the profile of the passage of legislation pertaining to the monarchy. Had the legislation proposed real changes it is likely that the level and coverage of any debate would have been very different.

ROYAL FINANCE - THE BASICS

There are essentially five sources which provide funding for the monarchy:

1 The Civil List – This is essentially the 'expense account' for the monarch which funds the cost of performing the official tasks of being head of state. It is paid by the Government and also covers the expenses of those members of the Royal Family undertaking official duties.

2 Grants in Aid – these are additional payments by the Government which cover the cost of maintaining the Occupied Royal Palaces – those in which the monarch actually lives and works – and of providing official royal travel by air and rail as well as communications and information costs.

3 Duchy of Lancaster income – this is in effect the monarch's official 'salary'. It consists of the profits – quaintly termed the 'surplus' – generated by an investment portfolio known as the Duchy of Lancaster, the net amount payable to the Privy Purse being £12.9million in 2011-12 (£13.3million in 2011). Based upon the remnants of a mediaeval estate reacquired and 'reassembled' – in part – after the Restoration in 1660 and added to since then, it is not actually owned by the Queen. She cannot sell any or all of it but is entitled whilst monarch to the annual profits from it. As a result, the income so derived tends to increase year on year – it is not a fixed sum.

4 Direct payments made directly by Government departments and the Crown Estates These are miscellaneous payments made directly to the Royal Household and have in recent years amounted on average to around £5million a year. They include such costs as equerries and other support staff seconded from the military, the cost of administering the 'honours' system and diplomatic service costs of royal foreign visits, etc.

5 Personal Income and Wealth – (the 'Privy Purse') – this is personal to the Queen and consists of the income from assets owned by her as a private individual – it is never publicly disclosed, and income from it is regarded as part of the overall , and rather quaintly termed 'Privy Purse' income. Any estimates of it can only be purely speculative.

THE SOVEREIGN GRANT ACT 2012

With the passing of the Sovereign Grant Act, which comes into operation in 2013, the first two on the above list, the old 'Civil List' and the various 'Grants-in-aid', will, in effect, be consolidated to form the 'Sovereign Support Grant', which is intended, as has been the case with the Civil List and Grants-in-aid, in order to meet the costs of performing the duties of monarch. This will be assessed using as a benchmark 15% (though Parliament can at any time in the future vary this percentage, up or down) of the annual profits of the Crown Estates using the figure from two year's prior to the year in question. The 'bare' (there are various additional sums) Grant for 2013 has thus already been set at £31million – which apparently includes a sum of £1milllion to pay for 'activities associated with the Diamond Jubilee' – and for 2014 it will be £36million. Under the old system, reviews were ostensibly on a ten-yearly cycle, and the new system is intended to 'run' on an ongoing basis unless Parliamentary review is deemed necessary. Whilst this may appear a purely retrograde step, the old system was in practice, very lax. 'Reviews' were given a low profile in the parliamentary schedule, often 'buried' by other events and also affected by the UK's rather irregular electoral cycle.

The new system does at least set in statute a greater degree of ongoing formal parliamentary accountability which a future government, if so minded, could use to great effect in imposing budgetary restraint. Some have alleged, and certainly in the early stages of the proposals for the new system, that it would remove the monarchy from proper parliamentary accountability and take us back to the situation which prevailed before 1760. This is not the case, but the UK's deferential system has always tended to keep the process at arm's length, in order to preserve the pretence of monarchical 'independence' and to boost royal pride which has rather been eroded by democratic developments in the last two or three centuries. The loss of the a regular review is on the whole, however, a very retrograde step. A bit of plain honesty which bluntly reiterates Parliament's supremacy at regular intervals would not go amiss.

The Duchy of Lancaster income and any private wealth is unaffected by the Act. For the rest of this chapter reference will continue to be made to the 'Civil List' and to 'Grants-in-aid' as for obvious reasons they provide an understanding of the system which has prevailed in the past. The new Act, by 'merging' and re-labelling them does not in essence change the nature and purpose of the funding which still derives from the Exchequer. The Crown Estates profits are used as an assessment device, not as the funding source itself.

THE PRIVY PURSE
The Duchy of Lancaster income and the income generated by the Queen's personal assets together constitute what is known as the 'Privy Purse'. Tax is paid on this income but only on a voluntary basis (the latest agreement being the 1993 Memorandum of Understanding between the monarch, the heir to the throne and the then Conservative government). It is somewhat disingenuously asserted that some of the Duchy of Lancaster income is spent on 'official' expenses. It would seem that this referred simply to the 'Parliamentary Allowances' paid to members of the Queen's family which are now reimbursed by her after the 1993 agreement. For the taxpayer to pay such incomes was by then judged to be politically insupportable. The Sovereign Grant Act has finally severed any notional obligation of Parliament to pay such 'Allowances', putting an end to the practice of the Queen then reimbursing Parliament. The Queen now pays these annual allowances to her children and assorted relatives – the so-called 'working royals' herself is a personal matter, though Parliament continues to pay the Duke of Edinburgh his £359,000 a year directly. More generally, to imply that the Queen really needs to dip into her own pocket to meet official expenses due to the inadequacy of the present arrangement is rather misleading. There is no real obligation to fund these official 'hangers-on', and if they are deemed indispensible to the operation of the nation's monarchy, then there ought to be full transparency as to what they cost and on what precisely the money is spent.

The Privy Purse (a 'Purse' sounds so quaint and innocuous, doesn't it), encompasses the Queen's personal wealth – estimated by the *Sunday Times* Rich List in 2011 as being £300million. Such a figure is very, very hard to confirm. The UK has no system of transparency of personal wealth as for example exists in some Scandinavian countries, Besides, with the widespread use of trusts money may not be held by, for example, the Queen as such, it may have originated as 'her' money but placing it in a trust keeps it at 'arms-length'. 'Official' wealth, such as those items held in the Royal Collection, is excluded, but that doesn't mean that the Queen doesn't perhaps have items of her own which are (possibly very) valuable. The private estates of Sandringham, Balmoral, and so on, for this reason, may or may not be included. It is also still a moot point as to whether, even today, the monarch is able to hold items other than land, in their own right. It has also long been speculated that Bank of England Nominees Limited exists as a handy 'front' for wealth held by – amongst others – the Queen. BOEN Ltd can 'hold securities on behalf of certain customers', and whilst apparently dormant at the time of writing, this of itself does not preclude it from acting as a nominee shareholder, and is also handily exempt from the usual notification provisions. (see Appendix: Bank of England Nominees)

THE HEIR TO THE THRONE
The heir to the throne derives his official income from the profits of the Duchy of Cornwall – £18.3million in 2012 (£18,288,000 to be exact). It tends to rise year on year as the Duchy's property portfolio profits rise, having been £17.8million in 2011, for example. This is of a similar nature and basis as the monarch's Duchy of Lancaster income and can only be received whilst the recipient is heir. Resignation, for example, would cause it to cease and be transferred to the next in line. It is taxed on a voluntary basis in the same way as that of the monarch. The voluntary nature of royal tax liability is ridiculous. They should be obliged by statute to pay tax as anyone else in the country. The reality now is that, forced into accepting that they should pay tax in 1993 (though monarchs had done so in the past, it was always done on a voluntary monarch by monarch basis), to now decide not to pay tax would in reality unleash a public furore which might – if they stuck to their guns – actually result in their dynastic demise, or at least would force the abdication of the incumbent.

Official expenses are also paid to the heir to the throne – £2,026,000 in Grant-in-aid from the taxpayer was, for example, paid to cover the cost of running Clarence House and official travel in 2007 (£1,584,000 in 2006). The figures fluctuate year on year but remain broadly consistent. The Prince of Wales can also offset expenses against his pre-tax Duchy income on the basis that it is claimed to be necessary to performing his – albeit legally undefined — role as heir. In 2012, the taxpayer funded him to the tune of £1,318,000 in respect of travel by air and rail – up from £1,080,000 in 2011, to which must be added £431,000 to run Clarence House, £62,000 to cover 'communications, plus £383,000 for costs of 'overseas tours' – a grand total of £2,194,000 (the Prince's overall Grant-in-aid figure for 2011 was £1,962,000).

The 1993 Memorandum of Understanding resulted from the poor esteem in which the monarchy was held by the public at the time, and their privileged financial position at a time of severe economic recession. Phillip Hall's book played a significant part in increasing awareness of the fact that the Queen paid virtually no tax unlike most of her predecessors, although admittedly they had all done so on uniquely favourable terms. This, together with the Windsor family's other financial privileges, intensified a growing hostility toward the institution at a time of considerable economic recession leading to business bankruptcies and house repossessions.

To prevent the very real possibility of a serious crisis of confidence in the monarchy, the government of the day, headed by Prime Minister John Major, drew up the agreement with Buckingham Palace. The arrangement that applied to 'the Sovereign', the heir to the throne, and 'the Consort of a former Sovereign' – the latter a definition which was designed to accord special treatment to the late Queen Mother (but could also apply to any surviving spouse of a monarch who had died or even abdicated).

Announced to the House of Commons on November 26th 1992 that a new agreement was in the process of being reached, and taking effect from April 1993, the Memorandum – dated February 11th 1993 – was purely 'voluntary', giving the monarch and the heir to the throne the option to bring the agreement to an end at any time should they so wish. However, whether such a move would be politically acceptable is another matter. Normal taxation rules are applied, although the exact rates that are paid are also 'voluntary' and the ability to deduct a great many expenses, notably in the case of the Prince of Wales, certainly helps to reduce overall tax exposure. The agreement applies to all income, and but it should be remembered that the privileged fiscal status of the Duchies themselves helps in itself to further enhance the income payable to their two beneficiaries.

HELPING THE AGED

The Memorandum contained special provision for the 'Consort of a former Sovereign'. It was tailor-made to grant an extraordinarily advantageous deal to a woman who despite having no official constitutional role had nonetheless managed to re-brand herself as a regal super-matriarch – the 'Queen Mother'. At the outset of her daughter's reign, the 'traditional' title, that of 'Queen Dowager' was still held by Queen Mary, widow of George V and in any case adjudged to be somewhat 'old-fashioned' by the elder Elizabeth Windsor. With her self-awarded title of 'Queen Elizabeth the Queen Mother', she was indignant at being asked to leave Buckingham Palace after her late husband's death.

The Queen Mother received an enormous Parliamentary Allowance which in the years up to her death amounted to £648,000 a year – untaxed until 1993, and almost certainly after that date too – plus her rent-free palace, Clarence House. Despite this generous assistance from the taxpayer she was, by the 1990s, known to have run up a seven-figure overdraft at her bankers – a fact disclosed by a former Coutt's employee. The terms of the 1993 Memorandum later enabled her daughter to acquire her estate free of the depredations of inheritance tax. This perk was worth many, many millions on the basis of her renowned collection of Impressionist paintings alone, including works by Monet and Sisley.

With tax liability only on that part of her estate not bequeathed to the Queen or Prince of Wales, this exemption was estimated to have saved as much as £28million[3]. Given that the taxpayer had enabled an estate of this size to be accumulated in the first place, surely a degree of reciprocal transparency would have been in order. However, a 'tradition' has developed which, since the early 20th century, keeps the contents of royal wills – and a will is are normally a public document – secret. In 2008 this convention, originally the result of an attempt to avoid a scandal involving the royal family, was the subject of a legal challenge. However, as yet, this deferential situation has not changed and royal wills remain inaccessible to the public.

An unsuccessful secret deal, designed to benefit the Queen Mother, was revealed in March 2008. An approach had been made by her treasurer, Arthur Penn, in April 1959 to the Prime Minister – to save her from what Penn claimed would be 'severe embarrassment'. At the time she was receiving £70,000 per annum, the same as previous 'Dowagers' under a 1936 Civil List deal (a sum roughly equivalent to £12.5million at today's prices). However, the 'Queen Mother's grandiose idea was to pursue the notion of 'service' which meant – in her 'reality' – a wide range of self-appointed roles for which she then expected to be officially – and lavishly – reimbursed. Accompanying this was an attempt to get 'rates' (property tax) exemption on her rent-free palace – Clarence House. However, this would have prompted Westminster Council to reassess the matter of the then exemption relating to Buckingham Palace, all potentially rather embarrassing.

Prime Minister Harold Macmillan suggested she might be treated as an ambassador, but this would have required Parliamentary scrutiny. Such examination was perceived by the parties involved as 'quite beyond the pale' and the matter was dropped. The Queen Mother's income remained at that level – admittedly boosted by her tax-exempt daughter – until 1971, but finally jumping – and paid directly by Parliament, don't forget – to £648,000 per annum in her later years[4]. Her habit of spending beyond her income in pursuit of her exaggerated self-importance would last her entire life.

As Phillip Hall demonstrated, money accumulated as a result of a whole series of favourable tax deals over the generations was being kept in the family. Given the exemption from inheritance tax in respect of 'Sovereign to Sovereign transfers' and those from a 'Consort of a former Sovereign', any 'transfers' – which can mean gifts, bequests, in fact any shifting of assets between these privileged individuals – can be made tax-free. It is interesting to speculate whether, strictly speaking, the Queen is actually able to hold wealth other than in the form of landed property. Monarchs were only able to hold land on their own right after the passing of the Crown Private Estates Act in 1800, but in the absence of specific legislation to permit money or chattels to be held independently, it could be argued that such a clear distinction has never been legally established. Hall does not speculate on this, simply describing the Queen's private and personal wealth as 'non-landed assets...not covered' by the above Acts.

2 MONEY AND THE MONARCHY

Monarchs are allowed to not only become very rich – for example, the Queen's secret 1952 investment income tax exemption – but also to transfer that wealth undiminished between generations. There is another reason they get so rich – public apathy born out of ignorance. Few are properly aware of the degree of financial privilege, and many, rather surprisingly, seem not to mind if members of the Windsor family get a special deal. Years of propaganda that presents the royal family as 'special' helps make this somehow acceptable, and the inherent complexity of the arrangements – and relatively poor accountability (although this has now been to an extent addressed by the new Sovereign Grant Act) – does not help.

When the new royal tax regime was announced to Parliament in November 1992, the Leader of the Opposition, the late John Smith drew attention to the anomaly of the exemptions relating to inheritance tax – although he seemed not to have noticed the fact that the word 'transfers' used in the document could involve a more general privilege in respect of gifts. He also appeared to confuse the private assets with the Royal Collection, the colossal art resource 'held' by the Sovereign 'for the nation'. Perhaps rather conveniently, the Royal Collection Trust was established at the same time as the tax deal, helping to give the impression that the Queen was being so very generous: Smith commented that

> I welcome the proposal to establish a Royal Collection Trust, which will maintain the benefit of the Royal Collection for the nation. However, although it is accepted that assets held by the Queen as Sovereign should not be liable to inheritance tax, will the Prime Minister explain why all private assets passing from one Sovereign to the next should also be exempt? Although private assets such as Sandringham and Balmoral could well be regarded as having at least partial official use, which could be recognised, is it necessary to exempt all other private wealth from inheritance tax?[5]

The Prime Minister evidently felt, however, that it *was* necessary. John Smith also overlooked the fact that the monarch claims expenses for the 'public' use of parts of her private residences when there, so it was 'recognised' and incurred no royal expense at all. The entire arrangement had been a rapid response to the situation brought about by the Windsor Castle fire and the unexpected public furore. The

Government – and the Royal family itself – had, it seems, been taken aback by the unequivocal public refusal to pay for the damage. Low approval ratings in the wake of family scandals and marriage breakdowns that year had damaged their image, plus a feeling that the Windsor family were immune from economic recession facing the rest of the country. While the nation had experienced a housing crash and an explosion in business failures and redundancies, the royal family appeared to be doing rather too well, and all at the taxpayers' expense. The Government felt obliged to act fast to address what risked becoming a potentially destabilising crisis of confidence in the monarchy.

Born of hasty expediency, the 1993 agreement was not as well-considered as it should have been. Constitutional reform campaigners had by then attained a higher profile but the government were anxious not to let the situation get too far out of their control. Further examination of the position of the monarchy could have had broader repercussions with which the government were decidedly uncomfortable. Times were changing. The Windsor Castle fire had been the catalyst for a review of royal taxation arrangements, but an alternative means to finance the repair bill had now to be found. Reluctantly, the Queen agreed to open Buckingham Palace to the paying public for a few weeks in the summer months The Queen also agreed in 1993 to bear the expense of reimbursing the Parliamentary allowances to the 'minor' royals – the royal children and their spouses, other than the heir to the throne and her husband, the Duke of Edinburgh. These so-called 'hangers-on' had been increasingly criticised for enjoying a privileged lifestyle at public expense, and to further distance them from public scorn they were encouraged to pursue careers of their own. This was not entirely successful. Dogged by accusations that they were trading on their royal connections, despite royal protestations to the contrary, subsequent events were to prove the accusers correct.

NEW LABOUR, NEW ERA?
By the time New Labour was elected in 1997, Tony Blair had committed his party to a manifesto promise to carry out a number of constitutional reforms – but no suggestion of reform of the monarchy appeared on the agenda. A commitment to challenge the hereditary element of the House of Lords did not extend to the House of Windsor. Perhaps it was felt that the 1993 agreement would suffice for the time being. 'New Labour' was committed to change, but seemed in no mood

to challenge the privilege and lack of proper accountability enjoyed by the royal family. It was also a very different party from 'Old' Labour having dropped its commitment to public ownership, enshrined within Clause 4 of its constitution.

A Labour government that had by 2006 found itself in trouble over 'cash for peerages' allegations, still found the idea of supporting a wealthy extended family entirely acceptable. Buying a seat in the legislature may have been wrong, and inheriting it had become unacceptable as well, but there seemed no inconsistency in continuing to inherit the throne. Meanwhile, a new breed of national and international super-rich was being feted by a government that indulged them with titles and non-domicile tax status. Britain, with accessible and very highly valued real estate and a booming financial sector in the City of London, had become a tax haven for those who wished to benefit from City trading and the property boom but could keep their remaining wealth elsewhere free from the Exchequer.

However, by 2007 patience with the fiscally privileged super-rich was wearing thin. New Labour's ideological schizophrenia was clearly evident. Exemplified by Peter Mandelson's earlier boast that they were 'intensely relaxed about people getting filthy rich', it sat uncomfortably with demands for many of the poorest in society just a few years later to repay the government as a result of bungled administration of the working tax credit system. A Monaco-based tax exile like retail entrepreneur Sir Philip Green received his knighthood for 'services to the economy' but did not wish to pay tax in the UK in return. Meanwhile, the 'average' person wasn't earning anything like an 'average' wage[6]. Household debt was rocketing – £1trillion in mortgage debt by mid-2006 – and with credit cards taking the strain where low wage growth could not keep up. The apparent high wage growth was in reality boosted by a tiny privileged minority in the City of London. The economy depended on spending to keep afloat, and easy credit had filled the gap. By 2006 inflated housing asset values were providing the Chancellor with an annual boost of around £40billion to the economy through equity release.

Meanwhile, by 2007, the Duchy of Cornwall reported a rise in the annual income of the Prince of Wales – the profits of the Duchy – to £15.2million. Given the unique way in which the heir to the throne's income is treated, with deductions for official expenses and a voluntary tax regime, it makes direct comparisons with ordinary mortals difficult, but does demonstrate a degree of institutionalised privilege that is hard to beat. It is salutary to bear in mind that, were the Prince to continue to receive his Duchy income for another decade, and at even conservative rates of annual increase, he will have by then received around a quarter of a billion pounds from the Duchy since the year 2000 alone.

However, the days when monarchs and their offspring were totally unaccountable are over, and the Prince of Wales's Duchy accounts are now carefully presented in order to gloss over the fact that he does so well financially from a public source. Soothing public relations language seeks to explain how a man with no real defined job and a multi-million pound income could claim to be conducting an almost frugal lifestyle. By the time of his marriage to Camilla Parker-Bowles in 2005, Prince Charles was well advanced in his long-term 'election' campaign for acceptance as the future King. His charitable works had by now been expertly honed as an established institutional shield with which to excuse his wealth and privilege. Those who dare to criticise him tend to be accused of envy and churlishness – and for failing to appreciate his charitable efforts. How could anyone possibly doubt the good intentions of a man by now slickly restyled as the nation's leading 'charitable entrepreneur'?

After her Golden Jubilee in 2002 the Queen was beginning to scale back some of her appointments and Charles was assuming some of these duties as well as, it seemed, some of the more constitutionally important work. On an official level, too, this also makes for potential conflicts as the heir assumes some of the monarch's duties yet retains the privileges of his vague and unstructured role as heir. In most organisations this kind of 're-structuring' might well be matched by a review of the financial picture. Not so with the British monarchy. This was a form of 'retirement', but on full pay. The Queen was, by 2007, doing progressively less and yet this was not really being reflected in the money the monarchy was consuming. By 2012, the Queen's Diamond Jubilee year, little had changed, with the monarch and her ninety-one year old husband determined to keep the show on the road, though with a further general scaling-down of their commitments.

OFFICIAL GOVERNMENT EXPENDITURE ON THE MONARCHY

(£ million)	2012	2011	2010	2009	2008	2007
Queen's Civil List*	13.6	13.7	14.2	13.9	12.7	12.2
Parliamentary annuities†	0.4	0.4	0.4	0.4	0.4	0.4
Grants in aid‡	18.7	18.4	19.7	24.1	22.6	20.6
Expenditure met directly from Govt. departments and Crown Estates§	?§	?§	?§	4.6	4.9	4.8
Total (£ million)	**32.7** (37.5)§	**32.5** (37.3)§	**34.3** (39.1)§	**43.0**	**40.6**	**38**

*This figure is a combination of the £7.9million Civil List level set by Parliament to which is then added the amount of 'Draw-down' from the Civil List Reserve, which had been accumulated as a result of the high allowance for inflation originally allowed for when the amount was last reviewed in 1990.

†Parliamentary annuity (£359,000) paid directly by Parliament to the Duke of Edinburgh.

‡Royal travel expenses by air and rail and the cost of maintaining the 'Occupied' royal palaces. To this figure, in more recent years, has been added a separate category, that of 'Communications and Information', to include such items as the cost of the Palace Press Office, and the increasingly sophisticated royal websites – as well as running the royal Facebook pages and Twitter.

§Curiously, recent financial statements have omitted this figure – hence the '?'. Therefore, for the purposes of comparison, a notional figure of £4.8million has been added (a rounded average of the preceding three years) to provide the alternative figures cited in parentheses below the officially quoted figure, and which constitutes the 'real' figure rather than the 'official' one. Such payments have been maintained, it is just that it has now been decided to exclude them from the recent figures. The explanation provided in the 2010/11 accounts is rather odd: 'In previous years, Head of State expenditure met from Public Funds was presented in this report, which included expenditure met directly by Government Departments and the Crown Estates. This expenditure is not under the direct control of the Royal Household and has been excluded from this report this year in order to *align the presentation* [Author's italics] with that which will be adopted in the future for the Sovereign Grant'.

This means that such expenditure is still being made, but it seems to have been dropped for what are no more than stylistic reasons – ie: to make the figures look better. The money may not be under the Royal Household's 'direct control' but they certainly still get it. A cynic might think that they dropped it in order to stop the figures from looking any bigger than they already are. After all, a quick glance is enough to see that the Royal Household is getting through more money year on year, principally by emptying the Civil List Reserve before the new Sovereign Grant comes into operation in 2013. This money was overpaid years ago – they didn't need it as inflation was low, but now they're taking it anyway. So, in future, this 'other money from government departments, etc.' will still be being paid but we'll probably have to get a Parliamentary question to elicit it – and of course that means it will appear relatively un-noticed and separate from the main announcement of the royal accounts – so nobody will notice it…

In case you are wondering what those 'other payments' actually are, it covers the cost of the administration of the honours system, the cost of royal Equerries (upscale mid-ranking 'flunkeys' on loan from the military to accompany senior royals), orderlies and 'other support', plus the cost of ceremonial occasions, maintaining Holyroodhouse Palace in Edinburgh (the Queen's official Scottish residence), and payments towards some of the Queen's overseas visits (Diplomatic Corps costs, etc).

THE NEW VERSION – THE SOVEREIGN GRANT – FROM 2013:

(£ million)	2014	2013
Sovereign grant	36	31
Security	100	100
Combined Duchy profits	33 (est.)	32 (est.)
Parliamentary annuity (Duke of Edinburgh)	0.4	0.4
Costs met directly by Crown Estates and government departments)	4.8 (est.)	4.8 (*est.)
Total (£ million)	**174.2**	**168.2**

NB: As the Grant is set as equivalent to 15% of Crown Estates profits two years back, the figure for 2014 will be equivalent to 15% of the 2012 Crown Estates profits figure, and so on, and the Sovereign Grant will therefore increase accordingly, year on year. *see proviso above re 'presentational alignment'.

2 MONEY AND THE MONARCHY

The latest Crown Estates profits were released in late June 2012 – a 16% increase, thus enabling us to judge the rate of increase in the Sovereign Grant – giving a 'bare' Sovereign Grant figure of £36million for 2014. At this rate, Parliament may feel it necessary to question the 15% 'yardstick' of the Crown Estates profits. The Crown Estates are really State property, and given the considerable growth in exploitation of offshore mineral extraction and the sale of offshore windfarm licences, is the state simply handing over too much to the monarchy for their expense account? The above figures also include very conservative rates of increase in other elements, from Duchy profits and the secret 'security' costs, the latter for instance not having been uprated by critics in estimates for some time. If the Sovereign Grant is seen to increase too fast, perhaps this may prompt Parliament to review this percentage 'benchmark' sooner rather than later.

EARNINGS OR EXPENSES?

The first and most fundamental error that is made is to regard the annual Civil List payment made to the monarch – £14.2million in 2010, for example – as income. It is not an income, but is a payment made to cover the expense of carrying out the official duties of the monarch. However, given the grandiose style of Britain's monarchy and despite a surplus in recent years, the current Civil List payment is regarded by the Palace as insufficient to meet the full extent of its commitments.

The fact that a surplus has built up – the Civil List Reserve – a result of past over-generous inflation-proofing provisions – and part of this is used each year to boost the basic Civil List figure, tends to suggest that the monarchy as a whole has tended to stretch its spending to meet available income. However – and this is a fundamental failing with the new Sovereign Grant Act – nobody has ever stopped to ask what the monarchy should actually be doing. It is always easy to claim to be 'financially overstretched' by the simple of expedient of failing to match one's activities to one's budget. Also, the fact that the Royal Household has been able to tap the Reserve itself has reflected the generally 'hands-off' climate of official Government accountability that has prevailed, though the Sovereign Grant Act now addresses this situation.

However, more generally, if the monarchy costs so much to do so much, the logical alternative is to save considerable sums simply by doing rather less – and in a less lavish fashion. Of course any head of state – hereditary or elected – is going to cost money, and a republican system would have its Civil List equivalent. However, given the cultural baggage which accompanies hereditary monarchs when compared to their elected presidential equivalents, nations feel, to a lesser or greater degree, the need to treat those who inherit the position of head of state rather more lavishly. Whatever the reason – and deep-seated cultural hard-wiring is no doubt at the base of it all, one significant aspect may be the feeling that national self-esteem is projected via the wealth and status of a nation's monarch. This does not apply to presidents of democratic western powers – we will ignore those from systems with little if any connection to democracy – we seem to manage happily with men and women on generally modest salaries who, whilst they might enjoy an exalted lifestyle whilst in office, return to something approaching 'normality' once they leave it, and certainly do not inherit wealth from it. For the UK monarch and heir, it seems necessary to pile on wealth, generation upon generation. It seems illogical, inefficient – and grossly extravagant.

The cost of the monarchy does not, of course, stop at the Civil List figure itself. Many additional payments are required to keep it operating in the manner to which it has become accustomed. The overall official figure given as being the 'cost' of the monarchy in 2006-7, for example, was £38million, which is the Civil List figure plus the 'Grants-in-aid' paid by the Government to cover the expenses of maintaining and operating the Royal Palaces and travel by air and rail. The 2007/8 figure was £40million, and with minor fluctuations the annual figure has for some years approximated to this amount. Grant-in-aid for the palaces covers those classed as being 'Occupied', that is, being used on a day to day basis by the monarch or heir to the throne as official residences.

GRANTS-IN-AID

A typical breakdown of Grant-in aid payments made to the Royal Household in recent years is as follows:

(£ million)	2012	2011	2010	2009	2008	2007
Property Services*	12.2	11.9	15.4	16.1	15.7	14.5
Royal Travel†	6.1	6.0	3.9	7.4	6.4	5.6
Communication and Information	0.4	0.5	0.4	0.6	0.5	0.5
Total (£ million)	**18.7**	**18.4**	**19.7**	**24.1**	**22.6**	**20.6**

*This is the cost of maintaining and servicing the 'Occupied' Royal Palaces

†Royal Travel by air and rail. Travel by car is paid for out of the Civil List budget. These figures are taken from the Royal accounts summaries – slight variations may occur due to subsequent following year corrections, or 'rounding up' in summaries – eg. Royal Travel for 2007 has also been stated as being '6.0'

Money is given to the Royal Household to spend rather than simply providing appropriate premises maintained directly at public expense. This state of affairs is curious. The Crown Estates exists to maintain all other similar state property – with the anomalous exception of the Duchies of Cornwall and Lancaster – and they would be the obvious body to assume responsibility rather than to delegate it to the Royal Household, and even the Sovereign Grant Act has allowed this situation to persist. When Royal Palaces are not being used officially – the official term 'Unoccupied' is used – they become the responsibility of the Historic Royal Palaces Trust, a charitable body which is alleged to cost the taxpayer nothing. This is however, disingenuous. In practice it can be little more than a temporary 'mothballing' role for those buildings which it does not open to the public long-term. Costly works can be held over until the properties are 'Occupied' and the taxpayer can pick up the tab – as for instance in the case of Clarence House. The inefficiency of this arrangement is clearly evident. There is also a clear matter of principle. If these are demonstrably state properties, which are by implication deemed valuable to the nation, then the nation should undertake the full responsibility for them on a continuous basis. Whilst the Sovereign Grant Act does now transfer responsibility for Palace maintenance to the Royal Household, there is no question that, ultimately, it is the State with whom the buck ultimately stops.

Unification of the administration of 'Occupied' and 'Unoccupied' Palaces would make for a more efficient use of public resources. The only loser in the arrangement would be the Royal Household itself which is able to exercise a degree of autonomy in respect of how this public money is spent. More importantly, perhaps, it also provides the Palace with a significant element of 'sympathy leverage', with tales of falling roof tiles being 'spun' to claim financial penury – and by definition a claim that they are not 'wealthy'. Scrutiny and accountability are still held at arm's length by the present arrangement. It also helps enable the fiction to persist that the monarchy is not spending taxpayer's money directly on the properties they occupy – and they also thereby get to feel they are still 'in charge' and not that annoying democratic upstart, Parliament.

SECURITY – HOW MUCH?...CAN'T TELL YOU – IT'S A SECRET...

'Security' costs are extra. The perennially secretive nature of the British system means that no figure is ever announced. Some costs of military 'support' and 'ceremonial' attendance are however released, but are so small as to fail to convince even a casual examiner that they really convey a true impression of the real figure – if indeed anyone has ever wanted, or actually could, in such a secretive climate, ever assess the true situation. Educated speculation in the past has put the overall security figure at around £28-30million[7]. Given inflation, expensive new technology and the heightened security regime necessitated by the current national and international climate, in particular the events on and following September 11th 2001, the estimated figure of £35million for the early 1990s would clearly seem to be decidedly insufficient, and figures of up to £100million have now been suggested. A former royal security chief let it be known that the real figure in the distant days when Diana, Princess of Wales was the Palace's responsibility was around £50million, so £100million would now seem pretty accurate. Indeed, as time goes by, it may perhaps now be becoming rather an under-estimate. The independent roles of Princes William and Harry can only have increased the figures in question, not to mention the increased independent lives of Princesses Beatrice and Eugenie, for example – especially with their father recently pushing for quasi-official 'roles' for them, and the consequent need for tax-payer funded security. Others benefit too. When 'non-royal' (that's the impression always given) Zara Phillips married rugby player Mike Tindall, 'security' cost the taxpayer around £400,000. One hundred million pounds a year is a lot, but now seems a very reasonable estimate. While operational details need to be confidential, the justification for such obsessive secrecy is unconvincing. If the estimates are disputed, it is for the government to reveal the truth to the public.

It is interesting to note that the official 'explanation' to be found in the royal accounts is that 'Head of State expenditure excludes the cost of Police and Army security and of Armed Forces ceremonial as figures are not available'. 'Not available', is how simply and succinctly the secretive British system phrases its perennially secretive attitude to the monarchy. While Freedom of Information applications have thrown small glimpses of light into this twilight world, remember that the monarchy is exempt from the requirements of Freedom of Information legislation. In other words, they can let you know what, and how much, if *they* want to reveal anything, but not if you want them to. The taxpayer pays heavily into the mystery security 'pot', and should be entitled to know exactly how much goes into it.

The fact that the cost of the monarchy's security also covers members of the extended royal family means that it is possible for the bill to spiral enormously. The cost of providing both security hardware and a round-the-clock security presence for a large number of individuals and their families – not only in respect of their official residences but also in their many private homes, and whilst travelling – means that this cost has an elastic nature that can stretch almost infinitely. In July 2006 it was revealed that the taxpayer would be meeting a bill estimated at nearly £2million simply to provide 'security measures' – including the construction of a bungalow to house royal protection officers – at an occasionally used residence of the Prince of Wales' wife, the Duchess of Cornwall, at Lacock in Gloucestershire. Apparently needed by the Duchess 'to escape the pressures of royal life', it is hard to see why the taxpayer should be required to pay either the capital cost of the work or the ongoing cost of maintaining a police presence there. It could reasonably be argued that any security cost incurred in respect of those other than official members of the royal family whilst on their official duties should be borne separately on a private basis by those individuals themselves.

Security is provided by the Police and the military and is thus apportioned between the Home Office, the Ministry of Defence and council tax-payers of individual Police Authorities. The contribution of council taxpayers in areas in which there is a particularly high regular royal presence, such as Gloucestershire and Norfolk, can be considerable. Whilst the royal family own many residences privately – eg Sandringham, Balmoral, etc., the taxpayer also pays a contribution for the 'use' of these properties when the Queen is 'working from home'.

As for glitzy public events, from weddings to funerals, though 'carriage processions' are listed – at a seemingly very reasonable £69,000 for 2003, for instance – the cost of the enormous contribution made by 'Armed Services Ceremonial', is omitted. A figure of £77,818 was released by the Ministry of Defence (See Appendix) in respect of MoD costs incurred, including aircraft 'flypasts' for Prince William's wedding in 2011. Such figures do seem rather low. The MoD are keen to emphasise that their personnel were already conveniently 'in the area', so no extra cost was incurred in getting them to the London. 'Security' was provided through the Home Office, and not disclosed. Overall, a general lack of transparency and the rather selective figures that are quoted leads one to suspect that the total could be very high indeed. This no doubt suits the Palace too. No wonder, for instance, that the Queen was keen to give her late mother a State Funeral. Without its public 'State' label the event would have been an expensive one indeed for the Windsor family.

OTHER COSTS...

To these figures must be added the profits of the Duchies of Cornwall and Lancaster. For the year 2012, that of the former amounted to £18.3million and the latter £12.9million, a total of £31.2million. As the only remaining Crown Estates properties not surrendered by the monarchy in return for the Civil List in 1760, only their profits are available to the monarch and heir to the throne and they have no access to the capital held therein. On this basis, the income from what are state assets – this matter will be examined in depth later in this book – is foregone by the state so can be regarded as yet another cost of the monarchy.

2 MONEY AND THE MONARCHY

Whilst there should be a clearer dividing line between the 'private' and 'public' life of the monarch, there is still likely to be a 'blurring' of the duties of Royal Household staff. This is evident, for instance, when a sizeable proportion of the official Palace staff decamp – at public expense – to accompany the Queen on her holidays. There are likely to be personal aspects of the Household's duties which 'overlap' with public aspects. The royal role and lifestyle inevitably leads to a diffculty in clearly separating the two aspects. Far greater transparency is necessary.

THE REAL ANNUAL COST OF THE MONARCHY

The failure to combine the various declared – and undeclared – costs of the monarchy means that the 'official' figure which is always quoted is very far from the reality. Selectively, the Civil List and Grants-in-aid figures are combined to produce the 'official' version, which taking an average of the five year's figures in the period 2006-2010, for example, gives a figure of £39million a year. This is the origin of the Palace's popular claim made that the annual cost per capita of the institution approximates to 'the price of a loaf of bread'. Not merely rather disingenuous, it is also, quite simply, not true. To the quoted figure must be added the 'secret' security costs, regarded as approximately £100million per year. In addition, the combined incomes paid to the monarch and heir to the throne from the profits of the Duchies of Lancaster and Cornwall – unincorporated Crown (State) bodies, that can really be regarded as constituting part of the Crown Estates but are not included as such, are lost to the Exchequer – a combined sum of £31million in 2011.

	(£million)
Civil List plus Grants-in-aid*	39
Security	100
Combined Duchy profits	31.2
Parliamentary Annuity (paid directly to Duke of Edinburgh)	0.4
Costs met directly by Crown Estates and government departments	4.8
Total	**175.4**

*The example given is annual average of 2006-10 period. From 2013 this will be replaced by the Sovereign Grant, equating to 15% of the Crown Estates profits for the year 2011. The

> figure for 2013 has already been set at £31million. It is not known if other miscellaneous costs usually paid directly by government departments and the Crown Estates, normally averaging around £4.8million a year, and separately accounted for until 2009, will be included. As is suggested above, these will still be paid but have been dropped in the last couple of years in order to 'align the presentation' with the new system. For this reason, a separate £4.8million has been added to the estimates to restore consistency.

The UK campaign group 'Republic' (www.republic.org.uk) quotes a total cost estimate of the monarchy as being £202.4million – this figure includes an element of costs to local councils occasioned by royal visits amounting to £26million. Whilst councils do undoubtedly suddenly find cash to smarten up venues just before a royal visit, much of this cost is likely to be that of policing rather than pots of paint, most of it met by the local police authorities rather than the Metropolitan Police or Ministry of Defence. If so, then strictly this ought perhaps be regarded as forming part of the mysterious 'security' budget. The reality is that the perennial secretive nature of the UK system means that such figures are speculative, but they are not officially challenged as such and derive from many years of close and informed observation.

IT ALL ADDS UP…
Nor should the ability of the royal family almost unilaterally to impose further considerable cost on the nation be underestimated. The 2011 royal wedding was an expensive event for a nation in the depths of recession. According to a report by accountants RSM Tenon, the effect of the combined public holidays in the Easter period which included the one-off public holiday for the royal wedding, could have cost the economy up to £30billion. The Confederation of British Industry reckoned the cost of the extra Bank holiday at up to £6billion. For Andrew Cave, head of policy at the Federation of Small Businesses, it was 'a cost added to businesses at a time when they are already struggling'[8]. The government's Department for Business, Innovation and Skills had put the figure at only £2.9billion. Economic figures later in the year tended to back up the CBI's larger estimate.

TOTAL COST INCLUDING IMPOSED COSTS OF ROYAL PUBLIC HOLIDAYS

	(£ million)
Cost to economy of royal public holiday every ten years on annualised basis	300*
Annual cost of monarchy	175.4
Total cost of monarchy on annual basis	**475+**

*If we estimate the cost to the economy of a single 'royal jubilee-style' Bank holiday at a minimum of £5billion, using a figure estimated by the employer's organisation the CBI government's Department of Business, Innovations and Skills, then, for the sake of argument, reduce it by the estimated benefit to the economy of around £2billion, that leaves a £3billion cost. Assuming a royal wedding, Jubilee, or whatever, every ten years, then we are looking at an averaged £300million cost to the UK economy every year. If we then take our already estimated £175million annual figure of the cost of the monarchy, add the above costs to the economy, we're then looking at a total annual cost of over £475million a year. This calculation is, by its nature, very approximate. The figure will also be significantly boosted if 'royal' public holidays are declared more than once every ten years – eg. the 2011 royal wedding was followed a year later by the Diamond Jubilee.

Such analysis might be regarded as overly cynical – ignoring the rather more intangible supposed benefits, and the figures are admittedly only estimates, but it is necessary if we are to build up a broader picture. It is always alleged that the monarchy is 'good for tourism', bringing visitors to the UK who might not otherwise turn up. This has always been a rather vague assertion, after all visitors aren't really expecting to see the Queen unless they arrive specifically to see a scheduled public royal event – and are in any case very, very unlikely to do so. Let us not also forget the many who left the country to 'escape' the Diamond Jubilee, for example, and spent their money abroad, not within the UK. Overall, any benefit to tourism expressly attributable to the monarchy is realistically almost impossible to quantify – for or against. The only time people are allowed to visit Buckingham Palace is in the short period in the summer when the Queen isn't there anyway. Official tourist industry data has in the past acknowledged that the weather and prevailing currency exchange rates are far more influential in luring visitors to the UK – not the monarchy. So far, in just over the last decade, we've had a Golden Jubilee, a royal wedding and a Diamond Jubilee too. That won't exactly help our economic performance in bad economic times, both at the present and going forwards. Monarchist spin merchants might reinterpret the figures to suggest that the monarchy costs roughly what it earns, and thus breaks even, but then their institution undoes all its allegedly good work by dragging the UK economy down on a regular basis by holding a massive national party.

...AND FURTHER COSTS

Leaving aside the costs imposed by the institution versus any claimed tourist benefits, we can see that the real cost of the monarchy is thus likely to be well in excess of £175million (and excluding imposed public holiday costs noted above), to this can also be added the lost income from the present under-utilisation of state assets with restricted or zero access which are effectively controlled by the Royal Household. For example, a mere fraction of the Royal Collection – artworks and other treasures 'held' by the Queen on behalf of the nation – is available to the public, and represents a national asset that is greatly under-exploited. The process of policy and administration of this vast and valuable collection is far from transparent and properly accountable. Some Crown Estate properties are currently rented on extremely favourable terms by members of the royal family, and though they are increasingly required to match market rates their occupation of these properties precludes more commercially favourable use of benefit to the nation as a whole – or their outright disposal. Add to all this the extremely favourable tax regime enjoyed by the monarch and the heir to the throne – and any 'Consorts of a former Sovereign' – then the additional lost income to the Exchequer could be considerable indeed.

2 MONEY AND THE MONARCHY

THE QUEEN'S OFFICIAL INCOME

The Queen's official income, which she receives in respect of her position as monarch – and excluding the proceeds of her own very extensive private wealth – derives from the profit produced annually by the Duchy of Lancaster, technically payable to the Queen in her position as 'Duke of Lancaster', a title traditionally assumed on becoming monarch. The Duchy is a combination of landed estates and investments – and as such forms a substantial portfolio producing a very considerable annual income for the Queen. As with the Duchy of Cornwall, a convenient degree of vagueness has been encouraged as to the exact legal status of the Duchy of Lancaster. This suits the present poor level of accountability for what are state properties. (See Chapter 3: 'Nice Little Earners – The Two Duchies')

Ultimately, the Duchy is public (state) property. This is clearly demonstrated by fact that it was, as a result of the Crown Lands Act of 1702, specifically prevented from being sold, either whole or in part, by the monarch themselves. The income it produces is allocated to the monarch, although Parliament is entirely at liberty to vary or end the arrangement. The 'trust' nature of the arrangement is thus entirely in the gift of Parliament which acts in effect as trustee. The detailed regulation of the Duchy is governed by a number of specific Acts of Parliament – by which, for example, subject to the Duchy of Lancaster Lands Act 1855 and the Duchy of Lancaster Act 1988, it is now possible for land to be bought and sold and long leases granted – 'adjustments' – notwithstanding the basic principle that the assets of the Duchy are as such 'inalienable', that is, they may not be disposed of. Investment transactions of land already owned by the Duchy were, and still are, governed by the Duchy of Lancaster Act 1817. Financial assets held by the Duchy are covered by the Trustee Act 2000.

The Duchy of Lancaster had a current total asset valuation of £347,142,000 in 2006, an increase on that of the previous year's figure of £310,252,000. (Duchy of Lancaster 2006 – Report and Accounts of the Duchy of Lancaster for the year ended March 31st 2006) – and considerably more today; by 2012 it was valued at £405,340,000. Some commentators, such as Kevin Cahill, author of *Who Owns Britain*, feel that these figures, as with those for the Duchy of Cornwall, considerably underestimate the true value. The estate produced a total 'surplus' – the

> word 'profit' is deemed rather too unseemly when discussing such regal matters – of £10,628,000 in 2006, of which £10,469,000 was paid to the Queen. In 2007 she received £11,627,000, a healthy rise of over 10% – and by 2011 the amount had leapt to £13,382,000. This very considerable income (whilst it may be taxed, as the Palace are so keen to remind us – but only on a voluntary basis), is hers to do with as she wishes.

Since 1993, the Queen has been required to reimburse Parliament in respect of the assorted 'Parliamentary Allowances', in effect the 'official incomes' – but excluding their official expenses – of the various assorted royal children and other members of the family who act in an 'official' capacity. This, by the way, is the basis for the claim that some of the Duchy income meets certain 'official' expenses. Often 'spun' as an act of personal generosity – or even noble sacrifice – it was a recognition by the Government at the time that to go on supporting the various 'hangers-on' out of taxpayers' money could no longer to be tolerated, and the Palace had no choice but to agree. Whether the Queen pays for her offspring is now really a personal matter, and thankfully the Sovereign Grant Act has at last recognised this. Curiously, the 2007-08 Civil List Annual Report Summary, noted that the Duchy of Lancaster income that it is 'largely used to meet official expenditure', but no further detail was forthcoming. If it were true, then the Palace should reveal upon what 'official' items all these millions were spent. Despite the bland assertion that the Duchies accounts being 'published and laid before Parliament' each year, there is no breakdown of this alleged 'official' spending out of the Duchy income. When one is Queen, it is easy to claim that almost anything one does is 'official'.

Excluded from this arrangement is the Prince of Wales who gains his principal income from the 'surplus' – or profits – of the Duchy of Cornwall, and the Duke of Edinburgh, who gets paid a handsome 'annuity' direct from Parliament simply for being married to the Queen. 'The 2008 Civil List summary pointed out that the Duke's 'annuity' was intended to pay for his 'official duties'. However, this seems to be a recent re-interpretation, his duties are fewer, and, in any case, there is no proper audit. If the Duke does incur official costs, then let us see what they are – after all, we are ultimately paying the bills. The tenuous basis for this act of public generosity dates back to 1947, when it was regarded that Prince Philip's position would automatically preclude him from making a living in his own right, but is in reality simply a hangover from a previous age. Additional money was also granted as he had no 'private wealth' in his own right. The money, naturally, came from the long-suffering British taxpayer who, in the late 1940s and early 1950s, was still enduring post-war privations and rationing. The Queen was also not required to reimburse the considerable tax-free annual sum granted to the late Queen Mother, which in her latter years amounted to £648,000 a year.

Like the Duchy of Cornwall, the Duchy of Lancaster, as an unincorporated Crown body, pays no tax itself. Thus the profits which constitute the Queen's income are in turn advantageously boosted. Further advantage is gained from the ability to deduct the cost of unspecified 'official' expenses before the payment of tax. The change by which the Queen had to reimburse Parliament for allowances to her family was (and might still be) mitigated by the probably tax-deductible nature of these payments. The sum of £1,244,000 – less than a tenth of her annual Duchy income – could thus be ultimately reduced in its impact. The Queen's 'generosity' in agreeing to reimburse those allowances was not therefore quite as generous as originally suggested and still might now cost her less than might be thought – assuming she is almost certainly bankrolling her children (excluding Charles with his Duchy income, one assumes) to a lesser – or more probably greater degree.

A degree of 'overlap' between public and private life means that a benefit is almost certainly derived from payments made from public sources. The Queen's own personal wealth has accumulated appreciably for over half a century, helped greatly by her exemption from income tax – and tax on her investments as well, for by far the greater part of her reign[9]. The Queen met the cost of the Prince of Wales' divorce settlement – estimated at £17million – as despite his income from the Duchy of Cornwall, and his own personal assets, he seemed to have no ready cash with which to pay his ex-wife. It is also likely that some of the high property costs incurred by the Duke of York and the Earl of Wessex in recent years have been similarly reimbursed through this route. For a senior public figure, whether monarch or not, an income on this level, is simply grossly excessive.

THE CIVIL LIST – AND THE CIVIL LIST RESERVE

This has, until the Sovereign Grant Act comes into force in 2013, and replaces it by the Sovereign Support Grant, met the cost of performing the monarch's official duties, though of course to the Civil List figure itself must be added the Grants-in-aid. The Support Grant will, on the basis of its being equivalent to 15% of Crown Estates annual profits, be approximately the same as the current combined Civil List and Grants-in-aid. It is set according to the Crown Estates profits of two years previously – so the 2013 allocation, already set at £31million, will be based on the 2011 financial year, and so on. The Civil List was set in 1990 at £7.9million per year but expenditure averaged £6.5million a year in the ten-year period to the end of December 2000. This is due to an allowance being made for higher than ultimately realised levels of inflation. As a result, rather than simply renegotiating a more appropriate rate and returning the surplus to the Exchequer, an excess was allowed to accumulate, which has become known as the Civil List Reserve. Instead of being allowed merely to remain 'ring-fenced', or even returned to the Exchequer, a practice evolved whereby the Palace was able to have access to this fund. The Reserve stood at some £32.2million in 2006, and since 2001, the demands on the Civil List have increased, or, to put it another way, costs have been insufficiently reduced, and the Palace has begun to 'draw down' on this reserve. By 2007, it had fallen to £26million, down from £29.4 the previous year. In the words of the Civil List 2004-5, 'Since the transfer of additional expenditure to the Civil List with effect from 1st April 2001 Civil List expenditure exceeds the annual £7.9million payment and amounts have been withdrawn ('drawn-down') from the reserve each year rather than paid into it'[10]. Curiously, this all comes at a time when the Queen is reducing her duties considerably in reflection of her increasing age.

The Palace do not specify the exact reason for the need for this increased expenditure, and this somewhat lax approach to royal finance has been aided and abetted by the lengthy ten-year periods – rather than on an annual basis – when the Palace has 'reported' to Parliament. Critics are kept at bay with brief annual accounts, thus limiting the opportunity for Parliament to examine royal financial matters. The Palace itself considered these ten-yearly 'reports' to be 'more consistent with the honour and dignity of the Crown'[11]. This is a somewhat genteel way of saying that they were uncomfortable with searching questions relating to royal finances being asked too frequently.

2 MONEY AND THE MONARCHY

Rather than trimming the royal budget – overall already the largest in Europe – to meet available funds, the Palace has simply resorted to a regular pillaging of the Civil List Reserve 'piggy bank'. By 2010, the amount remaining was just £9.7million, down from £15.2million in 2009. It is highly likely that the taking of increasingly large amounts in the last couple of years has been simply that they knew the likely form of the new arrangement of the Sovereign Grant, and have thus been raiding the china pig, with the government's tacit approval, to make sure that all the remaining cash is spent by 2013.

When the Queen succeeded to the throne in 1952, the Civil List Act of that year set her remuneration. The Palace was forced to approach Parliament for an upgrading of this arrangement in 1972 as a result of the erosion of their financial position by a long period of high inflation. This accounted for the need for the Civil List Act of 1972, and another Act soon after in 1975.

The Civil List Reserve had become a handy 'buffer' against the need for the Palace to re-apply to Parliament on a more frequent basis for additional monies and, inevitably face demands from MPs to know exactly why so much more money is needed. The 'draw-down' – another of those rather quaint terms – for 2007 was expected to be £5.3million, a very considerable amount indeed. Such a practice allowed the Palace to exceed their budget and to then cover the overspend by dipping into the Reserve. The fundamental question as to whether the Palace's extra expenditure was in fact genuinely justified therefore escaped proper debate. The Sovereign Grant Act alters the position by applying a greater degree of scrutiny and in effect capping any excessive build-up in the manner which had occurred in the past. The inherent wish of most governments to avoid debates on royal finances at the best of times means that events, and the parliamentary timetable, can usually be tailored to restrict time available to avoid any likely criticism. Current arrangements tend to be simply left in place, relatively unaltered, for as long as possible. The hope is that the Sovereign Grant Act will improve matters.

'PIMPING ONE'S CIRCUMSTANCE'

At least the monarch can now no longer benefit in the outrageous fashion permitted in the past by the use of accumulated surpluses built up from Civil List money. As Phillip Hall notes, such savings made by the monarchy in the past have enabled them to profit very handsomely as a result. Most notably, Queen Victoria and her husband, Prince Albert, who himself carried out much of the negotiations, repeatedly pleaded poverty yet accrued very considerable savings through the Civil List. It is thanks to the lack of proper accountability at this time that the present monarchy have reason to be extremely grateful. Queen Victoria originally purchased the Balmoral, Sandringham and Osborne estates using money 'saved' from the official Civil List. The Queen's grandfather, George V, was also able to accumulate money from the Civil List, and a proportion of this was devoted to the acquisition of further land for the Sandringham estate. The estates at Sandringham – with an estimated value of at least £100million in 2001[12], (likely to have been an undervaluation then and vastly more today) – and those at Balmoral, are effectively large businesses in their own right and able to generate considerable income in respect of their commercial agricultural operation as well as, for example, the sale of shooting rights and visitor revenue.

Such practices would be totally unacceptable today, yet the royal family continue to benefit from them. Together with a generally very indulgent tax regime, it has enabled the Windsor family to develop its large fortune. This latter aspect, most notably in respect of the exemption from inheritance tax, enables the 'private' royal estates to be passed on undiminished when the intention of the exemption is really designed to prevent erosion of what are more properly the official 'State' assets such as the Royal Collection which are 'held' by the monarch on behalf of the nation in their public role.

This is a clear example of the need to properly differentiate the royal family's 'public' and 'private' lives. Were the monarchy to one day be replaced by an elected head of state, these facts should not be forgotten when ultimately apportioning assets. The process is not helped by the historic practice of setting the Civil List at the outset of a new monarch's reign – and no doubt when all concerned are mourning the sad loss of the new monarch's recently deceased predecessor. This pervading air of sympathy probably means that a fairly lenient atmosphere tends to prevail and so the opportunity to set in place a more realistic arrangement is lost. There is absolutely no logical reason why a more frequent review period would not be more appropriate. Sadly, the Sovereign Grant Act arrangement sets a kind of 'rolling' arrangement in place and now any review would probably have to be triggered by particular – and possibly rather exceptional – political or economic circumstances in which it would be deemed necessary to press for alteration of the percentage benchmark figure of 15% of Crown Estates annual profits.

2 MONEY AND THE MONARCHY

THE CROWN ESTATES INCOME 'SURRENDER' MYTH

It has often been claimed that the Civil List is in fact a generous 'sacrifice' in return for giving up the income from the Crown Estates. This argument is misleading. The original deal struck in 1760 sprang from the reality that the monarchy – by then subordinate to Parliament – could not, and indeed should not, bear the costs of such institutions as the judiciary and the Civil Service.

It was a recognition of the fact that the monarchy could not – and indeed should not, for constitutional reasons – any longer be required to shoulder the burden of running a rapidly growing and more complex civil administration. The Civil List arrangement made the monarchy accountable to Parliament, and the idea that the modern monarchy would bear an annual cost estimated at many, many billions of pounds today – the expense of operating the Civil Service, judiciary, etc – is blatantly absurd. The sum supposedly 'surrendered' – the 'net revenue surplus' of the Crown Estates – was £230million in 2010[13].

The persistence of the 'surrender myth' simply fails to take into account the fundamental changes that have taken place in the nature of government and the constitution in the succeeding centuries since the 1760 Act. The monarchy is no longer involved in the day to day business of government in the way it was in the eighteenth century. However, this did not stop the Prince of Wales from suggesting in 1994 that the royal family might be financed by reverting to this old arrangement. Ardent monarchists often suggest that because of the claimed 'surrender' of the Crown Estates income the monarchy somehow pays for itself many times over and that the taxpayer should in no way begrudge the considerable cost of the institution.

To persist in maintaining such a pretence simply reinforces an outdated notion of the monarchy's position in the constitution that is demonstrably out of touch with the present-day reality. The 'formality' of the 'surrendering' of the Crown Estates income in return for the payment of the Civil List at the outset of a monarch's reign has become, as Phillip Hall emphatically asserted in his book, just that, simply a formality. Official Palace literature tends to present a rather 'gracious' version of history and in the definitions used when dealing in particular with financial matters. Uncomfortable aspects of British history, breaks in the so-called 'continuity', or the development of democracy and accountability tend to be glossed over. No doubt in an attempt to preserve royal 'dignity' and 'honour' this approach also persists in the portrayal of royal 'sacrifice' with regard to the so-called 'surrender' of Crown Estates income at the outset of each reign:

> Before 1760 the expenses incurred by the Sovereign and Royal Household to enable the Monarch to fulfil his or her official duties were met from the income from the Crown Estate and from other hereditary revenues, supplemented increasingly by customs and excise duties and general taxation voted by Parliament. Under the new arrangement the income from the Crown Estate and other hereditary revenues was surrendered to Parliament by the Sovereign for the duration of the reign in return for the payment of a fixed annual Civil List[14].

It should be noted that the Sovereign Grant Act effectively sets in place a percentage of the Crown Estates revenue (15% at present, set two years back) as an assessment benchmark for setting the annual Sovereign Grant. It does not allocate that figure directly from those revenues, so there is no 'ring-fencing' of any Crown Estates revenues as such. There is, however, a sense that the government fell victim in the negotiation process – in which the Prince of Wales was closely involved and consulted – to a version of the principle of his long-held opinion that the monarchy should be financed from the Crown Estates profits. Indeed, he has long maintained that he feels the monarchy should get *all* of the money, not just a percentage equivalent.

ATTITUDE AND PRESENTATION...

It is indicative of the Palace's mindset that it refers above to '*the new arrangement*' – i.e. that dating from 1760. In any case, the concept of 'usage' means that it can be reasonably assumed that, over the course of nearly 250 years of such practice, that a clear precedent has now been established for the 'surrender' of the Crown Estate income. The token act of 'surrender' is now little more than a Ruritanian pantomime act redolent of the theatrical behaviour surrounding that of 'Black Rod' and the Speaker at the opening of a new Parliament. A written constitution would help to clarify areas in which crucial aspects of our constitution are camouflaged and confused by 'precedent' and flummery. What is perhaps most important is that Britain is

2 MONEY AND THE MONARCHY

a parliamentary democracy in which Parliament is supreme, yet no mention of 'parliamentary democracy' – within the context of which the monarchy now operates – is to be found in their literature.

The last few years have seen the monarchy's annual accounts presented in such a way as to appear almost trivial – quoted on a 'per capita' basis – so that the cost 'per subject' is no more then cost of 'a loaf of bread' or 'a couple of pints of milk'. Apart from the fact that the sum quoted excludes a very large proportion of the real cost, this almost insultingly simplistic and patronising approach has evolved as the degree of criticism of the royal family's privileged lifestyle has increased. The timing of the release of the annual royal accounts – and those of the Duchies – is also guaranteed to be quickly 'buried' by other events at that time of year. Parliament – not able, by convention, to discuss the matter, on the floor of the House – is in any case winding down as the summer recess approaches. In 2007, the Duchy of Cornwall accounts were published in the press on the day of Tony Blair's last day as Prime Minister, an event guaranteed to dominate the headlines. The Queen's Duchy of Lancaster income figures are barely reported at all – and their release date is normally always well into July.

...AND CRITICISM

The prevailing general news agenda at that time of the year is important. It is at the early part of the summer 'season' – and the news is more likely to be dominated by tennis at Wimbledon, and in 2006, for example, by the World Cup. The press may give prominent coverage on the day following release, but follow-up discussion is usually extremely limited – certainly not the much-needed opportunity to debate the matter at length in Parliament. What is perhaps more revealing is the curiously contradictory attitude that is so often displayed. Following publication of the Duchy of Cornwall accounts on June 26th 2006, journalist Stephen Glover launched a bitter attack on the heir to the throne[15]. While lambasting the Prince in strong terms: 'Even Alastair Campbell at his most brazen would hardly dare manipulate the truth quite as outrageously as Sir Michael [Peat – the Prince's private secretary] and his team. They must think we are idiots'...'To present the Prince as a hero for paying income tax, when in fact he shells out almost as little as legally possible, is a piece of shameless legerdemain'...'The massive piece of obfuscation that is Sir Michael Peat's report is a cack-handed attempt to pretend that Prince Charles and his wife have the [spending] habits of church mice'... But then in the following sentence, Glover concludes this attacking piece on the heir to the throne with the words: '...as monarchists such as myself must concede...' and '...If a high-spending heir to the throne is bad news for royalists', finally concluding with the limp warning that if the monarchy fails to mend its ways, the future will be 'much, much worse'. Meanwhile, on the same page, we find the *Daily Mail*'s editorial comments on the Prince's 'extravagant way of life...' and that this is '...handing ammunition to the enemies of the monarchy...'. Such is the contradiction displayed in relation to the institution. What is so evidently wrong with it is well understood, even by those who claim otherwise to support it, yet who for some reason dare not take their criticism any further. It is a curious inhibition – which the Australians have so concisely defined as the 'cultural cringe' – that generally prevents concerns about the monarchy progressing to any form of constructive action. It is, however, noticeable that criticism tends to be rather more virulent amongst the very papers who claim otherwise to support the monarchy and the accompanying social ethos.

Such a strange attitude embodies so much that marks the inherent contradictions evident in 21st century Britain. Our society is becoming more, not less, unequal. We seem to know what is wrong, but are seemingly reluctant to actually do anything about it. History shows that fundamental change in Britain tends to come not from the bottom but from the middle. Even the 'English Revolution' that ended the monarchy in 1649 was initiated not by the working classes but by middle-ranking landowners and Members of Parliament. It would seem that 'middle England' knows what is wrong, but until 'middle England' itself decides that the time for action has arrived, nothing will be done.

STRIKING IT RICH
On a personal basis, the accumulation of the royal family's wealth has been helped by the especially favourable manner in which the monarchy have been treated over many generations, both through specific tax exemptions, poor financial accountability, and quite sim- ply over-indulgence on the part of the taxpayer. The Duke of Edinburgh has done rather well. In the late 1940s, at the same time as his surname was conveniently 'rebranded' as 'Mountbatten' – a change from his rather Teutonic-sounding 'Schleswig-Holstein-Sonderburg-Glucksberg' original version – Prince Philip was allowed an extra sum by the government of the day simply to make him a bit wealthier. In financially straitened

post war Britain, the young naval officer was permitted money over and above his official allowance as the new husband of the future Queen.

This staggering generosity on the part of the then government had no rational justification whatsoever, but has enabled a man who has held no more than a middle-ranking naval position on the basis of merit – his other, higher ranks being purely honorary – and no proper job since, to accumulate a fortune estimated in 2001 at £28million[16]. At present, the Duke continues to receive a parliamentary allowance, which the Queen is not required to reimburse, of £359,000 per year, despite by 2012 being in reality unable to undertake many 'duties' at all – and in any case never having had a contractual duty to be required to perform any specific duties as such.

A SECRET DEAL

In those tough post-war years, as the recently created Duke was beginning to fill his new piggy bank with taxpayer's money at a time of acute housing shortages and widespread rationing, there was another ray of sunshine for the royal couple. While the British economy struggled to rebuild after six years of conflict, the young Queen was allowed to avoid paying tax on her investment income. This made possible a degree of wealth accumulation that was denied to her subjects, and might well have made them less than happy had they known about it at the time.

This was the result of a secret deal hatched with the Palace by Prime Minister Winston Churchill and Chancellor R A ('Rab') Butler in 1952. The arrangement enabled her to accumulate a truly enormous wealth base over the succeeding decades. Revealing the secret deal in 2001 – discovered by dogged investigation, not official announcement – Phillip Hall estimated that had she possessed an investment holding of some £2million in 1952 – a not unreasonable estimate, by any means – this sum would, if invested in the Stock Market with all dividends re-invested, have increased to a truly vast £1.4billion by the year 2000. On that basis, for instance, she would be easily able to afford her expensive hobby of keeping racehorses. Estimated by Phillip Hall to cost her around £600,000 a year in 2001, this pursuit has also become a money-earner in that, run as a business in its own right, her bloodstock interests can earn significant returns

Unlike members of the House of Commons or the Lords, the Queen does not have to declare her interests each year. As the *Guardian* newspaper pointed out:

...her subjects cannot question her or know about potential conflicts of interests. She could be investing in firms selling military hardware, performing controversial biotech research or she could just have a portfolio of blue-chip firms. The point is that we, her subjects, don't know, and probably will never have the means to know. However, the reason for the wild variations in valuations of her private wealth can be pinned on the secrecy over her portfolio of share investments. This is because her subjects have no way of knowing through a public register of interests where she, as their head of state, chooses to invest her money.... Although reports occasionally surface naming companies she has bought shares in (in recent years these have included Getmapping.com and the Poptones record label), these invariably refer to shares bought from her Privy Purse funds (earned by her Duchy of Lancaster revenue) and should therefore not be thought of as part of her private investment portfolio. In fact, the Queen even has an extra mechanism to ensure that her investments remain secret – a nominee company called the Bank of England Nominees. It has been available for decades to all the world's current heads of state to allow them anonymity when buying shares. Therefore, when a company publishes a share register and the Bank of England Nominees is listed, it is not possible to gauge whether the Queen, President Bush or even Saddam Hussein is the true shareholder[17].

Whilst the Iraqi dictator is no longer with us since this was written, the option still exists for possibly quite dubious international figures to take advantage of this arrangement. The use of Bank of England Nominees Ltd, the setting up of which was enabled by the Companies Act of 1976, is not of course the only potential vehicle in which the Queen's extensive personal wealth is held. Royal wealth was admirably explored by both Phillip Hall and the *Mail on Sunday*, whose Royal Rich Report, compiled in 2001, provides probably the most accurate estimate of current royal wealth to date[18]. It made an overall, though very conservative, estimate of some £500million – given the value of the Sandringham and Balmoral estates alone – but the overall picture is obscured by secrecy. Additionally, though many of the world's super-rich easily exceed this level of wealth. they do so from commercial ventures or from other sources that are a matter for their respective nations to address.

'Minor' royals, too, still manage to lead extremely favourable lifestyles. This is in part due to their being personally wealthy, an indirect result of the favoured treatment of the monarch which means that wealth gained through such treatment over many generations has enabled the Windsor family as a whole to benefit handsomely. Whilst inheritance tax exemptions apply to just three of their members, such wealth may then be transferred to trusts from which remaining members of the family benefit. There is undoubtedly a considerable 'trickle down' effect. The entire area is complicated by the blurred distinction between the monarch in her 'private' and 'public' capacities.

In the past, members of the royal family had few, if any links to business – after all, being 'in trade' was simply beneath contempt for those with blue blood in their veins. However, changes in social convention over the years led to increasing demands for younger royals to work in some capacity in order to deflect accusations of being drones living at the taxpayers' expense. In the case of the Earl and Countess of Wessex, popular pressure required them to step down after injudicious comments by the Countess were reported in the media. There was also disquiet about possible conflicts of interest resulting from the Countess's RJH public relations company whose clients included Rover Cars (then owned by BMW). It was possible that, perceived as a 'traditional' British brand Rover could gain an advantage by association during, for instance, the couple's official tour of the USA. Such an accusation was almost inevitable, and the risk of conflict ever-present when the job of 'being royal' is in itself pure 'PR'. (Hindsight enables us to see that MG-Rover gained little with the help of the Countess's PR expertise. Having been shed by BMW, what remained went bust and its assets – production lines, presses and models – were acquired at a knockdown price by the Nanjing Motor Company, shipped to China and refurbished). In an increasingly commercialised world and with more subtle marketing techniques accusations of members of the royal family exploiting their position will no doubt arise in the future. The use of titles is perhaps crucial. The Princess Royal's daughter, Zara Phillips, has appeared in Land Rover and Rolex advertising campaigns. She has avoided controversy by not having a royal title, relying instead on her proven equestrian skills, although the distinct identification with the advertisers' target demographic is evidence of a more discreet promotion by allusion to her lifestyle, social circle and royal origins.

ROYAL TRAVEL – A TICKET TO RIDE
As head of state, it is plainly necessary for the Queen to be able to attend both national and international events as efficiently as possible, and in a

manner appropriate to that of a Head of State. However, as is presently the custom, a number of members of the royal family act in a supporting role and are thus similarly required to travel in the commission of their 'official' duties. Such travel is an expensive aspect of the overall cost of the monarchy, amounting, for example, to some £6.4million in 2008 (£6million in the previous year)[19]. The fact that it is deemed necessary for even 'minor' members of the royal family to perform a supporting role means that a very large cast of 'performers' are required to be moved about the country and abroad on an almost continual basis in the manner of a sophisticated travelling circus. Instead of merely a head of state, for example, and – perhaps – a deputy being required to fulfil official duties, an entire extended family are transported in a process necessitating complex and expensive schedules.

Until the year 2004-5, the royal family disclosed the details of individual journeys costing over £2,500, but for 2005-6 this limit was raised to £10,000. This seems to be an entirely unilateral decision which avoids the inclusion of detail of many journeys which fall beneath this cost level and, coincidentally in view of the cost bracket, are most likely to comprise short-haul helicopter flights Official car journeys are normally paid for by the individual members of the family, except that the Queen may charge her journeys to the Civil List, whilst the Duke of Edinburgh must pay for his out of his Parliamentary allowance.

It is noticeable, therefore, that the Windsors have a general dislike of using cars for even relatively short official journeys, when a helicopter trip is quicker and can be charged to the travel Grant-in-aid. However, because car journeys are not listed, even if they do exceed £10,000, the use of this transport medium is not particularly clear. Details, for instance, are not available for trips involving staff who may have to drive, or otherwise transport, official cars for long distances to meet the Queen, for example, when she arrives another way. In addition, 'senior Members' of the royal family – there seems to be no official definition, by the way, of what constitutes 'senior' – are allowed to claim expenses for any travel 'between residences'. Any journey that begins or ends at an official residence – and private residences used for even only in part for 'official' duties, a conveniently broad definition – may be classed as 'official', with the taxpayer covering the cost. A whole world of conveniently subsidised travel is available to a family who have a host of privately owned homes – owned either personally or through a complex network of trusts.

TRAVEL COSTS: PUBLIC OR PRIVATE?

When dealing with the subject of 'working' members of the royal family, the distinction between the 'public' and the 'private' personae can be hard to distinguish. This means that working out which journeys are really necessary for their official duties can be an exceedingly complex affair.

Since any journey to or from an official residence, or any journey to or from an official appointment – not necessarily a 'return' trip – counts as 'official' and can thus be charged to the taxpayer, even having multiple residences scattered across the nation need not be an expensive problem for 'working' royal family members and their spouses. When an otherwise undisturbed few days of salmon fishing in Scotland is interspersed by an odd appointment at the other end of the country, the taxpayer will leap to help out. This is further clouded by the absence of any real requirement to disclose full diary details, so the pretence of 'working from home' takes on a new meaning when applied to the royal family.

The scale of some appointments may vary, too. Whilst not begrudging the appreciation doubtless felt by many of those on the receiving end of a royal visit, some journeys using expensive transport – notably helicopters, particularly pricey machines to operate – do seem a little out of proportion. Doubtless, the royals will plead time and diary pressures, but some journeys stand out.

In April 2004, for instance, Mrs Anne Laurence, the 'Princess Royal' – a term necessary, one presumes, to distinguish her from non-royal Princesses – used a chartered helicopter at a cost of £4,710 to travel from her home in Gloucestershire to a Pony Club Centre near Biggleswade 'to present rosettes' – and then back home again. No doubt a small number of children were very pleased, but perhaps the privileged members of the Club – or their parents – ought to have picked up the bill, rather than the taxpayer.

That same month, her brother Charles, the committed environmentalist, travelled from his home at Highgrove by chartered helicopter to Poundbury, near Dorchester, to show a few MPs around his model village, the flight costing £4,031. A keen fan of helicopters, the Prince wanted to be seen to reduce his use of them and in 2006 announced that he had decided to give up polo entirely because his hectic schedule would have meant using a helicopter to get to and from matches with its consequent damage to the environment. The refusal by the taxman to let him offset the cost of his polo ponies – he had alleged that they were only for the purpose of his charity work – against tax not long before the announcement may have played a part.

THE DEVIL IN THE DETAIL

In general, much interest usually focuses upon the more expensive journeys, but given that many of these are long-haul international journeys, the expense is therefore not that surprising. 'Smaller' journeys can be just as revealing in demonstrating the expense of what might otherwise be overlooked in the day-to-day business of ferrying members of the family across the land. Two factors should be borne in mind. Firstly, members of the royal family – contrary to the conventional received wisdom that they are almost ridiculously hardworking – spend much time 'working from home'. It is not clear – there are no publicly available royal 'timesheets' – as to whether this is 'official' public business, or attending to their own personal affairs: estate management, charity work, and so on. In addition, numerous appointments are often grouped together, some quite brief, and yet, overall, are quoted in numerical total without reference to actual time spent on them.

The Queen may purport to take piles of official 'red boxes' with her to work on at home, yet this does not necessarily equate directly to long working hours on official 'business'. Secondly, with so many residences the royal family have a habit of being invariably at the wrong end of the country when needed for official purposes for an appointment at the other. The Prince of Wales, for example, has his 'official' residence at Clarence House in Central London, but has several others as well: Highgrove, in Gloucestershire; Birkhall, not far from Balmoral, and the Castle of Mey on the northernmost tip of Scotland near Duncansby Head. As a result, itineraries will often require air travel to and from RAF Lyneham – not far from Highgrove – and Aberdeen. This can be mixed and matched with use of the Royal Train, an expensive favourite of the Prince, who has a famous dislike of early morning starts.

Charles' sons have inherited the family love of helicopters. In April 2008, William and Harry took the opportunity to use an Army Chinook heavy transport helicopter to reach a 'stag party' on the Isle of Wight.

2 MONEY AND THE MONARCHY

William also 'dropped in' on his then girlfriend Kate Middleton's home in the country by the same means. The claimed 'training value' to Prince William, then being controversially 'fast-tracked' through an RAF flight training programme was rubbished by a Squadron Leader who stated that 'the idea that this was a legitimate authorised training sortie for HRH is absolute bollocks'[20].

MIDNIGHT TRAIN TO RURITANIA

Long slow overnight train journeys enable the Prince of Wales to arrive refreshed at his destination on time for his morning appointments with a minimum of effort. Except for the effort of the taxpayer, of course, who has to pay for it all. The Royal Train, together with the use of scheduled rail for shorter journeys, cost £700,000 in 2006-7. Journeys undertaken, for example, include a period in June and July of 2005, when, amongst other trips, the Prince of Wales used the train in June to travel from Kemble – the local station nearest to Highgrove, his English country residence in Gloucestershire – up to Ayrshire at a cost of £24,427. The next month, his father travelled from Windsor to Perth in Scotland in order to host a dinner for the G8 Summit. That cost £28,913.

A few days later, the Royal Train took the Prince and his wife from their convenient local station at Kemble, Gloucestershire, in order to go all the way to...Wales. Just a short car ride away, but the rail journey alone cost the taxpayer £37,033. Other modes of transport – invariably cars – are inevitably required in conjunction with the Royal Train, but car journeys are best kept short as it comes out of the fixed Civil List budget, whereas train travel comes out of the additional and flexible 'Grant-in-aid'. A train journey taking the Prince of Wales from Aberdeen to Lincoln for a visit to the city centre in May 2006 cost the taxpayer £24,354. Hardly a 'supersaver' ticket, and it made the onward helicopter journey from nearby RAF Waddington to Buckingham Palace – Clarence House sadly lacks a rooftop heli-pad – seem cheerfully cheap at only £1,850. The environmental benefits of train travel are well accepted, but they are based on the premise that trains normally contain a large number of passengers travelling as part of a scheduled system. Few rail commuters treat themselves to a helicopter journey home from the station. One train for essentially one person and a small team rather defeats the object, becoming instead a ludicrous indulgence.

The Palace may claim that the Royal Train enables savings on hotel bills and security, but for such money one could stay in some fairly lavish hotels, and the security aspect may well be conveniently overstated. The train is very slow, plus on Britain's crowded main lines it is difficult to fit between scheduled trains, with track 'slots' having to be purchased from Network Rail to fit in where available. For this reason, it travels predominantly at night as a 'sleeper' on long trips – eleven journeys at an average of 655 miles per trip in 2006-07. In 2009, it was used just 14 times at an average cost of £57,142 per trip. Costs for rail can be considerable. A journey by the Prince of Wales in April 2004 from Aberdeen to Plymouth – to carry out a handful of appointments in Devon – cost £44,908, slightly more than the cost of the chartered flight that the Queen and the Duke of Edinburgh took in November 2004 to go on a State Visit to Germany. Their entire round trip, from Heathrow to Berlin and Dusseldorf, and back again, cost just £44,200.

The Royal Train is a real favourite of the Prince of Wales. For example, on April 20th 2010 he needed to get to London from Aberdeen (that means he was up in one of the family's Scottish castles – probably Castle Mey, right at the tip of the Highlands near John O'Groats) for a Reception and Dinner for the British Asian Trust. So he took the train – the Royal Train, at a cost to the taxpayer of £37,158. Later in the year he used it from September 6th-9th for quite a journey. Starting at Glasgow, his magical mystery tour called at Edinburgh, Carmarthen, Bristol, Newcastle, Todmorden, Manchester, Nottingham, Birmingham and London. It was a real travel miscellany, opening shops, visiting a farm, dinner at a monastery, and so on, finishing up in the capital for a conference reception. And the price? £52,644 – the ultimate 'rover' ticket. Not long after that, he was back, riding the rails like a true upscale interstate 'hobo'. This time, on November 4th, he was off to visit the Welsh Gardens at Carmarthen (again, so soon?, he was only there in September...), travelling from London at a cost of £18,672. The trip also included visits related to various of his own Princes Trust charities. (See Chapter 5: Charities and Brand Ownership). Another example of his Royal Train travel was that of January 24th 2011 when he went from Ayr (he always seems to be in Scotland when you need him) to appointments in Cambridge and Norwich, setting you, the taxpayer, back £22,216.

As with that other royal luxury travel accessory – the late royal yacht *Britannia* – the train has been explored for its commercial potential in an effort to offset some of its costs – and has similarly been found deficient in providing a satisfactory enticement. The Public Accounts Committee found that attempts had been made to let out the train in 1999-2000 'but there had been no expressions of interest'[21]. Thrusting business travellers obviously found the lack of 'conference and dining facilities, and the configuration of the train for overnight travel' less than appealing. A couple of royal divans in a tediously dull décor was unlikely to wow high-powered executive punters with time to spare – and only a vintage Roberts radio for entertainment.

The Royal Train lacks space for overnight use other than cosy evenings *a deux*, and for corporate clients the appeal of hosting a drinks party whilst parked in the sidings at Clapham Junction has been completely non-existent. Anxious to improve its 'green' credentials, Clarence House announced early in 2007 that public rail services would be used by the Prince – in that perennially handy get-out phrase – 'wherever appropriate'. It remains to be seen how this will affect the Royal Train. For the Prince of Wales in 2007-08, for example, it meant ten trips in the Royal Train at a cost of £299,412, while its total cost that year was £475,357. Scheduled rail journeys in that period totalled just £48,893. Truly a *'Britannia* on wheels', this rather delusional luxury item is envisaged to be remain in the royal toy cupboard but its long term future must surely now be in question.

ROYAL FLIGHTS

The royal air transport function is normally performed by 32 Squadron RAF, and it is perhaps a good idea at this point to clear up a number of basic misconceptions which have arisen over time in relation to royal air travel. No. 32, 'The Royal' Squadron, is so called on account of just one of its functions. It is the 'descendant' of what used to be known in times past as 'The Queens Flight'. It is not a dedicated service whose primary function is to ferry the royal family between engagements.

First and foremost it is a VIP transport service for senior military personnel, and it is also shared with the Government for use of the Prime Minister and senior Ministers. Following the Strategic Defence Review in 1999, it was concluded 'that the principal function of the Squadron was to support military operations' but it was acknowledged that it could use surplus capacity in peacetime for the transport of government ministers and the royal family[22]. The impression is still often given in the media that the aircraft are 'the Queen's' and that use by government Ministers is somehow an appropriation of 'her' aircraft by upstart officials. This is a gross distortion of the situation although of course the more pedantic may allude to the Queen's ultimate notional 'ownership' of the asset as head of state.

The aircraft are charged out to departments and the royal family alike at agreed hourly rates – with royal use being met by the taxpayer through the Grant-in-aid. In response to the general tightening up in respect of aircraft usage by the royal family, the decision was taken in 1998 for the Palace to acquire an aircraft for its own exclusive use. This resulted in the formation of 'The Queen's Helicopter Flight' on April 1st of that year with the acquisition of a Sikorsky S76C helicopter – to be operated on a ten-yearly lease basis – with the ability to carry up to six passengers. The Palace has recently got a new one, on a similar lease basis. Previously, Wessex helicopters operated by 32 Squadron had been used but these ageing machines were approaching the end of their working lives and in need of urgent replacement. Increasing royal preference for helicopters had also meant that scheduling frequent access to RAF helicopters was becoming increasingly difficult and it was more logical for the Palace to get transport of its own. 32 Squadron British Aerospace BAE 146 four engine aircraft are normally used for short-haul operation, together with the smaller HS125 executive jets, while for long-haul operations larger aircraft are chartered as required.

In June 2006, the Government appointed Sir Michael Gershon to investigate a more economic solution to the rather untidy arrangements that had evolved for the Royal Family and senior Government figures. Originally the plan was for two aircraft: a Boeing 737 for longer trips, capable of carrying a large entourage, and a smaller HS 125 executive jet similar to the type currently used by 32 Squadron, but the 737 was later pruned from the plans by Gordon Brown after he became Prime Minister.

The new arrangement in its original form with the two planes used exclusively by the Government and the royal family – and charged to them on a per-hourly basis as in the old arrangement – was expected to save the Ministry of Defence the cost of keeping them available for non-military use, at around £1.5million a year. Though widely derided in a rather facile and disingenuous fashion by much of the media as 'Blair Force One', the advantage would have been a more distinctive official

> state image. With increasing military commitments overseas, official MoD demand on 32 Squadron has grown considerably. When RAF planes had been too small or unavailable, situations arose with incongruously liveried charter aircraft being used on occasions – not just potentially embarrassing but with considerable security implications.

The Royal Train may be expensive, but when the royals start flying abroad then the costs really do start to mount up. Before the Queen or other royals actually go anywhere, it is usual for Palace staff to make a 'reconnaisance' visit just to check that everything is safe and tidy. This sort of thing, to the Middle East or India, for example, usually sets the taxpayer back around £15-20,000 a time. Folowing that, the real thing, however, really does get expensive. Charter flights and a tour lasting four days in November 2010 for the Queen and the Duke of Edinburgh travelling from London Heathrow to Abu Dhabi and Muscat and back again cost £356,253. And that's just the travel costs.

Occasionally, the Prince of Wales needs a change from the Royal Train. For a visit to Kew Gardens in Surrey to open the Qu'aince Garden on April 8th 2010, he grabbed a charter flight from Aberdeen (Yes, Scotland again) then flew straight back to Aberdeen. That cost £13,391. Surely – even with 'extras', Ryanair might have been a lot cheaper! His younger brother, Andrew, the Duke of York, has a legendary love of flying. In his role as 'UK Special Trade Representative' he covered more miles than Star Trek's starship 'Enterprise'. Or at least he did until he was persuaded to step down through being an embarrassment to the nation. While the good times rolled, he could be found on taxpayer funded tours around the globe – like the one from April 13th-24th 2010, a tour of Italy and Central Asia. A series of chartered flights took him from Farnborough to Rome, then on to Milan, Ashkabad, Almaty, Astana, Atyrau, Kiev, and finally back to Farnborough. It cost in total £121,810. Another trip saw him off to the Middle East on May 3rd-11th 2010, travelling from Farnborough to Kuwait, Bahrain, Riyadh, and back to Farnborough at a cost of £88,612. In October 2010 the Duke of York was off to the Far East calling in at Hong Kong, Singapore and Vietnam, with a mixture of charter and scheduled flights costing around £90,000.

Further down the royal pecking order, others still get a chance to see the world. As honorary Colonel of various Canadian regiments, the Duke of Kent was off to inspect the troops between May 19th-22nd 2010, this time on a bargain scheduled flight from London Heathrow to Calgary, Toronto and back to Heathrow – it all cost £11,668. Jetting off to see fellow royals getting hitched is another reason to charge the taxpayer. In June 2010 the Earl and Countess of Wessex (you'd forgotten about them, hadn't you?) had to fly from Farnborough (not a commercial airport but it's very handy for their home at Bagshot Park, Windsor) to Stockholm in Sweden. That trip cost £14,916.

There are lots more journeys listed at the back of the royal accounts, featuring all of your favourite royals, all travelling to a host of different locations – unless they cost less than £10,000, in which case they're not deemed worth listing separately. That's a lot of money. Over the last five years, that averages nearly £6million a year to keep the royal family members moving around the country – and the globe. Are all these journeys really necessary?

KEEPING IT IN THE FAMILY

Merely being related to the Queen brings with it great advantage, and the closer to the monarch, the bigger the benefits. The Prince of Wales, as heir to the throne, gets his own special income from the Duchy of Cornwall, but the rest of the family have done very well over the years. The Duke of Edinburgh gets the following payment simply for being married to the Queen:

Duke of Edinburgh – £359,000 per annum. This is paid directly by Parliament, and this remains so with the passing of the Sovereign Grant Act. It is alleged that the 'annuity' is essentially a payment for expenses incurred in the performance of the Duke's 'duties'. That said, remember that the Duke was originally, on the occasion of his marriage, paid an allowance by Parliament which included an element to increase his personal wealth. He was basically broke, had a small Naval salary, and it was felt that someone marrying the future Queen ought to have a bit of cash behind him – and it was felt unseemly for him to have a job in the future. What that 'wealth-enhancing element' was, we don't know, and since the Duke's 'expenses' are never disclosed, this all remains a bit of a grey area. When the 2001 Royal Rich List estimated the Duke's personal wealth as being around £28million, one can speculate that the expenses incurred in performing his 'duties' (we have an unwritten constitution, and

2 MONEY AND THE MONARCHY

it doesn't actually require him to do anything) haven't been too great, and that the wealth-enhancing bit has stacked up rather well over the years. Not bad for someone without a proper job since the 1940s…

The following 'annuities' – often referred to in the past as 'allowances' used, until 1993, to be paid by Parliament direct to the lucky recipients:

Duke of York – £249,000
Earl of Wessex – £141,000
Princess Royal – £228,000
Duke and Duchess of Gloucester – £175,000
Duke and Duchess of Kent – £236,000
Princess Alexandra – £225,000
(2007 figures)

Following the 1993 Memorandum of Understanding agreed between the Government and the Royal Household, the payments were, though still made by Parliament, then reimbursed by the Queen from her Privy Purse income. The Sovereign Grant Act will, from 2013, end this practice and the payment of any such allowances will become the sole responsibility of the Queen. The exact terms and consitions of these payments has always been a little vague. If these are the equivalent of official salaries, it would be interesting to know on what basis these are taxed, whether on a PAYE basis with the Queen acting as 'employer', or as the equivalent of self-employed income with the ability to deduct expenses. In the words of HM Treasury's explanatory material on the new Act, the allowances are 'to relieve expenditure in connection with official duties', but as we don't see any detailed accounts to match 'duties' (which, don't forget are not constitutionally specified, or indeed required at all), it's rather hard not to be rather sceptical about the whole business. Are the payments are in reality more like official salaries than rather vague 'allowances' with the accompanying claims that they are designed simply to meet expenses? After all, travel costs are paid through the Civil List Grant-in-aid.

However, don't feel too sorry for the Queen for having to take on the great burden, since 1993, of supporting the family. These days she receives well over £13million a year from the Duchy of Lancaster (a state body, don't forget), so these payments aren't really affected in practice despite all the changes over the years – and they may, in any case, be tax deductible. The family also get access to the royal expense account too, so that all can perform tours and visits, both at home and abroad, to continue to help make them feel truly 'royal'. So the Duke of York, for instance, can still decide to go on a royal tour in place of his mother and the country will pay for his entourage, including the valet with the special ironing board – and the luxury hotels. This is despite having stepped down from his supposedly trade-promoting 'role'. So, instead of travelling the world as the UK's 'Special Trade Representative', with all expenses paid, he now simply travels the world as a senior royal 'stand-in' – with all expenses paid, naturally…

When first instituted, these 'allowances' were set a very high level compared to incomes as a whole, and whilst they may now appear to be rather less lavish, they are still pretty good given that the recipients get the money regardless of qualification or competence, but on a pay scale related to the heirarchy of birth. In addition, all the lucky beneficiaries have received – and continue to receive – excellent housing deals, described collectively by Labour MP Alan Williams, of the House of Commons Public Accounts Committee, as 'the best housing benefit scheme in Europe'.

TOP SECRET

A tradition of privilege and a deferential attitude in general has meant that the monarchy has managed to gain 'opt outs' from much legislation, as for example, the Freedom of Information Act and the Race Relations Act. The recurrent obsession with secrecy does result in seemingly absurd examples in situations where the monarchy is involved, however tenuously. In the case of the rather quaint tradition of the distribution by the Queen of Royal Maundy Money, the fact that the cost of manufacture of the coins in question is withheld as being commercially sensitive and not to be divulged seems frankly ridiculous. No doubt the world market for Maundy Money is a ruthless and competitive one, and any hint of such information would be tantamount to commercial suicide. Quite why the cost of making a handful of silver coins for the monarch to distribute as token 'charity' should remain a state secret is something of a mystery. It was thus listed alongside items such as the Ministry of Defence's Roll-on-Roll-off Strategic Sealift programme as being too sensitive to reveal. If nothing else it is an appropriate symbol of the culture of secrecy which surrounds so much related to the monarchy[23].

2 MONEY AND THE MONARCHY

ACCOUNTABILITY? BUT WE'RE ROYAL...
Legally, there is no requirement for the Queen and the Prince of Wales to present their accounts. The National Audit Office is unable to scrutinise the Duchy incomes, for example, and so far the government has declined to implement such a procedure. In reply to an invitation by Liberal Democrat MP Norman Baker in October 2005, to adopt such a process, the Chancellor of the Exchequer, Gordon Brown, was not forthcoming. Stating glibly that 'There is no obligation for Her Majesty the Queen and His Royal Highness the Prince of Wales to produce personal accounts', it seemed that there was no desire for greater openness in respect of two people who had the unique benefit of the profits of two publicly owned estates generating multi-million pound incomes[24]. By contrast, for instance, the US President's tax return is a public document.

The House of Commons Public Accounts Committee has, however, in the last couple of years, adopted an increasingly assertive and less deferential attitude in respect of royal finances, most notably in respect of the Duchies of Cornwall and Lancaster. Patience with indulgent perks and long-accepted situations that increasingly contrast with the scrutiny focused upon other areas of the public realm is wearing thin.

The new Sovereign Grant Act does, however, introduce a welcome step forward in that, from 2013, the Royal Household's accounts will be subject to audit by the Comptroller and Auditor General and to full parliamentary scrutiny by the Public Accounts Committee. It is also interesting to note the beginnings of change in attitudes to those who run for public office. The 2012 London Mayoral election campaign raised the possibility of candidates being pressured – or pressuring each other – to disclose personal financial details. Perhaps one day soon this may lead to those who are born to public office, rather than just running for it, having to be a bit more transparent.

BRITANNIA WAIVES THE RULES

The case of the *Britannia* is an interesting example of the particularly indulgent way in which the post-Second World War British monarchy was treated in sharp contrast to the privations endured by the population as a whole at the time. A nation which underwent two major currency devaluations in 1947 and 1949, as well as being in receipt of US Marshall Aid funding, which by the way it did next to nothing useful with, unlike France and Germany for example, still felt it necessary to splash out on a new floating palace. This maritime emblem of conspicuous consumption was exceptional in its size and standards of luxurious appointment and made previous royal yachts seem positively meagre by comparison. The new 'yacht' *Britannia*, built at John Brown's shipyard on the Clyde was launched on April 16th 1953 and commissioned on July 11th 1954, was, however, a far cry from its 160-ton displacement namesake predecessor. Hansard records the debate in the House of Commons on October 28th 1953 in which a Mr Bence, MP, was told that it could be converted to accommodate 200 hospital beds at a cost of £12,000. The new *Britannia*, nothing less in reality than a small ocean-going liner, was agreed to by a reluctant Parliament on the promise of its being able to fulfil the dual role of a hospital ship in times of crisis.

However, despite Suez and subsequent conflicts, no such function ever materialised. Its sole foray into the real world of international humanitarian activity was its participation in the rescue of foreign nationals from civil war fighting in Yemen in the 1980s, the vessel just happening to be in the area at the time. Scarcely used in its final years, the *Britannia* was, from its inception, the embodiment of a distorted view of Britain's post-war role. Previous monarchs had managed happily with much more modest vessels, but the *Britannia* was built to perform the UK's new global 'Commonwealth' role.

Imperial Britain had managed without such a vessel during the very heyday of Empire, yet embarked on the process of building one just as faster and more reliable long-haul aircraft were becoming available, and the Empire was disappearing. The vessel was, in effect, sold to the country under false pretences, a gratuitously extravagant pleasure craft used largely for private royal holidays and honeymoons by assorted family members rather than Commonwealth visits. It is unlikely that there was ever any real intention to use it as a hospital ship – originally envisaged, as a sweetener to a sceptical Parliament, allegedly to be convertible as such in just twenty-four hours!

With the pressing need for support vessels in the run-up to the 1982 Falklands campaign, consideration was given to the luxury vessel fulfilling that much-vaunted alternative hospital-ship role. However, there was a slight problem. *Britannia* ran on the wrong fuel. Its particularly quiet turbines had been designed to operate on 'furnace fuel oil', a heavier grade fuel than ordinary diesel. Specifically to cater for the sleeping habits of its royal passengers, this was typical of the no-expense-spared attitude that pertained from the earliest stage of the ship's design and construction. It meant that it would be operationally incompatible with the long-distance refuelling needs of the rest of the fleet. The Windsor family could breathe a sigh of relief – no need to strip the boat of its lavish interior fittings and it would be ready for the Queen's annual holiday jaunt to Scotland after all. Only well after the Falklands War had ended, in 1984, was the 'yacht' converted to run on diesel fuel, like the rest of the fleet – naturally at great additional public expense – though the prospect of its ever being needed to be used operationally was now perhaps even more remote than ever.

Britannia also had another, rather less well-known function. In the event of a nuclear war, it was envisaged that the royals could hastily embark on the old boat and take to the waters off Scotland, where they could lurk safely out of sight of Soviet radar, sheltering in the many lochs. A bit like the traditional royal summer holidays. Risking getting holed up like the German battleship Tirpitz during the Second World War might not have seemed like a barrel of fun, and given that *Britannia* was unlikely to have been very radiation-proof either, its use as an upscale escape craft was hardly in James Bond's 'Dr No' territory. Seeing out one's final days moored up in an isolated loch in the Western Isles under leaden, fall-out laden skies, as the Geiger counter ticked and the gin ran short, in the company of Princess Margaret and a pack of snapping corgis, would seem like the ultimate definition of hell. Were they really serious?

THE TIDE TURNS

By the 1990s, attention focused on the royal family's privileged lifestyle, and the ultimate expression of this was the *Britannia*. Boat owners have a definition of the object of their affections as 'a hole in the water into which one pours money', and at nearly forty years old, the ageing vessel was living up to this reputation. It was now was costing more than ever to maintain and the Ministry of Defence – who had traditionally paid the bills – was increasingly keen to rid itself of the burden. For example, in just the seven years from 1983 until 1990 it had cost an astonishing £44,131,000 in repairs. From 1990 until it was finally decommissioned in 1997 – with its last major outing being the handover ceremony in Hong Kong, on June 30th of that year – the royal yacht *Britannia* was used on 'export promotion' activities for an average of just nine days in each of the last seven years of its 'working' life.

Given that, based upon the costs of the vessel in the 1980s, its average annual cost was approximately £9.34million, then its daily rate was in effect £76,725. Was it really worth all this to keep a floating corporate party venue afloat? In 1997, in response to questions from Labour MP Alan Williams, the Defence Minister, Nicholas Soames, was forced to concede the truth about the *Britannia* that would, in effect, seal its fate. Far from the extravagant claims that the vessel – when not bearing the hard-working royals between successive foreign tours and engagements, and holidays of course – was tirelessly cruising the high seas in order promote British business abroad, it had in fact scarcely left harbour at all. In the course of the last two years of its 'working' life the royal family had used the vessel for a total of just forty-six days and it had been used for just sixty-three days in its 'export promotion' role. Even this could be largely accounted for by overall sailing time to and from engagements, with its royal passengers or corporate revellers leaving the vessel half-way and returning by air.

RARE AND COSTLY PLEASURES

In its heyday, the *Britannia* was not required to justify itself in the way that was later claimed as a justification for its retention. Not for the 'swinging 60s' royal party people did their precious vessel also have to prostitute itself as a travelling trade stand. Hansard records Labour MP and long-time royal critic Willie Hamilton asking on May 3rd 1961 what the vessel had been used for in the preceding 12 months. Princess Margaret, the Queen's sister, used to get to the West Indies, her perennial holiday destination. Next, the Duke of Edinburgh took it to Cowes on the Isle of Wight so he could use it as a base during the regatta. A little later, the vessel took him, and the Queen, on their traditional summer holiday around the Orkney and Shetland Islands. Following this, the Queen Mother used it to go to Tunisia, after which the Queen and the Duke were back on board as they were off to Italy for a State visit – followed by a cruise round Italy to Venice. The *Britannia* was getting used to the warm Mediterranean waters, as the Duke and Duchess of Gloucester then sailed in her to Athens to unveil a Commonwealth war memorial, after which they embarked on a tour of the eastern Mediterranean to visit other Commonwealth war graves. All very leisurely by today's standards, and not a single export order signed. At least assorted Windsor family members had a good time. By 1961 the annual pay bill for the *Britannia* was £200,000 – a lot more in today's money.

By the mid 1990s, the royal yacht wasn't being used quite as much, as in the aftermath of the Windsor fire the family had to be careful not to be seen to be having too good a time, and holiday snaps of royals sipping cocktails on *Britannia*'s quarter deck in sunnier climes wasn't going to go down too well with the tax-paying public or their unemployed compatriots. In 1995 the *Britannia* was used just once on a trip abroad, for a three night stay at CapeTown and Durban. The following year, there were just two foreign trips, both one-night stops at Amsterdam in the Netherlands and at Palm Beach in Florida. The longest trips in 1996 were in fact two fifteen-day excursions, one to the Isle of Wight so that the Duke of Edinburgh would have a suitably comfortable berth from which to observe the sailing at Cowes Week and the other to the Western Isles of Scotland, for the Queen's traditional summer holiday cruise. On the basis of the daily rate mentioned above, these holidays alone cost nearly £2.5million.

In an era of increasing scrutiny, there were also by now questions as to whether the royal family might ought to now be liable for incurring a tax liability for the royal yacht as a 'benefit in kind'. A financial journalist writing in the Independent suggested this could mean a tax bill equivalent to 20 per cent of the yacht's value each year. Other countries seemed to maintain their exports without the need for royal yachts – and Parliament was no longer prepared to tolerate such conspicuous privilege.

NEW LABOUR, NEW BOAT?

The story of the final months of *Britannia*'s 'active' service is revealing in that it occurred during the period in which New Labour was feeling its way in its first months in power. The fate of the vessel had for some time become something of a political football. The case for its retention – let alone a replacement – was difficult to make on rational grounds. By 1996 Conservative prospects of re-election were not looking good, so they were tempted to force a possible Labour administration into financing a replacement yacht. As Labour MP and later Paymaster General, Geoffrey Robinson later recalled, John Redwood had used the vessel in his leadership bid in the summer of that year with the rather jingoistic slogan 'Tories keep royal yachts, not scrap them'. In January 1997 the then Defence Secretary, Michael Portillo, had announced that the government were considering spending

£90million on a replacement for the ageing *Britannia*. Robinson's view sums up the ambiguity of the New Labour approach – 'We were opposed to using taxpayer's money, though not opposed in principle to the royal yacht'[25].

Labour's manifesto pledge not to use taxpayer's money to fund a replacement had appealed to the voters, although Tony Blair was worried about Portillo's replacement undertaking. The more 'hard-line' school, backed by Gordon Brown, won the day. New Labour's answer, when they came to power, was to investigate the possibility of seeking private sector finance (PFI) to pay for a new yacht, both in order to appease the Treasury, and to take advantage of the protestations of high-profile business leaders that such a vessel would be – as they claimed the current one had been – 'good' for Britain's export trade. Geoffrey Robinson was detailed to put together a plan to secure the necessary funding from business figures such as NCP tycoon Sir Donald Gosling and P&O chairman Jeffrey Sterling. The latter, however, favoured the traditional business case – the boat should be built and maintained at the public expense. It was all very well to take advantage of its projection of Britain's 'image', but he saw no reason why the taxpayer couldn't finance it – a not entirely consistent 'free-market' solution. Gosling, however – later to rent his own yacht to the taxpayer in March 2008 for the Prince of Wales and the Duchess of Cornwall to tour the Caribbean – was admittedly more amenable to contributing.

The problem was that the sums of money discussed – around £50million, about one-fifth of the amount spent by the Sultan of Brunei on his own yacht – would simply not be sufficient to construct a vessel of the type envisaged. Geoffrey Robinson also described the attitude of the Cabinet Secretary, Sir Robin Butler, who insisted that the new yacht should 'preserve the cachet' of the original. Therein lay the problem. The *Britannia* possessed the 'cachet' that business seemingly wanted to take advantage of precisely because it wasn't commercial, yet if big business were to pay for it – and exact some kind of reciprocal and visible sponsorship element in return – that 'cachet' would thereby be lost. To save money, a major refit, with new engines and equipment fitted in the old hull, was suggested. in order to retain the superficial appeal of the old boat. The Palace, meanwhile, played a somewhat disingenuous policy of discreet non-involvement – a classic Palace ploy – making it clear that the Queen wasn't asking for a new yacht, but would go along with whatever decision was taken. However as Geoffrey Robinson described 'To keep the cachet it would be essential for the new boat to be known as the royal yacht and that the Queen and senior members of the royal family would wish to continue to use it. The Queen, then, had the whip hand. If she disassociated herself from the project it would not succeed. We would just have another luxury yacht available for charter'[26].

The plan was thus to spend £50million, update the old 'yacht', and put in place a structured plan in which it would be leased out to business users for at least six months of the year at a rate of around £70,000 a day. For corporate 'suits', the days of free use of 'HMS Taxpayer' to seal already-agreed deals and sip gin and tonics on the quarter-deck as the sun set were over. Now they'd have to pay for it. Trying to justify spending on such a scale when the benefits were tenuous was far from easy. The admission that the *Britannia* was really not paying its exceedingly expensive way sealed its fate. Its much proclaimed 'business use' was virtually a myth. The various high profile business backers who appeared to protest their royalist credentials and venture that they might be prepared to get their chequebooks out for the monarch never materialised. Though Sir Donald Gosling was prepared to underwrite part of the annual 'business use' to the tune of over £5million for at least five years, this seemed like an admission, if ever there was one, that the real degree of commercial interest was poor. A few 'business interests' may have wanted to trade upon the royal provenance of any new vessel, but Robinson still couldn't get a more general 'bankable commitment' from the private sector to charter the boat at the going commercial rate.

The £50million refurbishment would still have to be paid by the taxpayer, and the 'sponsors' would want their names on the side. Robinson considered the placement of 'discreet plaques' on the vessel but it was all beginning to sound a bit tacky – and with not very much 'cachet' at all. All this and a not very enthusiastic Ministry of Defence were being expected to pay £5million a year to crew a combination of a royal pleasure boat and high-end business trade stall. 'On the limited number of occasions that *Britannia* had been used for commercial purposes – the ceremonial signing of large export deals that had already been clinched – the arrangements had worked very well'[27]. Of course they had. It had cost British business nothing in the past, but a genuine commercial deal in which it would have to pay dearly for its dubious pleasures was far harder to sell to them. At this point, however, 'events' took over. The death of the Princess of Wales seemed to play a major part in sealing the fate of the *Britannia*. Geoffrey Robinson summed up the mood: 'The impact of Princess Diana's death touched every part of British life, not least the monarchy itself. A new royal yacht, a refurbishment of *'Britannia* or whatever, did not seem to fit the post-Diana atmosphere. Back in Whitehall I told Gordon [Brown] that we should let the project drop. He agreed at once. I telephoned the MoD. They responded with unrecognisable alacrity that that had been their view all along, as I knew. When I phoned him, Sir Robin Fellowes said the Palace felt the same way'[28].

However, even in the face of such agreement the royal family didn't want to let go of 'their' prized 'yacht' without a struggle. Mrs Anne Laurence, the Princess Royal, wanted it to be scuttled – a solution scarcely justifiable on environmental grounds alone. She felt the vessel would suffer the 'indignity' of the public having access to it and feared that the extravagant care lavished upon it would not be maintained. The Duke of Edinburgh agreed. Even the Queen shed a tear at the vessel's decommissioning ceremony. There had been no such display of emotion at the funeral of her daughter-in-law. The Public Accounts Committee had examined the whole area of royal travel in the years following the Windsor Castle fire in 1992. Parliament was looking at Government spending on the royal family in an area that, aside from the vote on the Civil List, had hitherto been discreetly kept relatively free from the spotlight of parliamentary scrutiny. From grace and favour apartments to international travel, money had hitherto been a vulgar matter upon which it was not really the done thing to dwell, a cultural 'sophistication' which doubtless suited the Windsor family admirably, but now views were changing.

The *Britannia* was by far the largest item on the royal travel bill, and increasingly hard to justify. As the Falklands War experience had exposed the nonsense of the 'hospital ship' excuse, the Palace and sympathetic politicians had been forced to come up with a new way to explain why the royal yacht was so indispensable. In the increasingly market-orientated atmosphere of the time, its allegedly vital contribution to the country's trade balance was now touted as the reason for its retention. However, as with so much claimed free-market buccaneering – such as the recently privatised railways – it depended upon lashings of public money to make the sums add up. The 'good for business' myth was a very recent invention, in reality a tenuous veneer with which to perpetuate an imperial fantasy world. Germany remains Europe's leading economy, a position gained during the period of *Britannia's* existence, but somehow managed all this without a royal yacht.

BRITANNIA – CLOSING DOWN SAIL

The *Britannia*'s last major official outing was its appearance at the ceremony to mark the return of Hong Kong to China when the colony's lease expired on June 30th 1997, an appropriate theatrical prop for this imperial farewell performance. It was a fitting and graphic symbol of the end of the British imperial delusion to which the country had clung for too long. In a peculiar form of inverted symbolism she had appeared in a period in which Britain's maritime decline began and the Suez crisis marked a diminished world role.

The new generation of super-yachts were now the toys of the corporate super-rich. Computer magnates and Russian oil oligarchs possessed craft which, with their helicopter pads and satellite dishes, made the Windsor's vessel, with its funnel, black topsides, polished brass and teak look as quaint and antique as a Victorian pre-Dreadnought battleship. What is more, Parliament and the taxpayer had had enough of paying for it all. Instead, the *Britannia* would become a feature of theme-park Britain, along with red telephone boxes, Beefeaters and Routemaster buses. Following decommissioning at Portsmouth on December 11th 1997, the yacht became a floating heritage centre and conference venue, berthed permanently at Leith near Edinburgh. The *Britannia* defied financial reality to the very end. No proper tendering process sought to reclaim even a small part of its true cost to the taxpayer over the five decades it had spent as a royal pleasure craft. Just during the period 1983-1990 alone, this Ruritanian cruise liner cost £65.3million to maintain, but the final irony is that in this supposed age of freedom of information and accountability, the final price realised for this floating palace became a state secret[29].

Interestingly, in January 2012 a letter by Conservative politician Michael Gove was leaked which he suggested that a grateful nation might wish to buy the Queen a new royal yacht as a Diamond Jubilee present. Needless to say, it provoked a re-run of all the usual arguments, from the vital need for royal yachts as an export tool, promoting a nation with a fine seafaring tradition, etc. etc. The usual old establishment seadogs and tycoon suspects – like Sir Donald Gosling – reappeared from the woodwork to offer to help pay for it, and no doubt hoping for trip or two in it as well. In fact, the plan for a new yacht had been filed as 'Project FSP21' back in 2009, and that time its 'alternative guise' was to have been a kind of hybrid educational and research vessel. However, for a coalition government struggling with the recession and public sector cuts, this was an embarrassing story they could well do without. It did little for Gove's political reputation, common sense prevailed and it was buried as soon as possible. If the Queen desperately wanted a new yacht – and there was no suggestion that she did – then she would have to buy one herself.

THE WINDSOR CASTLE FIRE

In 1992, restorers at Windsor Castle left a powerful spotlight switched on – and rather too close to valuable wall-hangings. The resulting fire caused millions of pounds of damage. It was an event which was to be a catalyst for an abrupt change in attitude by the public towards the monarchy. The then responsible minister, Sir Peter Brooke, under whose aegis the building fell, ventured somewhat over-generously that the public would be more than happy to pay up for Her Majesty's tragic loss to a building that the Queen – as Sovereign – always liked to claim she 'owned', but did not wish to take responsibility for the damage.

The government was unprepared for the public reaction. The public disagreed strongly. No, they did not wish to pay. Although one could argue that, strictly speaking it might have been the public's responsibility, what really rankled was that prior to the fire the royal family were keen to treat the properties as their own. As the *Times* journalist Janet Daly commented at the time, 'While the castle stands, it is theirs, but when it burns down it is ours'.

A solution was devised, a handy ad hoc arrangement by which the Queen would open up Buckingham Palace – for a few weeks in the summer when she was never around anyway – and use the admission ticket proceeds to pay towards the repair bills for Windsor Castle. Buckingham Palace is 'owned' by the Queen, but only in her public role as monarch, with the taxpayer generously funding its upkeep at a cost of millions of pounds every year. The public could pay to see something they already paid for anyway and which involved no sacrifice at all to the Queen. The move was meanwhile spun outrageously by the Palace as a selfless gesture of the greatest generosity.

2 MONEY AND THE MONARCHY

Once the repair bill had been paid off in this way, did the Queen not say: 'We have paid for the repairs, but are still collecting cash at the Palace gate. What shall one do?' Not exactly. The Palace kept silent and continued to collect admissions from the lengthy queues visiting this state-funded building during the short summer period when the paying public were graciously admitted. The proceeds had been unilaterally diverted into another fund for the restoration and upkeep of art treasures held in the Royal Collection. Not an unworthy cause, perhaps, but it was generating earnings out of a state asset without any accountable process, a fact only discovered by the Public Accounts Committee in 2000. The sums involved were considerable. Ticket sales at both Buckingham Palace and Windsor Castle had, between 1993-94 and 1998-99, amounted to a total of £25.9million[30].

The status of the 'ownership' of much, if not all, of the contents of the huge and unique Royal Collection is something of a 'grey' legal area. (See Chapter 6 – The Royal Collection) The benefits to certain specific departments – such as the Royal Collections Trust, in conjunction with its 'commercial' arm, Royal Collection Enterprises Ltd, purveyors of tickets, mugs and associated royal artefacts for the delectation of visitors – are enormous, yet the fundamental question of quite why the Palace should be so entitled to such revenues, whilst the assets that produce the profits are in public ownership is rarely asked.

In Robin Simon's words: 'The Queen takes the money – or the Trust, chaired by the Prince of Wales, takes it. The State pays for the Palace and owns it, as well as the Royal Collection, which it also supposedly owns. But the Government gets none of the money'[31]. The Palace may claim that these commercial returns offset costs to the taxpayer, but if that is the case then they should follow a more direct path back to the Treasury. It is not for the Palace to make unilateral decisions about revenues derived from what are ultimately public assets. However, the nature of the relationship of government staff and ministers when dealing with the Palace is such that deference often obscures the picture, and matters are not perhaps dealt with as assiduously as would be the case elsewhere.

When the Queen lamented that 1992 had been an 'annus horribilis', was it as a result of the fire, her children's assorted marital woes, or the fact that a general downturn in the public's hitherto easygoing nature had led to the Palace having to cut a deal with the Government to agree she should pay income tax for the first time in her reign? The event is

> significant in that it marked a hardening in public attitude to a family that had done rather too well in comparison with the Queen's subjects, many of whom had lost businesses, been made redundant or had had their homes repossessed in the economic downturn.

ROYAL FINANCE – GENEROUS AND OPAQUE

Financial support for the royal family still remains a complex subject. Even the Sovereign Grant Act, designed to simplify and clarify the process, fails to address some of the basics. The hierarchy of birth is deemed sufficient to justify financial reward. The Sovereign Grant Act did not return to first principles in assessing what would be an appropriate level of funding for the monarchy. Instead, it contrived at a process which would in effect yield the same as that under the previous system. However, where it is to be welcomed is in respect of the fact that under the Act the Sovereign Grant will now be subject to Parliamentary audit:

> Clause 2 provides that Sovereign Grant expenditure will be subject to audit by the Comptroller & Auditor General from 2012. The Treasury will set the form of the accounts and the C&AG will audit them. The Grant accounts will be laid before the House and will be open to full parliamentary scrutiny, including by the Committee of Public Accounts. The C&AG will, in addition be empowered to carry out value for money studies of Royal Household expenditure.

Examination of royal finances used to be infrequent, usually agreed at the outset of each reign and then reviewed on a ten-yearly basis. Even then, a combination of deference and political reluctance to raise the monarchy as an issue has tended to militate against too much criticism. The long review period has also led to instances where developing trends during the period are not accounted for. Inflation is a classic example; the failure to adjust built-in allowed increases led to the large Civil List surplus. During periods of low inflation, the built-in allowances were not needed but were automatically added. Letting the fund grow rather than returning surpluses to the Treasury was illogical.

A proper review of the ageing Queen's reduced duties has not been carried out – the existing Civil List figures are based upon a younger monarch with more official commitments. For the Royal Family as a whole, the system of allocation of responsibilities is untidy, and has just 'evolved'. Payment by results, or actual time spent 'on duty' has never been considered. Some official appointments may last just a few minutes, while with others, days may be entirely taken up by royal 'duties'. Holidays are long and much time may be spent on personal affairs. The sheer complexity of the process – not made any clearer by a fog of arcane language and an aura of deference – has made it difficult to assess if the millions spent by the taxpayer over many decades could in any way be construed as providing value for money. It is to be hoped that the Sovereign Grant Act will at last give Parliament a proper chance to address the matter.

No attempt, however, has yet been made to address the disproportionate scale of the incomes paid to the monarch and heir to the throne from the Duchies of Lancaster and Cornwall. Neither, indeed, whether these are really appropriate at all, and whether they ought not now be replaced by defined official salaries. Perhaps deeper scrutiny of the Sovereign Grant in Parliament will herald a new era in which these payments will soon be questioned.

COMPARATIVE COSTS OF EUROPEAN HEADS OF STATE

MONARCHIES

	(£millions)
United Kingdom	175.4 (39*)
Belgium	9.7
Denmark	10.5
Luxembourg	7.8
Netherlands	88.3
Norway	23.9
Spain	7.4
Sweden	10.2

*This is the officially quoted figure but is so ridiculously inaccurate that it has not been used here, excluding as it does the cost of security, lost Duchy profits, etc.

A little explanation is needed in respect of all these figures. In the case of countries such as Belgium, for example, the monarchy resides in a total of five official residences, all owned and maintained by the state. There is thus no transfer of money to the royal family to spend on properties which they don't actually 'own', whereas the UK likes to maintain this pretence. Fundamentally, the problem is that there is little overall transparency. If the taxpayer is funding everything, then the taxpayer ought to know where their cash is going. In the case of other monarchies, perhaps all these figures are slightly questionable to some extent. The inherent nature of monarchies is their fundamental lack of accountability, and a fair element of deference – as prevalent in Delft or Esbjerg as in Dorking – means that they have traditionally made the most of this. We must assume they still do, and in some cases these international figures could well be bigger than they really are. It is noticeable too that on per capita basis the Dutch seem to do rather badly, as they have after all a very much smaller population than the UK.

PRESIDENCIES

	(£millions)
Austria	3.5
Finland	11.5
France	90*
Germany	21
Ireland	1.8

*Executive presidency – all others are non-executive. (Figures for foreign monarchies and presidencies courtesy of Republic – www.republic.org.uk)

More explanation. Firstly, and most importantly, France is a special case as – like the United States of America – it has an executive Presidency in which the President has day to day involvement in the political process and hence close working links with government ministries, with much higher associated staff and administration costs, and so on. All the other presidencies are non-executive in nature. Non-executive presidencies are rather more like their European monarchical counterparts in that they perform largely ceremonial functions but with certain limited constitutional powers which are exercised on few occasions. With the exception of the UK, all of these countries have written constitutions, with their monarchy's relationship clearly defined within that legal context.

All comparisons are by definition rather inexact. The exact scope of offices may vary from country to country – all constitutions are different. In addition, exchange rates and purchasing power differences can lead

2 MONEY AND THE MONARCHY

to significant variations and mean that precise comparisons are hard to achieve. In general, larger countries have correspondingly larger commitments and hence bigger head of state budgets. What is clear, however, is that, on the whole, monarchies – which are despite their constitutional position, largely ceremonial – do seem to cost rather a lot. Do not forget, too, that these figures are the overall cost of the office or institution, of which actual payments to office-holders as salaries or equivalent are only a part. As a result, royal families do much better in the long run. With an hereditary position, it's a job for life and family members can also get handsome salaries too. In 2007, for example, the Belgian King got an official salary of £1.4million, while his wife got £754,000, with two princes getting £533,000 and their sister £184,000. The same year, the Netherlands' Queen Beatrix got an official salary of just over 4million Euros. So, year on year, generation on generation, they can 'earn' quite sizeable amounts.

An elected president, by contrast, might be in the position for just one term, probably no more than five years, and then only for a possible maximum of two terms. Whilst they may get a decent pension and there may be the possibility of directorships, or perhaps a high-flying position with an organisation like the UN, they simply don't get the opportunity to accumulate and retain wealth on the scale of a royal dynasty. In 2012, the German President's official salary was €213,000 (£171,465), not very different from that of the British Prime Minister.

HOW MUCH, AND FOR WHAT?

There is still much confusion in the public's perception of what the monarchy costs, and, indeed, is actually worth. The frequent 'but they do so much for charity' and 'they bring in all the tourists' responses are, at best, almost impossible to quantify – let alone accurately, and at worst, dangerously misleading. Estimates made are usually coloured, to a lesser or greater degree, dependent upon the monarchist, republican or political persuasion of the estimator. Objectivity is frequently way down on the list, and when mixed with genuine confusion, uncertainty, and lack of official transparency, it is little wonder that any figures – assuming they can be trusted at all – vary so greatly.

Let's not forget that the real point of a head of state – monarch or president – is to act as 'chairperson' at the head of the constitutional pile. in basic terms, constitutionally, they have, dressed up in law – or in the case of the UK, law and custom – the 'casting vote'. Most of the UK head of state's powers – the old 'royal prerogative' powers – are now in practice ceded to the Prime Minister. They are the nation's top 'meet and greet' exponent, the chief representative on the international stage, save in the political sphere. That said, the role of head of state will differ depending upon whether they have democratic legitimacy or are hereditary monarchs, and the degree of neutrality implicit in their position. Ultimately, a nation gets its head of state in two ways, either via an electoral process (outright election or subcontracted to an electoral college), or through birth, which in practice means retaining an official royal family as, in effect, a state stud farm which produces 'heirs and spares' on an ongoing basis.

The British prefer the latter, and seem to also believe that they need to pay them a lot of money in return for it all. However, people – even royals – are only human, and keeping an extended family in luxury can place many stresses on both the incumbents and the system. It truly is a genetic lottery. A nation can get a useless monarch with a dangerously deep sense of duty, someone who would rather be anywhere else, or a dullard with all the charisma of a damp sponge. Money seems to take the unpleasant edge off what can be a rather Faustian bargain. If the price is right, many things can become rather more endurable. That said, involving an entire family on an official generational basis is fraught with problems, just one of the many of a system which hires automatically through birth and fires only upon the death of the incumbent. The public purse is compelled to pick up the tab for a large extended family all of whom are instilled with a profound sense of status and self-importance irrespective of any objectively judged attributes or skills.

It is certainly easier to establish clearer dividing lines when you have a presidential system, although as in the American system, for example, the spouse and any family may assume – though admittedly just for a few years – a high public profile. That said, incumbents usually manage such a profile to suit their presidential style. In the British system, an extended family is accepted – and paid for – almost without question, but for those beyond the monarch – and possibly the heir – there remains the sense that they are just expensive passengers with little or none of the responsibility. So why reward them?

Perhaps were people more clearly informed about the entire system they might be rather more questioning, and the British system has

2 MONEY AND THE MONARCHY

been adept at encouraging opacity and deference. A proper process of accountability is needed. In the early 1970s, at the time of the renegotiation of the Civil List, Lord Houghton proposed the creation of a new body – the 'Commissioners of the Crown' – in order to oversee all aspects of expenditure on the royal family. This proposal had broad support both within Parliament and elsewhere but foundered principally on the fact that making royal finance clearer by grouping it together would reveal the actual total amount. That really says it all. For once, a minister would have actually been answerable to Parliament on matters relating to royal finances. The Palace, rather predictably was not very happy with this proposed *glasnost*. Indeed, the Queen's reaction was so hostile that Lord Cobbold, the Lord Chamberlain, insisted that her views should not even be relayed to government ministers and the MPs who were actually sitting on the Select Committee which was then examining the proposals to reform the Civil List[32].

The Sovereign Grant Act has, in fairness, introduced a degree of parliamentary accountability, and it is to be hoped that in future this will encourage the opportunity to ask more searching questions about royal financial matters. However, where it failed is that it never asked more fundamental questions about what a twenty-first century monarchy ought to do, how 'big' it ought to be, and hence how much it ought to cost. Nor was there any examination why resources are devoted to the remaining members of the royal family. These 'peripheral' royals – with the possible exception of the heir to the throne – have no formal constitutional role whatsoever, merely a numerical ranking in the order of succession, and any functions they perform rest on no more than precedence and 'mission creep'. The UK constitution does not actually require them to visit places, shake hands with people and in engage in inane conversation. They do it essentially to justify their existence and the fact that they all to varying degrees benefit from the millions which we spend on this institution. This extensive cast list is little more than a hangover from an imperial system staffed by Queen Victoria's large extended family. The Duke of York was recently reported as being keen for his daughters to have more of an official role (and with it expensive security details and other official expenses). Famous for little more than a predilection for absurd hats, we must ask what – other than a ridiculously deferential system – encourages 'Princess Beatrice' and her sister 'Princess Eugenie' to think that they should be automatically entitled to a state-subsidised lifestyle? Imperial delusions persist. Although he has now been required to step down from his role as 'Special Trade Representative' the Duke still travels the globe at public expense.

APPROPRIATE AND ACCOUNTABLE
Proper transparency would be best achieved by more transparent parliamentary accountability and the payment of a straightforward, appropriate and normally taxed official income to the monarch – and the heir to the throne as the monarch's deputy. Should they need their own private staff to squeeze toothpaste or walk the corgis, this should be purely at their own discretion and at their own expense. For the purposes of their official duties, a fully staffed dedicated office and all necessary facilities, from travel to other support, would be provided through a specific publicly-funded allocation. The head of state – the monarch – would have a single, official residence of an appropriate nature. It should also be possible to further separate the incumbent's family and personal life from their official role. It has now become something of a cliché that upon the annual publication of the royal accounts the cost of the monarchy is presented to the public as being equivalent, on a per capita basis, to a 'loaf of bread' or a 'couple of pints of milk'. This rather patronising approach seeks to minimise what is still an important item of public expenditure and is in any case extremely selective, omitting as it does security and other costs. Whilst the figure itself may pale in comparison with the costs of health, education and defence for the population, it represents, uniquely, a situation where one family is maintained in a life of privilege and wealth at the public expense based entirely on their birthright. At the same time, the presentation of those costs seeks to trivialise what is still a very considerable sum of money.

As with so many aspects relating to the monarchy, the terminology which is used tends to assist in making the process almost impenetrable to an outsider – of dubious legal relevance and nearer to the language of an historical fantasy. Why, for instance, the use of quaint, Ruritanian terms such as 'Grant-in-aid' for the cost of maintaining official residences and for air and rail travel? This does little or nothing to relate popular concepts of an institution to the public which finances it. It serves to emphasise both its bizarre status and threatens the integrity of what is a fundamentally important institution of the head of state. This is not a merely decorative edifice, it is a very real component of our constitution, and as such deserves to be properly appraised and rendered truly accountable, before the next succession takes place.

THE SOVEREIGN GRANT ACT – A LOST OPPORTUNITY

It had been long apparent that the 1972 Civil List Act was no longer a suitable means by which to regulate the funding of the monarchy, those arrangements having become, in the words of HM Treasury, 'opaque and unsustainable', the ten-yearly review periods having required 'periodic parliamentary intervention and hazardous inflation assumptions'. It was realised that were the system to continue unaltered, then, sooner or later, a fairly hefty increase in royal funding would be required to keep the Windsor clan in the manner to which they had become accustomed. This would mean that the government would be faced with the prospect of having to hand out a considerably increased sum of public money at a probably most politically awkward time of budgetary restraint and outright cuts in the rest of the public sector, some thing which would certainly not go down too well with hard-pressed voters and redundant public sector workers. This, the Treasury realised, was 'simply not an option', and so the coalition government devised the Sovereign Grant Act. Assuming similar levels of funding in the future, and given the fact that royal spending had, it claimed, fallen by 50% in real terms over the last 20 years, then the search was on for a means by which to provide a non-contentious and enhanced funding solution.

Monarchists often trot out, as detailed previously in this chapter, the old argument that the monarchy could revert – however undesirable and indeed impossible in the modern democratic reality – to living off 'their' Crown Estates revenue. This, it was decided, could form the basis of a new funding process, not by actually using Crown Estates revenue as such, but by using a percentage of the annual – using the figure of the financial year of two year's prior – revenue as a yardstick to produce a 'suitable' annual amount. By a fairly unsophisticated bit of reverse-engineering, 15% was decided upon as a handy equivalent figure – but one which could be amended in future as necessary. Already, as the Crown Estates profits were released in late June 2012, it was possible to calculate the 'bare' Sovereign Grant for 2014 – £36million – as the figure is based on the Estates' profits for two years back. This is a big increase on the already set £31million figure for 2013, which itself included a £1million element to go towards the costs of the 2012 Diamond Jubilee. Even now, there is widespread misunderstanding about this money. For instance, London's 'Evening Standard' newspaper announced on June 21st 2012 that the growth in Crown Estates profits for the year would mean a '16% pay rise' for the Queen under the new system. It is in fact a 16% increase in her official 'expense account', but the remark typifies the misconceptions that tend to abound in this area. Any 'pay rise' for the Queen will be demonstrated by the Duchy of Lancaster profits for the year.

The more perceptive of you will have spotted – and this all slipped through Parliament pretty well un-noticed, as is traditional, by the way – that at no point was there to be a general debate as to what might be an appropriate scale of funding for the constitutional monarchy of a economically struggling, deficit-laden European nation. No, it was simply taken for granted that things should remain basically the same, and that the Windsor family should continue to live in the manner to which they have become accustomed, with the level of the Civil List and Grants-in-aid continuing largely unchanged. Yes, there was a debate in Parliament, but its place in the parliamentary timetable ensured that it would be almost totally overlooked. It took place just a few days before Parliament shut up shop for the summer, on June 30th 2011 – right in the middle of the Wimbledon tennis schedule. It was, and not wishing to be unfair to those – some of them MPs who have long stood up to be counted as critics of the institution – who participated, shunted into the shadows, when it was known that attention would be focused almost anywhere else.

The overall tone of the debate sadly epitomised much that surrounds those who criticise established elements of our constitution. A slightly supercilious, condescending and lightweight tone prevailed, fulfilling the requirement of a debate but not ever really getting serious. It felt like the end of school term before the summer break as, indeed, given its proximity to Wimbledon fortnight and the end of the parliamentary term, it actually was. Once again, the traditional 'cultural cringe' manifested itself whenever matters royal are aired in Parliament. Labour MP Dennis MacShane suggested that a 'wider debate' was needed but sadly this certainly wasn't going to be the time – or the place – for it. Any attempt by him, and fellow MP Paul Flynn to 'get serious', was diffused by the rather patronising feel of the proceedings. Serious questions were simply not encouraged that day.

Conservative Jacob Rees-Mogg – described by Speaker's wife Sally Bercow as a 'time-travelling Tory toff' – ludicrously opined that he wished for the 'precise opposite' of 'full transparency' in respect of royal tax affairs, despite the fact that they weren't actually debating royal tax anyway. He also trotted out the crazy idea that a future monarch could opt not to surrender the Crown Estate income at the start of their reign. Read the pathetic, brief proceedings in Hansard if you must, but it sums up the sad, deferential and sorry state of affairs of a supposedly democratic twenty-first century nation that still seems afraid to have even a proper debate about an institution that has public money thrown at it with few questions asked.

Some very questionable assertions were made – and never challenged. This was a brief, sparsely attended nod-through event in which everybody was supposed behave and not make a fuss. No attempt was made to challenge the huge earnings – detailed later in this book – of the monarch and heir from the Duchies of Lancaster and Cornwall respectively which effectively still state-subsidises an extended royal family. Instead, just a trivial bit of fine-tuning in relation to the status and entitlement of the Duchy of Cornwall income, chiefly to bring it in to line with modern gender legislation. Instead of a total of over £30-odd million a year being handed over to the lucky duo, no questions asked, why not institute properly thought out and appropriate figures to be paid as annual allowances? No, that would be truly unthinkable.

So, rather than asking whether or not the British monarchy might at present, as the comparative figures for other European heads of state suggest, be actually rather over-indulged by the taxpayer, and in these straitened times be required to downscale their entire operation, the show was to remain on the road in its extravagant, quasi-imperial-style form. Instead of the equivalent of 15% of Crown Estates revenue, why not 10% – or even 5%? These would still be handsomely large amounts in their own right. The whole nonsense of handing over Grants-in-aid for upkeep of the palaces to the Royal Household could have been replaced by putting them, as the state properties they really are, under the control of the Crown Estates and just let the monarch occupy them as a tenant – which is all they really are anyway.

FUTURE FINANCING

To preserve a notion of 'tradition' why not use the Duchies of Cornwall and Lancaster to form the basis of the financing of the monarchy? The existing Duchy incomes are now quite disproportionate and far in excess of what is required by the monarch and the heir to the throne in respect of their public remuneration – in effect their official 'salaries'. The two combined Duchy incomes – around £30million by 2010 – would in fact be an appropriate figure for the entire operating budget of a scaled-down monarchy.

Considerable savings could be effected by the simple expedient of removing the minor royals – and their corresponding expenses – from 'official' duties entirely. These 'duties' are not essential to the nation and in many cases might justifiably be paid for by the many charities and other private bodies which they currently represent. They have evolved on an ad hoc basis, with family members taking advantage of their position to push their own particular self-styled 'causes'. The Duke of York, having lost his position as the nation's 'Special Trade Representative', still seems to pursue his own version of the role in an semi-unofficial capacity and still wishing to be able to claim expenses for it – and has also wished his two daughters to have more high-profile, 'official' roles, and with it the state funded security presence, travel funding and so on that would accompany them. Anyone else trying this sort of thing on would be regarded as being virtually delusional, but we still seem to tolerate it in our royal family.

The present vague status of the heir to the throne needs addressing. It is easy to forget that in Britain's unwritten constitutional system he is the heir, but that's about all. Like the Prime Minister, he has no job description, no legally defined role which he is required to fulfil and with which to comply. Within this vague set-up he is now gets in excess of £18million of public money a year with which to do what he likes. He has evolved a lifestyle which seeks to avoid too much political controversy despite sailing very close to the wind at the same time. As we will see later, the world of 'charity' has become the facade behind which such largesse can be accommodated and made acceptable to the country as a whole. He is not, under our present system, an official 'deputy' to the Queen. The fact that he – and indeed other family members – stands in for her on a regular basis, and can claim expenses for doing so – is no more than an informal arrangement. Such a situation is both confusing and inefficient. It is time to remove all members of the royal family from the public payroll with the exception of the monarch – as head of state – and, perhaps, institute the heir to the throne as an official 'deputy', with an agreed contractual constitutional role. No-one else. Nobody. Period. If they have partners or family members them these should be allowed to pursue separate careers subject to full disclosure of interests or they should be maintained purely at personal expense. As would be butlers, valets and so on. At present the situation is vague in the extreme and a very grey area exists in terms of the borders between 'private' and 'public'.

Why do we have so many royal 'households', maintained at great public expense, and with different family members perform overlapping functions, for example? The absurdity of the monarch and heir being given state aid to spend on 'Occupied' royal palaces adds to the confusion, and is, one suspects, more a sop to royal pride so they can pretend they are 'really' theirs. Although officially described as 'legally inalienable property', and by the Treasury Solicitor in 1971 as 'non-surrendered Crown Property', the plain fact is that the monarch cannot dispose of them, nor in any case, afford to maintain them themselves. The status of the Palaces as anything other than 'State' property is no more than a contrivance. If the so-called 'surrender' of the Crown Estates income is now no more than a formality, perhaps it is time similarly to acknowledge this fact too in respect of the Palaces.

More sensible would be to recognise them for what they are – state properties – and for the government to pay directly for their upkeep and cut out the entire 'Royal Property Grant-in-aid' pantomime. The present situation permits a degree of 'buck-passing' in terms of responsibility for maintenance. In 2007 the Royal Household complained that the Palace 'Grant-in-aid' was insufficient and that loose tiles and pieces of stonework were falling into the courtyard at Buckingham Palace. The 'Keeper of the Privy Purse', Sir Alan Reid claimed that an extra £1million was needed to fix the crumbling structure. By 2008, the Palace was talking in rather more dramatic terms, arguing that they now had an estimated 'backlog' of repair work to the assorted 'Occupied' Palaces of £32million. This may, in one sense, be valid. After all, all old buildings need fixing on a regular basis. It also avoids another fundamental issue; why are there so many 'Occupied' Palaces in the first place? European monarchies generally manage perfectly well in just one or two official properties which are, unambiguously, maintained by, and remain the property of, the State. Maintenance priorities should be determined by the State, as the taxpayer is ultimately responsible for them, and not allowed to become a bargaining counter on the part of the Royal Household more generally. The new

Sovereign Grant Act has failed to properly address this area. There is now an urgent need for a reduction in the 'Occupied' property portfolio. For example, by 2008 £500,000 of repair work was to be carried out on two of eight properties in 'Lower Yard' at Windsor Castle. These are in reality 'tied cottages' for the 'Military Knights of Windsor' – retired military who carry out occasional ceremonial duties. What is needed is a wholesale re-evaluation of both the property and such roles. Why are we still providing subsidised housing for such Ruritanian 'jobsworths' at all?

The whole business is still dogged by a lack of transparency, camouflaged by a wheedling Palace PR approach which paints a picture of a threadbare monarch shuffling about in the evening gloom at Buckingham Palace switching off lights. Yet in 2010, the Independent newspaper revealed that whilst the Palace was begging for an extra £15million to patch up the building they were still allowing a cast-list of pantomime-titled employees to live rent-free in these state buildings. As the Commons Public Accounts Committee pressed – sometimes unsuccessfully – for more details, characters like the 'Mistress of the Robes' and the 'Surveyor of the Queen's Pictures' were two of six members of the household living free at the taxpayers' expense. Royals too, were benefiting, with Princess Alexandra – whose usual residence is the bargain leased Thatched House Lodge in picturesque Richmond Park – being able to stop over in one of the West End palaces if a taxi ride home doesn't appeal. Not only this, it was revealed that the Palace had tried to hang on to £2.5million from the sale of a small 'ransom strip' of land next to the Palace Gardens Hotel adjoining Kensington Palace. Ministers wanted it, given rightly that it was from the sale of state property, but the Palace claimed, curiously, that it was the Queen's personally[33].

All this comes at a time when an ageing monarch has considerably reduced her activities yet the costs still continue to rise. The present levels of financial support are hard to justify, and result from a haphazard historical process. Serious reform is long overdue. A clear and considered appraisal of what should define 'official' duties – and exactly who should need to be doing them – is essential.

With regard to the Duchies, a clear statutory incorporation of them into the Crown Estates – to resolve any present anomalies or doubts as to their exact status – should be implemented. The current relationship of the Prince of Wales, as heir to the throne, to the Duchy of

2 MONEY AND THE MONARCHY

Cornwall would, as a result, disappear, as would that of the monarch to the Duchy of Lancaster. Both should be replaced by straightforward official salaries. this would also make for a much easier differentiation between what at the moment is often a rather blurred mixture of earnings and 'expenses'. Were the monarch, for instance, to receive a similar amount as the Prime Minister, for example, who receives a salary of £188,848, that might be seen as an entirely reasonable level of remuneration. Being generous, and we have been for a very, very long time, and to preserve some kind of comparative league-table hierarchy, perhaps something in the region of £250-300,000 a year? Indeed, they would derive a potentially much higher benefit since their term of office – life-based as opposed to being dependent upon election at regular intervals, means that they might be likely to receive such an income for far longer. Let us not underestimate, too, the fact that we have as a nation, permitted to monarchy to get very, very rich, through tax exemptions and outright indulgence, over the generations, to accumulate very significant wealth personally. Witness, for example, the huge estates including Balmoral and Sandringham, and remember the millions likely to be sheltered behind Bank of England nominee companies, which are effectively invisible.

For an international comparison, we could look to the example of the German head of state – a non-executive presidency with constitutional duties not dissimilar to the hereditary British monarch. It is also a nation that has succeeded impressively well without a tottering institutionalised pyramid of flummery and privilege at its constitutional apex. The Federal President received an official salary equivalent to £133,330 in 2007, a far cry from the Queen's £11,627,000 that same year.

THE HEIR TO THE THRONE
The heir to the throne could be paid on a basis similar to that of a Cabinet Minister, whose combined income – ministerial plus that as an MP – totals £133,997. While his Duchy of Cornwall income has to cover some of his official duties, it should be remembered that those duties are not formally defined, and are hard to isolate from his other personal interests. It is, in any case, at over £17million gross a year, a hell of a lot of public money.

Perhaps a more appropriate method of assessment might be to remunerate the heir on the same basis as an average salary of the several military ranks which he holds and of which he is evidently so proud and in the ostentatiously medalled uniforms of which he frequently appears. A four-star General, for example, would have received £142,205 in 2005[34] – and his other positions are on similar grades. Given that the Prince of Wales is estimated to have a personal fortune of at least £4million – and that is probably a very considerable under-estimate – thanks to the royal family's favourable treatment in the past, he might expect a return on that sum of, say, £300,000 per annum. Combined with the official salary as heir, that would provide a reasonable income, approaching half a million a year before tax.

Not only that, but the income should be dependent upon the heir to the throne accepting to abide by the same requirements of political neutrality in terms of conduct which applies to the monarch. After all, whilst Charles may be keen to 'deputise' for his mother he still wants to be able to express often contentious opinions. He can't have it both ways, and a clear contract should make this crystal clear.

THE 'INDEPENDENCE' MYTH

In the past, the Prince of Wales has been emphatic in his assertion that he should have a high degree of 'financial independence', and has made it clear that without it he would be unwilling to take on the position of sovereign: 'I think it of absolute importance that the Monarch should have a degree of financial independence from the State. I am not prepared to take on the position of sovereign of this country on any other basis'[35]. Yet as the monarch is indisputably the ultimate state employee, who else *would* pay them?

To collude in such a pretence of 'independence' is simply to accept the elements of the political versus court 'game' that has insulated the British monarchy from reality for so long. True financial independence for a monarch is a carte blanche for absolutism, the very antithesis of parliamentary democracy. The Duchy of Cornwall – the Prince's present source of income as heir – is not independent from Parliamentary scrutiny. He has no access to its capital – and the Civil List and its accompanying payments are granted by Parliament. It would seem that he is happy to benefit from the income at present, and at the present level he really can't complain. Nor can his mother with her own Duchy of Lancaster income. These are sums of money which would might make even Fred Goodwin (formerly 'Sir'), the disgraced banker, blush slightly. One suspects that as long as they receive their present extremely high incomes they are prepared to overlook the obvious fact that the money is not really 'independent' at all, but is granted through the ultimate consent of Parliament.

The money from the Duchies is paid conditionally upon the incumbents in their official capacities – not simply as private individuals. The idea of 'independence' is simply nonsensical. Lots of cash and infrequent, preferably, non-existent reviews is their ideal. The reported wish of the Queen for greater accountability and the need to rein in spending increases which accompanied the Sovereign Grant Act was simply an acknowledgement that to act otherwise would be politically unacceptable in a period of spending cuts and high unemployment.

The Prince of Wales used to argue that he ought to be entitled to his 'independence' by taking back the income from the Crown Estates. One hopes that with the passage of time he has learnt that is an impossible demand. Phillip Hall neatly sums up the situation:

> The answer, or 'advice', that any government would give a monarch who demanded back 'his or her' Crown Estates would simply be that, regrettably, it was not possible in the modern era. And that would in itself settle matters. It may be true that government ministers and civil servants have usually been careful to maintain the formality that a new monarch can reverse the so-called bargain of 1760. But it is no more than a formality. For the monarchy's own sake, the government of the day (of whichever party) would seek to protect the monarch from the consequent embarrassment of such a step back into the eighteenth century[36].

OVERPAID, OVERINDULGED...

The monarch and the royal family have been indulged for generations, able to accumulate considerable wealth and enjoy a lifestyle of institutionalised privilege and influence at public expense. Tax concessions, high official income for leading members and favoured access to public resources persist. This process has continued during the reign of the present Queen, subject only to occasional and limited review. Much of this has been achieved by voluntary agreement rather than legislation, a process kept apart from our elected representatives. Royal finance is still beset by misunderstanding and a general lack of transparency. The picture is complicated by a haphazard process of evolution of the financial structure which supports the monarch and the royal family, and is accompanied by a traditionally deferential attitude on the part of Parliament as a whole. The Government of the day tends to lapse into a default defence of the status quo despite often broader general consensus for reform. Criticism is discouraged, or, at the very least, proper debate. Even the Sovereign Grant Act may fail to provide the necessary level of acountability if it is not accompanied by a more assertive attitude on the part of Parliament.

PUBLIC NOT PRIVATE

The blurring of the distinction between holders of royal titles and their role and status as individuals adds to the complexity. When, for instance, the Queen conveys a title to the heir to the throne, whilst it may be done by her in a 'personal' capacity, this is through her official position as monarch, not simply in a private family capacity. After all, these are officially recognised titles rather than just family nicknames.

Members of the royal family perform duties in their titular roles – as 'Earl of Wessex' or 'Duke of York', for example, yet little thought is given to the fact that inherent conflicts of interest may arise as a result. In times past, this was of less importance, but in what is now a more market-orientated environment this can, and increasingly will have, serious implications for both office-holders and the taxpayer unless the situation is reviewed. The titles are themselves firmly in the public domain, and hence ownership of them is not personal to the holders themselves but possessed, in our modern Parliamentary system, by that embodiment of power, the 'Crown in Parliament' – the state – a combination of the will of the people expressed through the elected government. Parliament is supreme, and although some prerogative powers still remain, they are mostly now exercised by the Prime Minister of the day, upon whose advice the monarch acts, whilst retaining few powers in their own right. The present monarchical line was established by Act of Parliament and, Parliament's supremacy, makes the monarchy by definition ultimately subordinate to it.

ROYAL WEALTH AND INEQUALITY

Financial 'independence' for a constitutional monarchy is a fiction. By accepting money from Parliament they accept a contract. As George Bernard Shaw once perceptively noted, in a slightly different context, having accepted the basic principle, all we are left to argue over is the price. Culturally, Britain has hitherto accepted a situation in which the monarch – and the royal family – have been able to become rich

2 MONEY AND THE MONARCHY

and to consolidate and retain that wealth, and have done so through a culture of secrecy and deference.

The royal family have been able to avoid the tough economic reality of the everyday experience of the majority thanks to a level of public indulgence that truly defies belief. Palace spin and a deferential public attitude in general keeps this expensive show on the road. Perhaps more than any other class or institution, the monarchy symbolises the notion of institutionalised privilege and inequality and sets a poor example for the nation. Britain as an offshore tax-haven for the world's super-rich with high levels of wealth and income inequality might be acceptable to a tiny minority but it is no solution for the mass of the population who are increasingly suffering from the effects of globalisation and world financial instability. As the wealth and privileges enjoyed by the super-rich attract increasing concern, the monarchy will not be immune to criticism. Rising unemployment and a long-term economic downturn will be a hostile environment for a privileged royal family who have never emerged from public scrutiny with more, only less. On any rational examination, the British monarchy will have to be prepared to make serious sacrifices, and the time for such a critical and far-reaching examination is long overdue. In this respect, the Sovereign Grant Act has failed spectacularly. The UK has long ago lost its empire, but it continues to cling to – and pay for – an imperial style monarchy. The scale of the UK monarchy in a sense reflects the scale of the nation's continuing delusion of its real place in the twenty-first century world.

WHO OWNS WHAT?

Firstly, and most importantly, we must establish exactly what belongs to the royal family and what belongs to the people. Attempts to answer even this seemingly simple question have not yet met with success. In 2000 the then Chancellor of the Exchequer, Gordon Brown ducked the issue in response to that very question – from MP Norman Baker – by talking simply about the Royal Collection[37]. It is time to cut through the veritable forest of evasion and the quaint and arcane language that merely conspires to obscure and confuse the issue. While the Crown Private Estates Act of 1800 enabled the monarch to own land in a personal capacity, the remainder of the picture is extremely vague. Generations of privilege, tax exemptions and conveniently blurred distinctions between money given for 'official' purposes and money given for 'expenses' or as outright income means that the Windsor family have accumulated serious amounts of money. The individuals may claim not to be as wealthy as some may claim, insisting it is not 'their' wealth but is in fact held within trusts and so on. The reality is that they benefit from money ultimately derived from public sources, and as such need to face serious accountability in respect of it.

A NEW CONTRACT
We should decide exactly what it is we actually expect the monarchy – and perhaps more importantly the heir – to do. Official income, taxed on an equal basis to all other citizens, should be paid in return for a properly defined full-time schedule. Activities other than outright official duties should not be remunerated. The present situation, in which royal 'duties' of the monarch, heir and extended family members – have grown into an extensive, ill-defined and costly process, should end. The so-called 'minor' royals should be removed from the public realm entirely, and the monarch and heir retained to perform a purely constitutional role. It would also help address the problems of a nation trying to cope in the modern world without a written constitution. Indeed, it would be a most desirable progression for Britain – or a future re-configured 'United Kingdom' – to define its constitutional position with proper Bill of Rights and a written constitution.

Such new financial and contractual clarity would be to the advantage of Parliament and the public, who support the entire operation. It would also benefit the royal family as a whole who would no longer risk being perceived as living a life of privilege at the public expense. The monarch and heir to the throne would, in this revised system, be able to fully devote themselves to fulfilment of their official duties and would thus be able to represent the nation in a more defined and focused manner, one which would be appropriate to the role and status of a modern European democracy. If this is unacceptable to them, then a republican alternative with a modest, democratically elected non-executive president would be the obvious solution, and which could be incorporated relatively easily into our constitutional system.

Royal failure to accept a very stringent reappraisal of their role and funding could have more profound consequences. It is easy to see that there is very considerable tolerance for the present Queen. As long as she remains on the throne, the status quo will prevail, with the generally conservative public willing to overlook the family's considerable wealth gained at public expense. However, for her successor, things could be very different. It is likely that the succession itself will mark a point of serious reappraisal. Many countries for whom the Queen is presently head of state may wish to end this arrangement at that point. The future of the United Kingdom could well be in doubt too with the possibility of Scottish independence. A lack of popular support in the UK itself might place the new monarch – George VII, as it is believed Charles Windsor would like to be called – on very fragile ground. Such doubt could well provoke a degree of instability which could threaten the institution itself, certainly calling into question its scale and cost. In such a situation, 'skipping a generation' might be possible, but the prospect of a profoundly down-scaled monarchy might not be deemed appropriate – either to the royal family or the nation. At this point, a republic might become perceived as a much more preferable alternative.

3
'Nice Little Earners':
The Two Duchies

The Treasury should review the working of the arrangements whereby surpluses from the two Duchies provide an annual income for the Households of The Queen and The Prince of Wales. As these arrangements have been in place for over six hundred years, such a review would hardly be over-hasty. Our work has revealed obscurities and potential conflicts of interest in the management and governance of the Duchies accounts. I cannot understand why these accounts are not subject to the same disclosure requirements as other accounts presented to Parliament. More information and explanation need to be given to readers of the accounts, not the least of which is Parliament. And the best way for Parliament to get that information and explanation is for the Comptroller and Auditor General to be given the power to audit the Duchies' accounts.
Edward Leigh MP, Chairman of the Public Accounts Committee, speaking on the occasion of the publication of its 19th Report of Session 2004–05, which examined the accounts of the Duchies of Cornwall and Lancaster.

On Monday, February 7th, 2005, the Public Accounts Committee had an opportunity, for the first time since the formation of the first of the two bodies in 1337 – to quiz representatives of the Duchies of Cornwall and Lancaster about their management and financial control. Historically, the function of these two estates has been the provision of an 'official' income – though admittedly rather more recently than is often thought – for the heir to the throne in the case of the Duchy of Cornwall, and for the monarch in the case of the Duchy of Lancaster. Whilst an official income for the head of state is entirely reasonable, the nature and scale of the present system of remuneration owes more to historical accident and official neglect than anything else. As for the heir to the throne, for a position with no defined constitutional role, and no 'job' other than that of merely 'waiting', the need for any remuneration at all is rather more questionable.

The incomes from the two Duchies are not intended to meet any of the costs of performing official duties – these are met by the Civil List and Grants-in-aid which will be in effect merged and replaced after 2013 by the Sovereign Support Grant. There has supposedly been some reliance on these funds, particularly in the past, for meeting some expenses which have, or allegedly have, a 'public' dimension. The use of such funds for what are claimed to be 'official' purposes has distinct propaganda appeal for the monarch and heir. These 'poor' royals are evidently so hard-pressed that £140million plus per year of official expenses – and that is excluding the money received from the Duchies – is simply insufficient for them to do their job. However, no concrete proof is ever submitted in respect of such expenditure which it has been claimed has had to be made. The system assists in perpetuating such stories with its high degree of 'blurring' between the private and public roles of the incumbents. Even their actual entitlement to these incomes is more than a little questionable, given the nature of the unwritten British constitution, resting more upon precedent rather than statutory entitlement.

HISTORICAL DEVELOPMENT
This book does not propose to describe the historic detail pertaining to the Duchies – this was thoroughly examined by Phillip Hall in his book 'Royal Fortune'[1]. The Duchies' promotional materials emphasise the obsolete mediaeval history which is in reality now little more than fanciful set-dressing. Whilst complex historical and legal justifications may be sought for the original right of the monarch and the heir to the throne to the incomes of the two Duchies, they now rest ultimately on the discretion of Parliament. Our present monarchy itself derives from legislation passed in the early 18th century – the Act of Settlement of

3 'NICE LITTLE EARNERS': THE TWO DUCHIES

1701. They inherit their position through a legislatively designated lineage – that of the 'heirs and successors' – of Sophia, the Electress of Hanover. In this way George I – unable to speak English and barely known beyond his homeland principality – became King. Even before that, Parliament had handed the throne to William of Orange – part of the present-day Netherlands, as a result of James II having decamped to France in 1688, following his unsuccessful attempt to reassert absolute monarchy. The Duchies, such as they were, had been inherited by these monarchs as merely one of a number of sources of income.

Following the execution of Charles I for treason, all the Duchy estates were sold off and dispersed which convincingly breaks any tenuous notion of 'continuity' linking them to the feudal estates of the mediaeval period. They were then 're-assembled' in a rather patchy and piecemeal fashion by Parliament, in a rather dubious attempt to restore the pre-1649 status quo – and the 1702 Crown Lands Act effectively confirms the state ownership of the Duchies. As such, it is for Parliament to decide whether the monarch and heir benefit from the estates' revenues rather than the assumption that there is some kind of 'right' to the money dating back to the Middle Ages.

The Duchies are now little more than convenient collective terms for large real estate investment portfolios far removed from their original namesakes. Some historical 'remnants' persist, such as religious connections with certain parishes, in relation to the Duchy of Lancaster, and even the now effectively obsolete title of the Chancellor of the Duchy of Lancaster itself – now little more than a label for a 'Minister without Portfolio' – and the right to *Bona Vacantia* revenue. Others, such as the responsibility for appointing magistrates in their respective areas have now been abolished. As demonstrated by the Public Accounts Committee in 2005, the de facto position would now seem to be that Parliament regards the Duchies as comparable to other Crown Estate property. As such they are ultimately able to legislate not only the amount of money which the monarch and heir receive from these bodies – but also whether they actually continue to receive it at all. Not surprisingly, the Duchies themselves protest their alleged 'special' status. They emphasise their mediaeval historical provenance and hold out against submitting to the standards of accountability applied to other public bodies. No doubt it is simply their connection with the monarchy which makes them feel they are above normal levels of scrutiny. The Duchies justification for special treatment is poor, but that has not stopped them persisting in such behaviour. They have sought in the past deliberately to conceal information in order to deflect criticism, with the second volume of the official history of the Duchy of Lancaster printed privately and its very existence withheld at the time of the extensive deliberations on the monarchy's finances in the early 1970s[2].

MAJOR REFORM IN 1760: THE CIVIL LIST

In 1760 – at the time of the accession of George III – a major financial rearrangement was agreed between the monarchy and the government of the day. The monarchy surrendered its rights to the Crown Estates and other Crown hereditary revenues. This stemmed from both the perennial inability of monarchs to live within their means – and their consequent pleading with Parliament to increase their income on a regular basis. It marked, more importantly, the point where the monarchy was brought properly under the financial control of Parliament. Since then, the Duchies have become defined sources of official income for their incumbents. Crown Estates revenue was surrendered in return for the payment of the Civil List.

The 1760 legislation was the recognition of a fundamentally changed political landscape in which the monarch was made accountable to Parliament and was relieved of a number of responsibilities which were transferred to Parliament – that of paying for the cost of a burgeoning Civil Service, the Judiciary, and the Government as a whole – estimated to be at least £15 billion a year at the present time. In addition to this, however, as the Labour MP Willie Hamilton, for so many years an outspoken critic of the monarchy, pointed out in his examination of the institution in the 1970s:

> ...a later Act of 1787 transferred all the 'hereditary revenues' to the Consolidated Fund, i.e. to the Government. Thus is the charade of the Crown 'voluntarily' surrendering the revenues of its private lands at the beginning of each reign in return for a fixed Civil List – to last for the duration of the reign – calculated to deceive the nurturing of myths about the 'hereditary rights' of the Royal Family to revenues from lands which are so patently public property – which have, since 1786, been publicly controlled and publicly developed by Commissioners appointed by the Chancellor of the Exchequer and answerable to Parliament – is beyond the credulity of the rational mind[3].

3 'NICE LITTLE EARNERS': THE TWO DUCHIES

The established formality is that in return for 'surrendering' the income from the Crown Estates for the duration of each reign, successive monarchs have received an agreed Civil List payment to cover the costs of performing their official duties. Though the exact scope and amount of this payment has changed since then, it is to meet the expense of operating the monarchy, and is not as some often believe, an income. The Duchies provide official incomes for their two recipients through their status as public officeholders, not as private individual. Were a monarch or heir to abdicate – as happened with Edward VIII – then that income would cease.

THE ORIGINAL DUCHIES

The Duchy of Lancaster, which provides the monarch with an official income, originates from an estate seized in 1399 by Richard II, from John of Gaunt. The latter had died, and the King took this opportunity to increase his landholding whilst Gaunt's son, Henry, was exiled abroad. On his return, Henry took back the property and control of the country as well. In his new guise of Henry IV, he set in place the arrangement used as the basis for the monarch's entitlement to the income from the Duchy of Lancaster. He intended it as a 'separate inheritance' to protect his family's future financial security in case they were deposed in the future. This is because at the time any property acquired by a monarch automatically became 'the Crown's'. Until 1800 a monarch could not hold property as a private individual separate from their official status.

The 'official' version of Duchy history tends to gloss over this important fact. The Duchy was never 'separate' as such but simply became a income producing asset – one of many – for successive monarchs irrespective of their dynastic origins. Henry's aim to 'ring-fence' the Duchy for his family thus failed from the outset. The Duchy was not actually incorporated by charter until 1461 but its provenance as an income producing Crown asset was established as much by precedent as by statute. Phillip Hall goes somewhat further, arguing that it was more a combination of neglect and convenience which permitted the monarch and heir to benefit from these estates with no real established basis for actually doing so: 'After 1830, governments may have found it expedient to allow the monarch to annex the Duchy revenues for his or her private use, but this was and continues to be an anomaly'[4]. The fact that the Duchy appeared to be expressly left out of the 1760 Civil List agreement, and its income 'surrendered' along with the rest of the Crown Estate may simply have been due to the fact that it wasn't really making any money at the time – an annual profit that year of just £16-18s-6d[5]. Even in 1760, £17 was by no means a fortune.

The Duchy of Cornwall, meanwhile, has its origins in 1337 when Edward III acquired the estate for his son, Edward, Prince of Wales, and it has since then been used to provide an income source for the heir to the throne. Whilst an heir is a minor, the income reverted to the monarch. Section 9 of the new Sovereign Grant Act makes alterations to this to take account of changed gender legislation so that a female heir, who, whilst not becoming the Duke, can still receive the money without the title – and without the Duchy income reverting to the monarch. Curiously, in the case of the Queen, she seems able – gender notwithstanding – to become Duke of Lancaster. (In future, if the heir to the Duchy of Cornwall is under age, and the revenue goes to the Monarch, the overall Sovereign Grant will be reduced by an equivalent amount). The Stuart Kings, habitually overspent and extravagant, were actually forced to sell off much of the Duchy assets to raise funds. Following the execution of Charles I in 1649, the estates were sold and dispersed; subsequently attempts were made to reacquire and 'reassemble' them after the restoration of the monarchy in 1660.

These and further acquisitions over the centuries have resulted in an historical 'patchwork effect' which means that the Duchies now no longer correspond to their original equivalents in terms of either their extent or composition. Today, the majority of the acreage of the Duchy of Cornwall – 28,539 hectares, or 52% of the Duchy's total of 54,764 hectares – is, for example, in Devon. Contrary to the popular 'country estate' image, Duchy accounts for 2005 showed that by far the largest proportion of its acs s, some 44%, are accounted for by commercial properties, agricultural land and forestry making up 28%, with residential properties and financial assets amounting to 14% each. Of greatest value are the 15.9 hectares in Greater London, which include the famous Oval cricket ground. Other holdings are spread over numerous English counties, 23 in all, as well as the Vale of Glamorgan, in Wales, and the Scilly Isles. The largest landholding of the Duchy of Lancaster is 6,847 hectares in Yorkshire – not Lancashire – while its highest value holdings are sites in the Regent Street and Strand areas of London's West End, including the ground upon which stands the famous Savoy Hotel. The alleged 'continuity' of these institutions in other

3 'NICE LITTLE EARNERS': THE TWO DUCHIES

> than name only is extremely misleading. The notion that they date back seamlessly and little altered to the 14th century is far from the truth. They remain now as little more than labels to cover their present-day status as investment vehicles providing incomes for their respective incumbents. The monarchy likes to regard them as essentially private fiefdoms but closer inspection reveals fundamental flaws in this view.

THE MODERN DUCHY OF CORNWALL

In the past, the Duchy of Cornwall was essentially a low-profile investment portfolio based around landholdings, and as such remained largely in the background fulfilling its role as provider of an official income for the heir to the throne. More recently, this remit has been defined – and somewhat altered – by the Duchy itself as 'a private estate which funds the public charitable and private activities' of the Prince of Wales[6].

This is significant on two levels. Firstly, the Duchy's definition of itself as a 'private estate' is very, very questionable indeed. Secondly, rather than being a simple income provider for the heir, this purpose has now become restyled with 'charitable activity' being the emphasised reason for its existence. This is not a legal requirement but the recent result of a concerted effort to make the provision of a large income for the Prince of Wales more publicly acceptable and accompanied by greater efforts to promote his charity work, particularly in times of flagging popularity.

The Duchy also explains its status by using a brief potted history of itself to justify arguing that 'the joint effect' of that history is 'to place the Duchy's assets in trust for the benefit of the present and future Dukes of Cornwall', an altogether very simplistic and selective view. There is no attempt to explain who the trustee – or trustees – might be, although the Prince of Wales's 'Duchy Originals' company website used to argue, curiously, that it was the Prince himself. Whether these rather conflicting descriptions of the status of the Duchy are entirely accurate will be dealt with later, but there is no doubt that the Prince has decided to exploit the commercial and associated public relations potential of this asset in a manner unthinkable in the past. A concerted public relations campaign, comprising books and media appearances which promote the Prince himself, the Duchy, the Prince's charitable interests and his 'Duchy

Originals' brand, combines to emphasise the 'softer' nature of the heir to the throne – benevolent, caring and concerned – but omits the hard fact that this all depends upon a public asset and the money produced by it. The image conveyed by 'Duchy Originals' product branding depends heavily on the high profile and royal associations of the estate from which it takes its name. The operation is far from being a cosy cottage industry. It is a sophisticated commercial operation with a multi-million pound turnover, its income derived almost wholly from royalty payments for the use of the Duchy coat of arms on product packaging – some £40million in 2005 – a figure that had grown to £53million in the following financial year. Sitting alongside competing products on supermarket shelves, the consumer might have been forgiven for assuming that their 'Duchy Originals' biscuits were an example of open commercial rivalry between the heir to the throne and the producers of similar goods; they enjoy a distinct and unique market advantage. Duchy products are endorsed by the heir to the throne – with Duchy Originals profits being donated to charity – and enjoy by implication a 'premium' status but with less overtly commercial overtones. As we will see later, this situation was somewhat altered by Duchy Originals' less than healthy performance as trading conditions became more difficult, leading in effect to a bail-out by supermarket chain Waitrose. However, they retain the Duchy name and the Prince continues to feature prominently on their website – and his charities benefit from the rescued company's profits.

PAYING TAX 'LIKE ANY OTHER BUSINESSMAN'
Today, the Duchy is rather more productive than its mediaeval counterpart. On June 26th 2007, when the Duchy published its annual accounts for the year, it revealed a 'surplus' – the net profits of the estate which constitutes the Prince's official gross income – amounting to £15,174,000 (£14,067,000 in 2006). In addition, the Prince also received some £2,026,000 (£1,584,000 in 2006) allocated by Parliament as 'Grant-in-aid', including £461,000 to maintain Clarence House (up from £355,000 the previous year), and £1,485,000 to cover the cost of air and rail travel. In 2006, for the first time, the Duchy of Cornwall accounts revealed the amount of tax the Prince had paid. This was not a legal requirement, but rather a public relations manoeuvre designed to deflect increasing concern at his very high – and rising – income

received simply for *being* the heir to the throne – as well as the very low level of financial disclosure actually required. He had paid £3,296,000 in income tax – a slight rise on the £3,263,000 it was revealed that he had paid the previous year. By 2007 this figure had risen slightly to £3,434,000 – and in 2012 he handed over £4,496,000 – not a bad overall tax rate on a gross income of £18.3million – thank heavens for all those deductions. It was clear that the Prince's advisors were concerned that, following the 2005 examination of the Duchies of Cornwall and Lancaster, were he not to reveal such facts, Parliament might demand greater disclosure in future and therefore sought to pre-empt such likely demands. The Duchy has made much of the fact that he actually pays income tax – not such a great boast, everyone has to do so by law, except for Charles and his mother who do so only voluntarily. It also glossily paints the Prince as an 'entrepreneur' rather than the reality, that of upscale 'state trustafarian'.

In explaining the 2007 figures, his communications secretary, Paddy Harverson explained; 'The Prince of Wales pays 40% tax just like any other businessman. He is entitled to write off business expenses…'. His words were, however, rather selective. Whilst it was true to argue that his tax was paid at a [then] rate of 40% the Prince is able to pay tax on a purely voluntary basis – and to deduct much as allowable expenses – in accordance with the 1993 Memorandum of Understanding. Responding to a 2007 television documentary, his office denied that he enjoys a 'unique and very privileged tax position'. Paying voluntary taxes is a privilege in itself.

TAX ADVANTAGES
He is not 'any other businessman', but a 'subject' of the Crown like no other. He is the heir to the throne with a colossal state income and a growing charitable 'brand', with his lifestyle and many projects directly and indirectly supported by it. Yet his deductions for 'official' and 'business' expenses, are effectively those of the self-employed. He also receives 'Grant-in-aid' payments from the taxpayer to cover official travel and the costs of running Clarence House. This means that he claims expenses from the state as Prince of Wales whilst also being able to offset expenses through the Duchy as Duke of Cornwall. Prior to the 1993 agreement, he made a voluntary tax payment of just 25%, and was also able to make notable savings by means of a one-off payment of £833,037 which neatly slid in 'under the wire' – in the

words of an MP – for tax purposes in advance of the new regime – a potential saving of nearly £125,000 in tax. The origins of this handy windfall are obscure, an earlier Public Accounts Committee question in 1992 failed to throw any real light on the matter, it having merely been explained by the Duchy as 'working capital accrued since 1983'[7].

The ability to deduct many items as 'business related expenditure' is extremely advantageous for someone with a lifestyle where notions of 'public', 'business', and 'private' are, to say the least, blurred. The Duchy itself is exempt from liability to capital gains tax – not unreasonable in that the incumbent is not allowed to sell any of the capital assets, although as will be seen later, the Public Accounts Committee was concerned at the movement of monies from the capital to the revenue account. However, what really disturbs other business people is the Duchy's exemption from corporation tax. The Duchy's justification for this is that it is 'not a separate legal entity for tax purposes' – unlike a limited company for example. In reality, the Duchy is part of the Crown lands and as a state asset cannot in effect pay tax to itself. It is the ultimate proof that it – and the Duchy of Lancaster – are actually state assets.

The Duchy thus enjoys a unique privilege against its competitors, from which it benefits in being able to achieve these considerable profits which then form the Prince of Wales's official income As long as the interests of a Crown body and an individual are so closely combined, where the profits of one translate to become the income of the other, this will continue to present an anomalous situation.

The Prince gets more than just an income from the Duchy. It is a ready-made business empire which can be used to offset his tax liability and an infrastructure which can help to boost his charities too. Whilst his staff have referred to his 'entrepreneurial' flair, there are those who have questioned that talent. Patrick Hosking, the *Times* investment editor, was critical of the Prince's alleged skill. Writing in the paper on June 27th 2006, he commented that:

> Analysis of the Duchy accounts indicates that the core business [property ownership and management] is shrinking, cash is flooding out rather than in and the overall empire is making only a negligible return on its assets. Only some highly successful punting on the stock market last year and the group's exemption from corporation tax prevented the profit-and-loss account from looking even less pretty[8].

Perhaps one should really be asking, as the Duchy is in essence a property company, whether or not more of the profits ought to be ploughed back into the business, and far fewer – if any at all – to the Prince.

DUCHY OF CORNWALL ASSETS

The Duchy's total assets were valued at just over £600million in 2007. By 2012 this figure had risen to £764million. Some regard the valuation as, to say the least, rather conservative. Well before even these latest figures, Kevin Cahill, the author of 'Who Owns Britain', had estimated the value of the estate as around a billion pounds. Property owned by the Duchy of Cornwall is by no means restricted to Cornwall, and neither are the Duchy and the county synonymous. Assets are spread over a total of 23 counties, amongst them an area of south London, in Kennington, which includes the famous Oval cricket ground.

This is a matter of concern to Surrey County Cricket Club, which currently pays an annual rent of £200,000 to the Duchy. The Surrey Trust, a charity which works to develop cricket has long wished to buy the freehold of the property, with rent paid by the Club to the Trust to be used to develop cricket and sport in the Kennington area – one of the most 'dense and deprived in London'[9]. The reluctance on the part of the Duchy to sell – although precluded in general from selling its assets, it is permitted by statute to make 'adjustments' to its portfolio, so such a sale is not entirely out of the question – is quite restrictive to the Club's potential growth plans. The rent for the ground is linked to the Club's turnover, so, ironically, the Duchy's ownership can act as a disincentive to more extensive commercial exploitation of the asset. The Club had borrowed to improve its stand facilities – including a £2million loan from the Duchy itself – as part of a deal in which rent would be pegged until 2009.

In keeping with the Prince's 'green' self-image, the Duchy promotes the bucolic aspect of its property portfolio, from Welsh slate roofed holiday lets to refurbished West Country small-business farm buildings, rather than larger offices and other commercial properties. The Public Accounts Committee, however, argued that the 'industrial shed' aspect was closer to the reality.

A 'PECULIAR' TITLE

With his special status as the heir to the throne – although itself not a constitutionally defined role with specific duties or obligations – the Prince of Wales is, like the Queen, able to reach his own, extremely favourable agreement with the Government. He can decide what sort of tax, and exactly how much, he donates to the Exchequer. But why should it be that the heir to the throne is treated as if he were the monarch?

The 1913 'Opinion of the Duchy of Cornwall by the Law Officers of the Crown and Mr Finlay', stated:

> 1) We are of the opinion that the same principles which render the provisions of an Act of Parliament inapplicable to the Crown unless the Crown is expressly named, apply also to the Prince of Wales in his capacity as Duke of Cornwall. This result arises from the 'peculiar title' of the Prince of Wales to the Duchy of Cornwall. In other respects the Prince of Wales, as being the first subject of the Crown is, like other subjects, bound by statutory enactments.

The 'title' in question applies in its legal sense to the right of the Prince to the dukedom of, and income from, the Duchy, not to the title of 'Prince of Wales' itself. All this was the result of the Duchy not wishing to pay extra tax following Chancellor of the Exchequer Lloyd George's 'People's Budget' which had just been passed. Prior to this, the Duchy had paid income tax, '[f]rom at least 1849…', in Phillip Hall's opinion[10].

So, 'peculiarity' derives not from statute but simply from a legal opinion which has yet to be properly tested. Even then, in 1913, the Duchy was advised that to insist upon its 'special' status might nonetheless attract adverse public criticism. Before the 1993 Memorandum of Understanding, the Prince of Wales had paid his voluntary tax – at a particularly favourable rate. Up to the date of his marriage in 1981 Charles had paid 50% of his income as a voluntary tax contribution, but this was halved to 25% once he had married Diana, Princess of Wales. Half-rate tax to newly-weds was not a concession granted to ordinary citizens. It should also be remembered that the 50% rate, compared extremely favourably with other higher-rate taxpayers of the time who might have been required to pay rates in excess of 80%. The 1993 agreement was – just agreed, not the result of legislation – intended to make the monarchy's tax position rather more transparent than it had hitherto been. The Queen had up to then paid almost no tax at all. Its popularity as a whole was at an all-time low and visible concessions were needed to allay further public criticism. Accusations of a lavish lifestyle have been aggressively countered by the Prince of Wales's staff. In response to a Channel Four documentary, Clarence House was keen to emphasise that His Royal Highness 'lives in a way appropriate to his role and position'. As heir to the throne, however, he no doubt aspires not only to be, but also to live, like a King. His multi-million pound income, numerous residences, many staff and regal treatment tends however to convey to many the impression of a lavish lifestyle.

'LE DUCHY, C'EST MOI'

The failure to fully differentiate the Prince's 'official', 'charitable' and personal activities needs further serious investigation. His official work, as distinct from that spent managing his 'personal' affairs (extensive charity interests and formerly his work on his commercial 'Duchy Originals' brands) is not adequately clarified. Only crude numbers of official appointments attended are disclosed. Perhaps a few royal 'time-sheets' might be in order. Given that the money is paid from what is essentially a public asset similar processes of disclosure should apply as with other public bodies. Without this, the taxpayer is in effect indirectly subsidising Charles' charities and commercial enterprises when they should be paying only for his official duties. Tax paid by the Prince in 2007 on the net surplus from the Duchy amounted to £3,434,000 (£3,296,000 in 2006), while his 'non-official expenditure' was some £2,614,000 (£2,181,000 in 2006). This latter amount could be regarded as the Prince's net 'take-home pay', though given the mixing of the public and private sides of his life much is already paid for. Even the greater part of the costs of maintaining his grounds at Highgrove House, for instance, are deductible on the basis that the public are allowed into them on occasions.

The Prince no doubt has additional investment income, (the 2001 Royal Rich Report suggested a fund of around £4million) and it is hard to believe that he was not left anything by his late grandmother. Perhaps one day the public will be able to see the will. The image of an otherwise almost penniless Prince of Wales, dependent upon his Duchy income, has long been disingenuously encouraged by his public relations team. Assuming investments of £4million, then given, say, a 5% annual return, his additional personal income might be around £200,000, not a bad earnings figure in its own right.

In 2007 the Prince intervened to help save a Scottish stately home, Dumfries House, for the nation. He was able to guarantee a £20million pound loan, suggesting that £4million may now be a considerable underestimate[11]. Whether he actually risked his own money though is questionable – it is likely that his charities actually provided the guarantees.

Prince Charles' life revolves around the Duchy. He is in a position to offset most of his living expenses against its income. It is hard to determine what he has to spend for out of his post-tax income. Following the 2005 Public Accounts Committee's less-than-deferential attitude toward the Duchy accounts however the 2006 accounts were slightly more revealing. For the first time the actual amount of tax paid was revealed. Following publication, PAC member Ian Davidson called for a full investigation into the Prince's income. He felt that the drop in charitable donations to £500,000 did not match the rise in the Prince's total income. This is quite apart from the £110million which the Prince 'directly or indirectly' 'helped' to raise for charity. This very statement, however, demonstrates how charitable work has become a somewhat misleading justification for a multi-million pound income level which is in itself very difficult to defend.

Charles' total income from the Duchy in 2010 was £17.3million – a very impressive figure – but even that shot up to £18.3million in 2012. In 2006-7 it amounted to £15.2million, with a 'residual' figure of just £2.6million of 'personal expenditure' up by £433,000 on the previous year. Between the net surplus and the residual figure is a sum of nearly £13million spent in 'supporting' the Prince of Wales. As with anything relating to the royal family differentiating between the 'public' and 'private' domains is far from easy, and this works to the advantage of the royal family as a whole. The intertwining of the Prince with the Duchy enables Charles to live 'off the estate' to a high degree. It means that he can claim, rather disingenuously, that he doesn't own his own home or has much in the way of personal investments. Even his cars – with the exception of his cherished classic Aston Martin Vantage Volante – are leased by the Duchy and includes its fleet of Jaguars, as well as a Toyota Prius hybrid eco-car. The latter was convenient not only to avoid criticism on environmental grounds

3 'NICE LITTLE EARNERS': THE TWO DUCHIES

but also the London congestion charge. The Bentley which he uses for certain appointments is not actually his but belongs to the Metropolitan Police – an 'essential' item of spending in the mysterious 'security' budget.

His principal home is Highgrove House, bought by the Duchy, for the Duchy, in 1980. This is when he is not staying in his recently refurbished 'official' residence, Clarence House in London, or in one of two Scottish residences both owned by family trusts. Highgrove is rented by the Prince for the appropriately princely sum of £336,000 a year. This was imposed by the 1993 tax agreement. Prior to this it had cost him nothing, the property being part of the Duchy estate itself. The new fiscal arrangements meant that he would have to pay tax on the property as a benefit in kind, so his financial advisors felt it best for him to start paying rent. The rent is paid, of course, to the Duchy, from the revenue surplus of which Charles ultimately derives his income...

The Prince's official income is impressive for a man with the 'job' of waiting around, without any defined duties, to inherit his mother's throne. His actual tax status is interesting, too, for it would appear that he is essentially assessed as if he were self-employed. The income is not a fixed annual sum – it is whatever the profits of the Duchy are. As a result of improved management, it has increased year on year. The increase has also resulted from financial practices which have caused the Public Accounts Committee a degree of concern. It is also boosted by the exemption of the Duchy – as a Crown (State) body – from corporation tax. Also, does the Prince pay National Insurance contributions – compulsory for thd belf-employed? For someone so dependent upon one income source it is questionable that he is actually entitled to be assessed as what is in effect self-employed at all, with all the advantages of deducting 'business' expenses. Perhaps the Duchy should employ him on a PAYE basis. This never seemed to occur to the Public Accounts Committee. His advisers claim that the Prince's 'openness' in his financial matters is greater than that of any other citizen, yet it misses the crucial point: No other person derives such a state-backed benefit – except of course the Queen with her Duchy of Lancaster earnings – on the basis of who they are by birth.

THE PRINCE OF WALES'S DUCHY OF CORNWALL INCOME

2012	2011	2010	2009	2008	2007	2006	2005	2004	2003
18.3	17.8	17.3	16.5	16.3	15.2	14.1	13.2	11.9	9.9

(£million)*

*This income equates to the net 'surplus' from the Duchy of Cornwall and constitutes the gross income payable to the heir to the throne. Deductions, including those for 'official' expenses, the duties which are purely voluntary and not constitutionally defined, are then made before voluntary tax is paid in accordance with the 1993 'Memorandum of Understanding'.

PROMOTING THE PRINCE

A development that has taken place increasingly in recent years is the assiduous promotion of the Prince's charitable works and environmental credentials. More and more, this has become a catch-all justification for his position, huge official income and luxury lifestyle. 'Sustainability' and 'charitable entrepreneur' are just two examples of the buzzwords that pepper the Prince's public relations material. The jargon may be increasingly used to deflect attention from one simple issue: the anomaly of a man who is indulgently treated simply for being who he is.

The Prince's elaborate website in its former incarnation used to have a 'Promoting and Protecting' section which highlighted the seemingly limitless talents of a man who it described as 'prescient in identifying charitable need', adept at 'promoting tolerance and greater understanding', as well as being 'a catalyst for facilitating debate'. (For a more commercial emphasis, one could have consulted the site's 'Opportunity and Enterprise' section. Since then, his official website has been noticeably scaled back – perhaps even they realised it verged on the preposterous). It was only just a shade away from the effusive praised lavished by North Korea on its 'Great Leader'.

For the Prince's 2007 Annual Review[12], increasing emphasis was being placed upon his environmental efforts, with the news that the Duchy had managed to reduce carbon emissions by 9% and that the heir to the throne's Household had a carbon footprint of 3,425 tonnes

3 'NICE LITTLE EARNERS': THE TWO DUCHIES

of CO2. With the exception of his Aston Martin, which was now only covering 100 miles a year, all the Duchy vehicles were running on bio-diesel. By 2008, even the Aston had been converted to run on bio-ethanol produced from surplus wine, and even the Duchy cattle were emitting less methane thanks their improved diet. In this and other respects, down to the impeccable 'green' credentials of the company which prints his annual accounts, it is at times almost stiflingly 'over-worthy', and hard to escape the conclusion that without the vast financial resources available through the Duchy, such assiduous standards would be much harder to achieve. It costs a lot to be as 'green' as the Prince of Wales, and one cannot help avoid the conclusion that in such respects a distinctly smug attitude prevails. With similar advantages, we could all afford to be as environmentally friendly. Although the Prince was urging his staff to cycle to work he had no such plans to do so himself. The previous year he had made the noble gesture of trading-in his Duchy-leased fleet of Audi cars in favour of similarly leased Jaguars on the basis that the latter would be less damaging to the environment. Curiously, by 2008 Audis seemed to be back in favour, probably more to do with a 'special deal' than emissions[13].

The Prince has also decreed that all royal lavatory cisterns will have water-saving devices – often little more than bricks – installed in his numerous properties. His office has emphasised his continuing commitment to reduce the amount of travelling that he does between his many appointments – often to lecture the nation on his 'green' credentials. Clarence House's 2007 commitment to use public transport 'where appropriate' was a belated nod to counter increasing criticism of a man travelling the country – and the world – by assorted luxury travel modes on journeys which were often perceived as hypocritical. Most memorably, perhaps, a British Airways flight in early 2007 to the USA, simply to collect an Environmental Award for which the entire First Class was reserved for his extensive entourage.

The Duchy of Cornwall now provides far more than a mere income. It has been progressively developed as a PR vehicle, a showcase demonstrator of Charles' 'entrepreneurial' competence, charitable interests and social compassion. As such it is a subsidized propaganda tool for a race-runner who already knows the result. However, despite the equivalent of an annual multi-million pound election campaign fund with which to prove himself as future King, it does reflect a growing insecurity on the part of a monarchy that now has to justify itself in a way that it did not in the past. The increased sophistication of this promotional aspect has developed in direct proportion to the degree of public skepticism of Charles as the next King.

CHARITY AND THE DUCHY

The Duchy of Cornwall has become a key component in the promotion of Prince Charles as 'charitable entrepreneur'. Without its financial support, he might well struggle to project that image. However, the link between monarchy and charity is a very close but increasingly questionable one. Charitable work has become one of the monarchy's main defences against their critics – it is hard to criticise those doing 'good works'. In a feature article in the Oxford Dictionary of National Biography, Frank Prochaska noted that, as monarchical authority declined, royalty recognised that patronage of charitable works was 'money in the bank'. Prince Albert realised back in the 19th century that charity was his family's route to popularity and acceptance. In a Mass-Observation survey in the 1960s it was seen that in the public mind 'the monarchy's humdrum social work had become as important in its survival as its "dignified duties"' Prochaska claimed that royal patronage and fundraising are worth between £100 and 200million to the voluntary sector annually, 'three or four times what the royals receive from the state'[14]. However, given that even a cursory examination of the total cost of the monarchy leads to a figure well in excess of £170million, the yield barely exceeds the cost. In any case, is one to seriously suppose that, in the absence of a monarchy, the British public would cease charitable giving?

'CASH FOR GIFTS'

Accusations of this high-rolling 'cash for access' culture surrounding the Prince of Wales were matched by a 'cash for gifts' market culture being carried on 'below stairs' too. The latter, a small-time but distinctly sleazy practice more worthy of 'Del Boy' or Arthur Daley was exposed; the 2003 Peat (Sir Michael Peat, Charles' Private Secretary) Report[15] provided details of the practices. Although St James' Palace had been investigating itself, enough detail emerged to tarnish the image of a Household that already suffered considerable adverse press that extended to lurid allegations of male rape.

3 'NICE LITTLE EARNERS': THE TWO DUCHIES

The *Independent* newspaper on March 14, 2003 commented that:

> We had no confidence that an investigation into the running of the prince's household carried out by the prince's own private secretary would put the serious charges to rest, and our lack of confidence has been richly repaid...it remains a deeply unsatisfactory response to the questions raised about the conduct of the prince and his closest advisers. These allegations are not all trivial tabloid tittle-tattle. In a constitutional monarchy in which the crown possesses residual political powers, and in which the royal family receives substantial support from the taxpayer, the heir to the throne should be treated as any candidate for high public office.

The same day, *The Times* suggested the creation of a 'civil service-style secretariat at St James's Palace [to] counter the murky impression fostered by recent scandals of a prince surrounded by cronies and disloyal sycophants.' Following the Peat Report, however, little really changed. St James' Palace, in effect, 'promised to do better in future', but then contradicted itself. A key figure in the affair – the Prince's close aide, Michael Fawcett – who the report decided had 'infringed the rules' by accepting various gifts, had to go. But not very far. He was almost immediately re-hired by the Prince as an 'outside contractor' with a generous financial settlement. It was alleged by the House of Commons Public Accounts Committee that this included rather favourable purchase terms on a Duchy-owned house in a leafy Surrey suburb. 'Upstairs', however, fewer questions seemed to be asked provided one wore formal dinner attire and carried an open chequebook. Wealthy donors to the Prince of Wales' charities have become a key element in boosting his image as the nation's leading 'charitable entrepreneur'. Entry into the elite world of high-end charitable giving, where a generous donation is the admission ticket to the British royal circle, conveys status and by implication, a high degree of legitimacy and validation. The potential rewards for donors can be enormous, while the infrastructure for this high-end culture is subsidised by the UK taxpayer for whom the benefits are often less easy to discern. While some charities benefit from this, they are often the Prince's own and the contributions may gloss over the fact that donors are people who are able, unlike ordinary taxpayers, to keep their millions well away from the Exchequer. Super-rich UK resident non-domiciles may pay little tax in the UK but write a cheque to one of the Prince's charities and enhance their image for 'generosity' – an honorary title may come their way too. The Prince's charities benefit whilst the NHS does not. The Duchy is the vehicle by which these charitable works are enabled and promoted and that charity increasingly serves to excuse the scale of the financial benefit to the heir to the throne.

Neither should it be forgotten that the Prince will one day be King and occupy a position of considerable influence. Money given to a future head of state also carries with it possible questions of probity. Someone who favours the Prince through charitable donation now could perhaps later seek to call in that favour over a matter of political importance and many important figures in the royal family's social circle may wield political power in regimes which do not share this country's ethical and democratic liberal values.

POTENTIAL CONFLICTS OF INTEREST?
When the Prince of Wales speaks in his 'official' capacity as heir to the throne, there are occasions when the particular event in question could be construed as promoting businesses not entirely unrelated to those in which he himself has a particular interest. This is not exactly rare, given that the Prince has such a broad range of interests. One example was the 3-year Invest in Fish South West project, a consortium involving the WorldWildLife Fund UK, Marks and Spencer and a number of commercial fishermen's organisations. The tax payer paid the £44,908 travel bill for the Royal Train which brought the Prince from Aberdeen to one of its major functions in Plymouth. Given that he is a high-profile commercial promoter of sustainable, regionally produced food himself, was the Prince rather not too close to the industry for the taxpayer to pick up his travel bill? Should he be speaking in an official capacity as a supposedly neutral public figure, while promoting a cause in which he might have a vested interest? An MP or a civil servant would have to declare such potential conflicts of interest, but no such similar requirement exists for members of the royal family.

Thanks to the taxpayer's support of the heir to the throne through the many official benefits which he enjoys, he has an unrivalled high profile and an official platform from which to promote his favourite causes – as well as the Duchy Originals brand. Not simply a 'charitable entrepreneur', he is also promoted by inference as a kind of business tycoon, although the company was undoubtedly helped by his Duchy of Cornwall money and infrastructure. Even so, it ultimately needed bailing out. However, it is his own charities which benefit whilst the 'entrepreneurial' label helps to foster the idea that he is a 'businessman'. This ignores the multi-million pound state benefit he receives. The direct link between the state and the Duchy income was not clear even on his own website – it was described merely as his 'private income'. The generosity of the taxpayer which gives him such a distinct advantage compared to his commercial competitors, is not spelled out at all. There was a distinct smugness in the Duchy brand which formerly stated that it 'continues to reflect the Prince's original commitment to creating a virtuous circle, whereby profits are generated for charity from a business that provides natural, high quality food and other products while helping to protect and sustain the natural environment' (Prince of Wales official '.gov.uk' website – This text was subsequently changed and of course the Duchy brand is now further distanced from the Prince himself – but by no means entirely). State subsidy is a key but conveniently omitted component of that 'virtuous circle'. And the profits go to charity. No doubt his competitors would be as generous if they were as lucky.

BUILDING A DUCHY 'BRAND'

In 1992, the Prince of Wales set up a company of his own which would operate in a sustainable fashion that 'encapsulates the uniqueness of the brand which aspires to create truly original and premium quality products every time'[16]. 'Duchy Originals' began by selling biscuits made from organically grown ingredients produced on the Prince's Home Farm on his Highgrove estate, but since then has broadened its range to a very considerable degree, encompassing food, drinks, toiletries and garden furniture. Whilst no-one would in principle dispute the aspirations of 'sustainability', 'environmental benefits', and 'added value marketing', the Prince's organic competitors might well be entitled to feel less than happy.

The privileged 'Duchy Originals' brand – augmented by the 'Duchy Collections' line – has grown into a significant market presence, both in the UK and abroad, with a range of over 140 products, but one which it should be remembered produces almost nothing itself. Only relatively recently did the company actually add amanufacturing element – a bakery at Launceston in Cornwall. In reality it earns its money almost entirely from royalty fees for the use of the company's Duchy of Cornwall coat of arms – on the wide range of products which are produced by other specialist manufacturers. The net profits are then donated to charity.

With a ready-made investment infrastructure, its large income, an impressive national and international profile backed by his family's own high-profile 'Windsor' brand, a minimum of scrutiny, and Duchy tax exemptions not enjoyed by his competitors, the advantages are many. Despite all that, the company had to be taken over. 'Duchy' products bear the Prince of Wales's distinctive 'feathers' logo – a title available to him only as heir to the throne, not in any other capacity. Such commercial use of such a symbol without the express approval of Parliament is curious and highly questionable. Interestingly, the Prince was not technically on the Board of management of Duchy Originals, although his Private Secretary was a director. In company law, however, he could have been regarded as a 'shadow' director, given his involvement and influence on the company. Irrespective of Duchy Originals' fate, it still enjoys a unique advantage in being endorsed by a member of Britain's royal family. Given that the Windsor's exist in the position they do at the behest of Parliament, it is curious that Parliament seems to remain very 'hands-off' in respect of the virtual appropriation of state assets, namely the continuing use of the Duchy coat of arms by the Duchy Originals company.

THE DUCHY, THE PRINCE, AND THE COMMITTEE

The Duchy of Cornwall produces considerable income for the heir to the throne increasing at a significant rate year on year. The Public Accounts Committee sought to examine both the actual scale of that income and whether it was in any way 'appropriate'. The Committee's Chairman, Sir Edward Leigh regarded it as nothing more than 'an accident of history', and called for the Treasury to investigate. Whether the Duchies of Cornwall and Lancaster 'produce too much, or too little, has simply never been questioned and it is reasonable to conclude that the whole business is getting rather out of hand', he said. Can it be true that the heir to the throne really needs a gross pre-tax income of over £17million a year whilst simply waiting to take over a job at some point in the future? Does someone who has inherited a public position through the accident of birth really need to gross one hundred times the earnings of the Prime Minister?

3 'NICE LITTLE EARNERS': THE TWO DUCHIES

The Public Accounts Committee's deliberations in November 2005 sought also to examine not only the benefit to the Prince from the Duchy, but the competitive advantages enjoyed by the Duchy itself in the sectors in which it competes. The deliberations were revealing on a number of levels. As stated both at the outset of the session, and at its conclusion, this was the first time in the history of the Duchies that they had been asked methodical and searching questions by Parliament. Perhaps the least that can be said is that such a review, indeed any review of any kind, was long, long overdue.

A SUPERIORITY COMPLEX

A simple report of the proceedings cannot convey the tone and the atmosphere when elected members of Britain's Parliament attempted for the first time to ask demanding questions about the Duchies. These are institutions which have never before had to endure the outrage of being grilled by 'mere' MPs – 'commoners'. The relatively closed nature of the Duchies administration has been examined by *Who Owns Britain* author Kevin Cahill, and reveals the links, in terms of schooling – Eton is very popular – marriage, and so on. There is a real sense in these reported exchanges that there are 'intruders' at the royal door. The conversational style is as telling as much as the information itself that is extracted – and much, it must not be forgotten, was refused.

One must read the transcript of the questioning to properly appreciate the level of *hauteur* – the quiet but ever-present arrogance, of two organisations that regard themselves as above the scrutiny of our democratically elected Parliament. They are now complex investment organisations which need to be fully accountable like all public institutions. As with so much in the royal arena, however, language and tone are employed to draw a distinction between matters royal and the rest of us.

Frequently, those questioned by the Committee adopted an almost pained tone, as though the Duchy income is spent in a fashion that denotes a degree of worthiness and personal sacrifice. In the words of the Duchy of Cornwall's Mr Bertie Ross:

> It is private income. It is entirely at his discretion what he wants to use it for. The point I want to make is he does use it for his official duties and private purposes. I would like to make a small point about those official duties because, again, the sum of the money is well used. It is to

support the Queen, charitable enterprises and national and traditional excellence. He is paying something in the order of £3.2 million worth of salaries alone for those purposes out of his own private income....
He is the biggest multipurpose charitable enterprise in the country.
[Author's italics]

The term 'charitable enterprise' conveys a strong sense that there is a 'you can't knock us, we do a lot for charity' response to any hint of criticism. And what, precisely, is 'traditional excellence'? Is it the deliberate practice of seeking to ensure continual enrichment and an opulent lifestyle at the public expense, to avoid normal taxation processes and to oppose accepted standards of Parliamentary scrutiny applying to estates in the public domain?

The Duchy is run by a body of eleven people – the Prince's Council – a non-executive board which is 'purely advisory' and to which appointments are made by the Prince of Wales himself. Likened by a member of the PAC to the non-executive board of a Plc, the description fails to do justice to the informal and unaccountable nature of the appointment system. In reality there is no official prescribed system of scrutiny at all. Described by one MP as 'a pretty rum kind of governance', it was suggested – just a suggestion – that it might be a good idea for the Duchy to voluntarily subject itself to the scrutiny of the National Audit Office. How indulgent we are to our hereditary monarchy. The income may be 'private', but it derives from an asset which – though the Prince of Wales' staff, curiously, assert is also 'private' – is by any rational definition 'public'.

'IT'S "OWNERSHIP", JIM, BUT NOT AS WE KNOW IT...'

We are truly in another universe when we enter the curious eco-system which supports the heir to the throne. The Public Accounts Committee's question asking 'Is his capital private?', raised an area which is dependent upon the niceties of legal language that might even confuse some lawyers. Sadly, the hearing had not the time to explore this fascinating area. The Duchy of Cornwall's representative, Bertie Ross, ventured his own unique definition – and no doubt one shared by the Duchy – that '[t]he estate is owned by the Prince of Wales as a limited owner'. This answer was not pursued by the panel, but ought to have been. The notion of 'limited ownership' is at best somewhat contradictory. One either owns something or one does not. The classic 'acid test', is whether the 'owner' can dispose of the property in whole or in part, subject perhaps to a charge on the property. They may only do so if they possess the 'title' to the property in question and can thus then pass legal 'title' to a purchaser. If not, then they cannot be regarded as being the 'owner' at all. The Prince cannot do this – so how can he be the owner?

The seeming ability of the Duchy to license out the rights of Duchy Originals Ltd to use the Duchy coat of arms on its packaging might well be challenged on this basis as they could well be exceeding their powers in this respect. Logically, Parliament ought to be required to grant permission in such a case. (See also Chapter 5: Charity and royal 'brand' ownership). Above all, it reveals a culture in which the Duchies are largely 'left to get on with it', free from proper Parliamentary accountability. The Crown Lands Act 1702 prevents the Duchy from being sold off, either entirely or in part – apart from later permitted minor 'adjustment' sales. No-one but the most misguidedly loyal staff could with any serious justification seek to assert that the Prince of Wales actually owns it. It is Crown Estate property and thus owned by the State. However, there is a curious reluctance to actually say this openly, no doubt for fear of upsetting the Windsor family. The picture remains clouded by a lack of full statutory definition, and ambiguities are allowed to persist. The legal case in 1913, originating from an Inland Revenue attempt to persuade the Duchy of Cornwall to pay tax, led to the notion of the Duchy of Cornwall being a 'peculiar' title in law. The Duchy pleaded Crown immunity yet as the Prince of Wales was most definitely not the monarch, how could it expect immunity as if he was? Answer: because of the claimed 'peculiar' nature of the title. Upon this tenuous claim would still appear to rest the 'special' status accorded the Prince through the 1993 Memorandum of Understanding.

One version of the Duchy's own view used to be expressed on the commercial Duchy Originals company website as being that it is 'held in trust by the Prince of Wales as the 24th Duke of Cornwall'. One could go so far as to say that the website's assertion was nonsensical. Surely '… in trust for…' the Prince of Wales would have been more appropriate, assuming the trust interpretation. Since the first edition of this book appeared, these exceedingly tenuous assertions have been quietly dropped. The Duchy's implication that the Prince holds the estate for himself was distinctly bizarre. It is unlikely to be a trust at all, given the

1702 Act, though if that were the conclusion then Parliament would logically be the trustee. For practical purposes it would seem that it suits the monarchy to promote an air of legal 'mystery' as to the real status of the Duchies and to rely upon general deference and Parliamentary inertia with which to fend off any critics. At the time of writing the Duchy of Cornwall website conveniently avoids the whole subject of 'ownership'.

As 'Star Trek's Mr Spock might have said of the legal rights of the inhabitants of some far-flung planet, '…this is "ownership", Jim', 'but not as we know it'. The Duchies do not belong to the royals, but are public assets which provide official incomes. Yet the orthodox presentation seeks to convey the pretence that this not actually the case. It is merely a sop to the notion – strongly held by the Queen and heir – that their official incomes are 'independent'. The reality is that they are not, nor in any case in a parliamentary democracy is that desirable, yet the pretence is allowed to persist to avoid denting their regal pride.

The fact that the Duchies are exempt from the payment of tax would strongly suggest that they are truly public entities – after all, as with the rest of the Crown Estates, it would be illogical for a public body to pay tax to itself. Not only that, but the profits from the two Duchies go to the monarch and the heir to the throne only as public figures – lose their positions and they lose the right to the money. This reinforces the notion that they cannot be regarded as private assets which cannot be disposed of by their incumbents. Despite this, a situation has developed in which no-one has really challenged the very basis upon which the Duchy of Cornwall, and the similarly unique Duchy of Lancaster, actually exist as unincorporated Crown (State) bodies.

They are 'public', yet the system colludes in endowing them with a favoured status, leaving them free from full accountability. It is a fairy tale, akin to the story of the Emperor's new clothes. To supporters of the present world of royal financial privilege, any claimed 'special' legal status is nothing more than the collective collusion in a myth. These are most definitely not private estates. Indeed, strictly speaking, they could not have belonged to the monarch on a private basis in any case before the start of the 19th century. It was not till then that an Act of Parliament in 1800 enabled any monarch – George III at that time – actually to own property in their own right. Prior to that, any land purchased by the monarch was automatically regarded as Crown land, the distinction between the 'private' and 'public' faces of the monarchy being so far less defined than today to the extent that, for practical purposes, there wasn't one.

3 'NICE LITTLE EARNERS': THE TWO DUCHIES

LOCAL INFLUENCE
The degree of power exerted by the Duchy of Cornwall over the southwest of the UK (including the Scilly Isles) is a matter of concern. The Duchy is a predominant but unaccountable landowner and landlord in the region. While it involves itself, for instance, in some aspects of affordable housing, it is unlikely that any local council would stand up to it in the event of disagreement. The Duchy is run by the Prince's Council, a body which is anything but democratic. The social and cultural power wielded by a small unelected coterie appointed – and headed by – the heir to the throne upon those living in a relatively closed community is considerable.

Resident workers, often poorly paid, may be directly or indirectly dependent upon the Duchy for their employment as well. Its status as a private 'fiefdom' was actually criticised by the Public Accounts Committee in 2005. The Council may make much of its 'Duchy Stewardship', with all its 'environmental integrity', yet it has considerable influence over important regional issues, including infrastructure development in the Scilly Isles and on the mainland, for example, at Penzance harbour.

Important, highly influential, yet totally undemocratic, the Duchy operates in areas which overlap with those normally dealt with by county councils and regional bodies, both of which have a democratic component, either by election or appointment by elected ministers. In the Duchy, the ultimate decision-maker holds his position by birthright alone. Whilst the Duchy may promote its benefit to the community, the degree of subtle, yet far from insignificant, power, assisted by a social and cultural deference that is historically embedded, should not be underestimated. It is not necessarily what the Duchy actually does that is questionable, but the fact that it is doing so as a highly influential but undemocratic and largely unaccountable body.

'REINFORCING RELATIONSHIPS'...
Back in 2007 there were concerns that the Duchy was exercising its considerable influence in order to further the commercial interests of the Prince's company, Duchy Originals. The Duchy's 2007 Annual Report referred to its 'Tenants' Marketing Initiative'. Set within the document's smooth corporate prose, this Initiative was 'designed by the Duchy to ensure a profitable and sustainable future for agriculture within its community of farming tenants', and its action plan included

the worthy aims of providing 'information and best practice', 'defined needs', 'seminars' and so on.

However, it then continued in a more questionable manner when it talked of *'Reinforcing the relationship with Duchy Originals* and identifying opportunities for collaboration' [Author's italics]. There was the potential for bringing undue influence to bear on farmers and other producers who, whilst able benefit from the relationship, nonetheless might have been tenants of the Duchy of Cornwall and might well feel themselves under pressure to accede to policies which are also for the benefit of the Prince's (then) company. Not only might they have felt 'tied' to the Duchy as tenants but also under implied pressure to contract to one company – Duchy Originals – rather than another[17]. All this underlined a culture in which, although 'feudalism' might have long been a thing of the past, a rather comparable atmosphere of hierarchical pressure might still prevail in this curious historical remnant in which the heir to the throne possesses real power and influence – and derives a very considerable financial benefit from it.

THE 'DUCK' TEST

The Duchies are, in effect, those parts of the Crown Estates not surrendered by the Crown in 1760. It is only the income produced by them which can, under the present arrangements, be regarded as 'private' in that it goes to only two specific people, one holding the highest public office in the land, the other waiting for a turn to hold it. The use of quasi-legal language, such as that contained in the 1913 legal opinion of the Duchy of Cornwall's 'peculiar' title does not help. It does little more than disguise a conceit, conspiring in a 'Looking-Glass' world where things mean what the royal family and their acolytes would like them to mean.

The fact is that the Duchies' profits go only to the monarch and the heir to the throne in respect of their public positions – they have no right to the money as plain Elizabeth or Charles Windsor. In that sense, by clear implication, the Duchies represent a form of trust. The positions held by the beneficiaries are ultimately in the gift of Parliament, since the monarchy as presently constituted exists by virtue of the Act of Settlement of 1701. When the income from a state asset goes to someone for them to then to call that asset 'private' is plainly ridiculous. The monarch and heir are merely the recipients of monies produced by state assets: the Duchies.

3 'NICE LITTLE EARNERS': THE TWO DUCHIES

The fact that the Duchies themselves pay no tax is a clear indication that they are deemed part of the state structure. Their profits are taxed only when they have been received by the monarch and the heir as income. The fact that they are not officially deemed part of the Crown Estates is no more than a hangover from the 1760 Civil List settlement which left them somewhat 'semi-detached' from the rest of the Crown Estates. This was because they were then – especially in respect of the Duchy of Lancaster – simply producing next to no income. The Crown Lands Act 1702 regarded them as part of the overall state structure. Thus, due to little more than an historical accident, and a degree of Parliamentary negligence, they have gradually been allowed to become almost a law unto themselves. The anomalous nature of this position has become noticeable relatively recently with more modern management practices leading to far higher profits being produced than was the case in the past. The Duchy of Cornwall was intended to provide the incumbent with an income in the manner of the landed gentry of the 18th century. It was not designed to be a corporate investment vehicle providing the means to boost the public relations campaign of an unpopular heir to the throne, and producing an income grossly in excess of any other senior public servant.

In his book *Who Owns Britain*, author Kevin Cahill states unequivocally that: 'The ownership of the Duchy is not in doubt. It belongs to Prince Charles as Duke of Cornwall until he becomes King'[18]. However, his 'definitive' statement is rather confused. The Prince of Wales is not able to act as any normal 'owner' at all. He is restricted by a number of Acts of Parliament which prevent any sale, either whole or in part except for minor 'adjustments' permitted by the Duchy of Cornwall Acts 1863-1982. The important point, though, is that the Prince of Wales gets the Duchy income only whilst waiting to become King. Once he has succeeded to the throne his heir gets the benefit in turn. That is not 'owning' the asset that produces that income. In the event of there being no direct male heir for the time being, then the Duchy income reverts to the monarch of the day. Kevin Cahill sees that fact, as in the case of George VI – who had only daughters – appointing trustees to administer it, as being clear evidence that the Duchy 'belongs, ultimately to the Sovereign personally'. This is to confuse the individual with the office. Now, the Sovereign Grant Act directs that in the absence of a male heir, the money can go to a daughter – who, whilst still heir – cannot as such become Duke of Cornwall.

Parliament is thus dictating where the money can go – they are really in charge, for the Duchy is ultimately state property.

The 1800 Crown Private Estates Act which allowed monarchs to acquire property in their own right, sets the point from which monarchs could thenceforth buy their private estates. The Duchies predate this, so could not have been privately owned by the monarch – they were purely 'state' property, and crucially, they remained state property, they were not acquired by the monarch personally. Under George VI, the Duchy was still being run by its Council, so was still being administered 'as usual'. The use of the word 'trustees' is misleading, they were really no more than delegated officials. The estate was still producing its 'profits', which the King was collecting. However, could the King have, for example, at this stage, theoretically disposed of the Duchy? The answer is most definitely 'no'.

The very existence of the present modern monarchy dates back only to the Act of Settlement of 1701, which established the present lineage, and the 1702 Crown Lands Act, which governed state property and of which the Duchies are a part, restricted what could be done with the Crown Lands. Parliament drew up the arrangement whereby the Civil List payments are made in return for the income from the Crown Estates income being 'surrendered' at the outset of each reign. Forget the fiction that a new monarch could choose not to comply with what has become a formality rather than the 'sacrifice' that some claim[19]. The eighteenth century monarchy was re-instated in a fundamentally different constitutional, social and cultural context than that of previous centuries.

The modern arrangement of the two Duchies providing incomes for the monarch and heir respectively was agreed to offset the surrender of the Crown Estates income, and was conducted on Parliament's terms – not that of the monarchy. As the saying goes, 'If it looks like a duck, and quacks like a duck, then it probably is a duck'. So, applying the duck test, the Duchies appear to be public bodies, part of the Crown Lands, enjoy the same fiscal status, and are evidently considered to be so by members of the House of Commons Public Accounts Committee. An honest recognition of this fact is long overdue and as a result they should be subject to the same scrutiny as the Crown Estates. The monarchy has been indulged for too long over these assets. The effective fiction of the idea that the Crown Estates are really the Sovereign's – and 'surrendered' voluntarily at the outset of the reign – perpetuates the misconception of an 'independent' income that is in reality simply granted by Parliament.

'PUBLIC' OR 'PRIVATE'?

The 2005 Public Accounts Committee hearing touched upon the concepts of 'public' and 'private' as it relates to the royal family. Despite its length the following exchange between Richard Bacon MP and Mr Clarke, one of the spokesmen for the Duchies, is important:

Q187: Mr Bacon: Can I ask a slightly different question and that is about the nature of the phrase 'public money' because we have been bandying this phrase around. The net surplus of the revenues from this landed estate are handed over to the Prince of Wales as his private income, and the same in relation to the Duchy of Lancaster, but they are monies from an agricultural landed estate in the same way as the Duke of Westminster has a landed estate or the Duke of Bedford or whoever else, so in what sense are they public money? Do you regard them as public money in that sense?

Mr Clarke: I think that is a very good question. I do not want to go back because I know time is limited, but when the Duchy of Lancaster was first created, Henry Bolingbroke created the first pre-nuptial agreement to the extent he actually inherited the Duchy before he was King and when he took over the monarchy he brought the Duchy to it, but he wanted to make absolutely sure it was dealt with as a separate inheritance outwith the estates he took over as monarch. So the Charter of 1399 was created and that Charter very specifically states that it is a separate inheritance under separate administration from the Crown Estates.

Q188: Mr Bacon: So, for example, Sandringham, we know, is privately owned by Her Majesty the Queen, whereas Windsor Castle and Buckingham Palace are properties of the state. Are you saying this would be regarded in the same way as Sandringham, as private property?

Mr Clarke: Yes.

Q189: Mr Bacon: Although the capital cannot be accessed in the same way as if it was private property?

Mr Clarke: No, the capital cannot be accessed, but it is like a statutory perpetual trust.

Mr Bacon: Thank you.

Richard Bacon was being sold a story that has little connection with the present reality. It is surprising that he actually swallowed Mr Clarke's version at all – who likened the position of the Duchy to that of Sandringham in terms of it being 'private'. This takes the meaning of the word onto a new plane altogether, and the idea that the Duchies are just 'agricultural landed estates' any more is ludicrous. Let's not forget that prior to the 1800 Crown Lands Act it wasn't possible for a monarch to create the 'separate inheritance' that Mr Clarke spoke of. So much for the credibility of a 1399 Charter. The words 'private, 'public', and 'like a statutory perpetual trust' seem to mean whatever those in the Duchies in their own special little world might wish. The privileged world of the Queen and heir is thus permitted to continue relatively undisturbed. The concepts of 'accountability' and 'royalty' do not sit easily together.

It should also be noted that, although the Sandringham and Balmoral estates are regarded as 'private', the circumstances by which they were acquired were as a direct result of practices that would now not be tolerated. Queen Victoria and her beloved Prince Albert saved considerable sums of money from the Civil List. As a result of Albert's pleadings of poverty they were given more than they needed but then hung onto the cash, and invested it in property[20]. The state helps to pay for an element of running costs even in royal 'private' residences. There might be a future potential capital gains liability in the same way that anyone running any part of their property for the purposes of a business and declaring it as a business expense – in the event of any of those properties being sold.

THE SUPREMACY OF PARLIAMENT

The present monarchy is a product of the Act of Settlement of 1701, and as such its existence and that of its predecessors relies upon legislation passed since then. It exists by the grace of Parliament, not through a Ruritanian muddle of mediaeval pageantry and claimed precedent. Parliament is now supreme, not the monarchy. The relationship between a 1399 Charter and a monarchy that was effectively created little more than three centuries ago is extremely tenuous.

3 'NICE LITTLE EARNERS': THE TWO DUCHIES

Given the fact that a clear line was drawn under the 'old' version of the institution in 1649 and the present line of succession defined half a century later, that would seem to sever any such pretence of 'continuity'. The mediaeval Charter quoted by Mr Clarke is a long way from a modern Act of Parliament, and his response was generally muddled – a mixture of half-truths and vaguely redolent of an Arthurian legend.

A 'SHROUDED SECRET SOCIETY'

Another extract from the Public Accounts Committee's delicate probing illustrates the attitude of the Duchy representatives to 'mere' elected Members of Parliament. Sion Simon, attempting to tease out information, pleaded:

> We would very much like to have a look at the books. Given that you are so proud of your governance, given that you are dashing backwards and forwards from the Treasury every twenty minutes asking them to check on the latest thing, why not just let us have a look, let them have a look?

The Duchy of Cornwall's Mr Ross replied:

> I am satisfied with the arrangement we have with Price Waterhouse auditing our books on the private side of the Prince of Wales's business and I do not see the difference between that and any other private business. It does the job and I am quite certain the National Audit Office would do the job just as well but this is a procedure which was set out for us to follow in the 1982 Management Act. I have not seen a strong enough reason yet to do it differently.

Note the use of the Duchy's version of the word 'private'. They operate, in effect, within their own definition of what is 'private', and thus see no reason to compromise their position and bring themselves under proper scrutiny.

MP Brian Jenkins summed up the Committee's frustration:

> The difficulty we have got here is we are what is called a public spending committee and we like to look at public monies. You like to look at this as a shrouded secret society whether it is a limited company or not. It is not even a limited company but some personal fiefdom you hold sway over.

In the face of Bertie Ross's continued refusal to provide information, he continued:

> ...we like accountability, we like openness, and we like transparency....
> I am interested in what the [British people]...think, what the people who have ultimate ownership of this territory think.

BONA VACANTIA

Just one solitary question from the Committee's Richard Allan (Q214) addressed this profitable perk enjoyed by the Duchies: '*Bona vacantia* – I just love the word – I think it was the same principle we used to use to plant flags on entire countries and claim them and now it only applies to unclaimed estates in certain parts of the UK...'. For many however the term *Bona vacantia* is not so light-hearted and has serious consequences. The literal meaning of the Latin term *Bona vacantia* is 'vacant goods' and in English Law it is defined as 'ownerless goods' or 'vacant property'. It covers procedures to be followed in dealing with three groups of assets: firstly, items of value which are found – so-called 'treasure trove'; secondly, the assets of those dying intestate, that is, without a will or surviving relatives; and thirdly, the assets of companies which have been declared bankrupt, are wound up, or for which no owner can be found. 'Treasure trove', with the rise in popularity of metal detecting, and the high value now placed on such archaeological finds, can now represent a substantial source of money.

In English law, the 'title', or legal ownership, of any property must belong to, or be 'vested in', an identifiable person or other legal body, for instance, a registered company. No property or goods can be regarded in law as being 'ownerless'. If legal ownership cannot be established by anyone else, the 'Crown' must administer those assets. Normally, in most of England and Wales, the Treasury Solicitor will administer such cases. However, there are two fundamental exceptions: Such cases arising in the Duchies of Cornwall or Lancaster – in the quaintly termed 'County Palatine' in the case of the latter – will be administered by the 'royal' solicitors, Farrer and Co. Any such proceeds go to the Duchies themselves – not the Exchequer as would normally happen. This rule applies to anyone – or company – dying or, in the latter case, be dissolved within the boundaries of the Duchies – including parts of

Kennington in South London, for example. The Duchy of Cornwall website states that 'Under Bona Vacantia, the estate of a person who dies in Cornwall with no will or surviving relatives passes to the Duchy of Cornwall'. This is true of any individual residing, or business registered within, Duchy 'territory' – not just Cornwall.

THE GRIM REAPER – BY ROYAL APPOINTMENT

The privilege enjoyed by the Duchies has important ramifications for all private and commercial occupiers deemed to be 'ordinarily resident' within their boundaries. Anyone who dies intestate elsewhere in the country leaves their estate by default to the 'Crown' – in practice the Exchequer – so that it automatically reverts to the 'public purse'. *Bona Vacantia* also includes other sources of money – 'Treasure Trove' and assets of companies for which ownership cannot be traced and thus even some pension fund surpluses. According to Inland Revenue & Customs, *Bona Vacantia* also covers the property and rights that were beneficially owned by dissolved companies, but the right of the duchies to this money has been conveniently ignored by the Duchy website.

In the not so distant past *Bona Vacantia* benefited the monarch and the heir to the throne personally. This anomaly allowed George VI, the Queen's father, to receive money from the estates of service personnel dying intestate as a result of active service during the Second World War. Perhaps he used the money to augment his impressive stamp collection. Phillip Hall suggests that the increase in receipts of these 'devolutions and forfeitures' led to the late King George Vl making in excess of £1million in modern values during that period[21].

The practice continues to this day. Should a serving soldier, for example, normally resident within the borders of one the Duchies, die on active service today in Afghanistan, not leave a will and beneficiaries cannot be traced, then their estate will go to the Duchy – not the Exchequer. Following concerns expressed some years ago, it has been the practice since the early 1970s for *Bona Vacantia*, to be paid into separate funds and given to charity. This process is, however, purely voluntary – die without a will within one of the Duchies and any property you leave could well go to the Queen or the Prince of Wales, and they can technically do whatever they wish with the proceeds. *Bona Vacantia* has generally applied to the proceeds of small individual estates, although the underlying principle of the monarch or heir benefiting financially from a subject's death is disturbing in a modern society. This historical anomaly is even more worrying when it relates to monies remaining in the pension funds of bankrupt companies.

BONA VACANTIA AND DISSOLVED COMPANIES

When a company is dissolved, its assets pass to the Crown – or the Duchies, if its registered address falls within the confines of these two bodies – under Section 654 of the Companies Act 1985. A company is, in law, a legal 'person' by which it is able to own assets and in debts or liabilities. Should a company go into liquidation and is then wound up, its assets are first used to settle its liabilities as far as possible. The company is then closed and ceases to exist. If, however, it is subsequently found to have owned assets that were not distributed prior to the dissolution, these assets cannot be returned to the now non-existent company. Prior to dissolution these assets could have been used to settle remaining debts. Instead, these assets, classed as *Bona Vacantia*, become the property of the Crown or that of the respective Duchies. In practice, occupational pension schemes usually take a long time to wind up, usually longer than it takes to wind up the company. If a surplus after payout is found to exist, it cannot be returned to a company that no longer exists. Such occupational pension schemes are those paid into by employers and employees ultimately to benefit retired workers. For decades investment performance in these funds was very good and thousands of these schemes did maintain surpluses. This surplus will then pass to the Crown or one of the Duchies – without any tax being deducted. In the case of the Duchies, this means that such tax-free sums contribute to the income of the Queen or the Prince of Wales. Although such money is put into a charitable benevolent fund, this is just a voluntary convention, a nicety that developed through pressure in recent years. There is nothing in law to prevent a future monarch or heir from spending it all on fast cars and wild living. Such is the unwritten British constitution.

All monies passing to the Duchies which are classed as *Bona Vacantia* do so without any Inheritance Tax liability. Although Prince Charles advertises the fact that all the money he receives in this way is repaid to charitable good causes – most probably his own – before

3 'NICE LITTLE EARNERS': THE TWO DUCHIES

this happens, a large slice is deducted as expenses (administration costs) for receiving and handling this money. In 2006/7, the Duchy received a total of £145,000 as *Bona Vacantia*. (£110,000 in 2004-5) as *Bona Vacantia*, 'before allowing for ex-gratia payments and other associated costs of £13,000 (£55,000 in 2005/06)', a considerable decrease from the previous year, though no further explanation is given. The Duke of Cornwall's Benevolent Fund, a traditional destination for such monies, received £75,000, a considerable improvement on the previous year when it received nothing (in 2004-5 it was given £30,000). In 2009 just £34,000 was received as *Bona Vacantia*. Two years later, in 2011, it had more than doubled to £75,000, but in 2012 it jumped to £552,000 – of which £86,000 was deducted as 'costs'. The fact is that *Bona Vacantia* receipts from the Duchy of Cornwall are allocated at the whim of the Prince. The accounts for 2005-6 state that 'in accordance with the wishes of His Royal Highness the Prince of Wales grants were made to educational and agricultural charities together with the restoration of churches and environmental charities as well as to a variety of other charitable causes'[22]. Such a description would fit that of the Prince's very own specific charities and which promote him as 'charitable entrepreneur'. It would be less self-interested if such money were independently administered or went to charities not connected with the Prince. Otherwise such funds appear to be used to support Prince Charles' own public relations campaign.

In the case of the Duchy of Lancaster, such money is likely to go ultimately to either the Jubilee Trust or the Duchy of Lancaster Benevolent Fund. The Duchy of Lancaster accounts for 2005 reveal that a total of £725,000, of which 3% was deducted as expenses, was received as *Bona Vacantia*. This was a much smaller figure for administration than that deducted by the Duchy of Cornwall, so there appears to be no consistency in the levy of costs between the two Duchies. Money goes – usually – to the Duchy of Lancaster Jubilee Trust, 'a separate registered charity', this being 'at the discretion of the Council'[23]. During the year ending September 30th 2004, a total of 327 intestate estates had been dealt with, as well as a total of 406 dissolved companies. The fact that such donations are made to charity at all is a very recent practice. The Board of the Duchy of Cornwall has refused a request by the Treasury Select Committee to allow them to examine the audited accounts, claiming that it is 'a well-run private business'.

'WE ARE NOT PUBLIC BODIES, WE ARE EXEMPT'

It is not only in the area of finance that the Duchies are permitted special treatment by the Government. Both are exempt from the mandatory provisions of the Freedom of Information Act. Any request for information on the Duchies is 'judged on its merits' – rather than automatically granted – under our still innately secretive system. When asked by the Committee whether the Duchies would be classed as public bodies for the purposes of the Freedom of Information Act the two representatives, Paul Clarke and Bertie Ross replied like Lewis Carroll's curious duo, Tweedledum and Tweedledee:

Mr Clarke: 'We are not public bodies, we are exempt'.

Mr Ross: 'We are the same'.

These smug responses sum up a protected little world which, because it is so closely attached to the monarchy, operates outside accepted levels of scrutiny. The Duchies are happy to take advantage of tax exemptions that apply to them as public bodies yet are unwilling to reciprocate when it comes to openness.

HYPOCRISY BEGINS AT HOME

The concept of 'sustainability' has become a prime concern in all aspects of modern business practice, and not least by the Prince of Wales himself. His website used to proudly boast that he:

> ...has shown a strong personal interest in environmental issues for decades. The main themes to which he most often returns are the need for sustainable development, for responsible stewardship of our natural resources and for global co-operation to protect our environmental heritage so that the world can be passed on to future generations in the best possible state.

The 2007 Annual Review highlighted the fact that the Prince 'ensures that sustainable development is at the heart of the Duchy of Cornwall's management approach'[24]. When challenged by the Public

3 'NICE LITTLE EARNERS': THE TWO DUCHIES

Accounts Committee, however, the Duchies' representatives were not prepared to divulge much detail about their investments in relation to ethics and sustainability. After a couple of evasive replies, Ian Davidson pressed on with his question:

Q262: Mr Davidson: I am asking whether or not you can give us a list of the properties in which you have money invested in order that we and others can make an assessment as to whether or not those investments are ethical and sustainable.

Mr Ross: It is a very judgmental issue.

Q263: Mr Davidson: Are you willing to give us the information?

Mr Ross: I will discuss what is ethical and sustainable if…

Q264: Mr Davidson: I am prepared to debate the issue. Will you make the information available about the investments in order that judgments can be made by you, me and third parties about what is ethical and sustainable?

Mr Ross: I do not think this is an issue which is relevant to this Committee.

This is an accountable democracy, where a Prince receives a multi-million pound income from a public asset, voluntarily pays some tax on it, and then his staff don't want to talk about an area which the Prince otherwise trumpets as one of his main concerns?

Q265: Mr Davidson: Sorry, I am asking the questions and you are providing the answers, that is the way in which the Committee works. I am asking you whether you will provide a list of the properties that are held by the Duchy in order that we can measure whether or not they come up to the standard about which the Prince speaks so often and so movingly.

Mr Ross: I think it is something I would need to have a great deal clearer understanding of because who is going to be the judge of what is ethical and sustainable.

> **Q266: Mr Davidson:** Public opinion. The Prince has spoken at great length on this. We would measure them against the criteria he has set himself. Can we have a report on the list of properties?
>
> **Mr Ross:** I do not see why.
>
> **Q267: Mr Davidson:** I know you do not see it but I am asking you, can we have it?
>
> **Mr Ross:** I do think it would serve any better purpose...
>
> **Q268: Mr Davidson:** You do not think that but I do. I am asking you – yes or no – will you make available a list of the properties? Are you refusing to do so?
>
> **Mr Ross:** I am not saying no but I still need to be persuaded there is a good reason to do so.
>
> **Q269: Mr Davidson:** If you are not saying no you are saying yes then. This is a simple yes/no question.
>
> **Mr Ross:** I am leaving the question unanswered because I cannot see the purpose of it.

A 'CARBUNCLE' OF ONE'S OWN

Was the Prince not concerned that his multi-million income might be derived at least in part by modern commercial properties, including large out-of-town industrial 'sheds' and other examples of the hard-nosed modernity rather than the bucolic idyll which he constantly espouses?

> **Q270: Mr Davidson:** Given that the Prince has expressed strong views on out of town supermarkets and things that he describes as 'carbuncles', can you tell us whether or not you own any of those?
>
> **Mr Ross:** The only supermarket which I am aware of is one that has been built at Poundbury which was subject to very stringent control.

3 'NICE LITTLE EARNERS': THE TWO DUCHIES

Q271 Mr Davidson: There are no other supermarkets or out of town superstores or anything similar?

Mr Ross: We have other out of town industrial properties.

Q272 Mr Davidson: Are they 'carbuncles'?

Mr Ross: They are ones we have purchased ---

Q273 Mr Davidson: Is that a yes or a no? Are they 'carbuncles' or are they not?

Mr Ross was certainly not being very forthcoming. When the question of the ultimate ownership of the estates arose, he sang his favourite song again:

It is a private estate. Under the terminology, it is a private estate.

Q327 Mr Davidson: Is it not in trust for the nation?

Mr Ross: The Prince of Wales and the Duchy of Cornwall are entitled to some privacy about this.

Q328 Mr Davidson: Is it not held in trust for the nation?

Mr Ross: It is a private estate.

One could have been forgiven for thinking that the record had stuck. And to what 'terminology', precisely, was he referring – the Duchy's own, unique version?

These and other questions during the course of just one, solitary February afternoon sought to shed light on two of the most privileged parts of our constitution. They exist to provide multi-million pound incomes to the Queen and the Prince of Wales. The incomes they produce are not fixed, but increase very significantly year on year, with the Queen, for example, enjoying a 10% increase in 2007 from the previous year. In the case of the heir to the throne, part is expended on ill-defined official duties. The remainder is solely for personal use, including the unashamed promotion of the Prince of Wales. It subsidises his charities and his business interests, providing an unfair advantage over competitors. The Duchies' privileged status enable them to develop bigger incomes year on year, and yet despite the fact that they cannot be regarded as anything but publicly owned bodies, they reject any attempts at serious scrutiny.

PUBLIC ACCOUNTS COMMITTEE RECOMMENDATIONS
The recommendations of the Public Accounts Committee to the Treasury[25], sought to address the curious position of the two Duchies. As regards the exemption of the Duchies from corporation tax and capital gains tax, the PAC wanted the Treasury to justify their 'favourable' tax position, and the competitive advantage which they enjoy as a result 'in the property and other markets in which they operate'. The Treasury, however, did not feel that this favourable treatment conferred any competitive advantage. It argued that trading was 'in the open market', subject to 'market forces and prices in the same way as the other organisations operating in this area'. No such examples, however, were given. The PAC felt that more transparency as to the principles underlying the Duchies' charitable and other interests was needed; as well as more clarity in respect of the division between the Prince of Wales's personal assets and those of the Duchy of Cornwall itself, together with an examination of the appropriateness of the levels of money paid to the Queen and the Prince of Wales.

To date, the entire matter of the Duchies has retained a low profile. In May, 2007, MP Brian Iddon's Early Day Motion in the House of Commons, signed by eight other MPs, noted that the Duchy of Cornwall was still not 'required presently to meet the disclosure requirements set out for public sector organisations and companies', and that despite the recommendations of the PAC's report referred to above these had yet to be implemented. It was left, the motion noted, to the campaign group 'Republic' to apply 'repeated pressure' on the matter. Such poor standards of accountability in a public body such as the Duchy, are increasingly both inexplicable and indefensible[26].

The Duchy of Cornwall, not altogether surprisingly, disagreed with much of the Committee's findings. They felt that there was no conflict of interest in the close involvement of the present incumbent in the running of the Duchy and accordingly no need to modify present arrangements in respect of its management. The Duchy felt that all this had been adequately dealt with by the Duchies of Lancaster and

3 'NICE LITTLE EARNERS': THE TWO DUCHIES

Cornwall (Accounts) Act 1838 and the Duchy of Cornwall Management Act 1863. This rather ignores the fact that 21st century Britain is now a very different place and that the Duchy has grown into a different institution from its previous historic incarnations.

The Duchy did agree to 'give further consideration to the way in which appointments to The Prince's Council are made'. They were also more forthcoming with regard to noting the role of the Treasury in respect of the future presentation of Duchy accounts. They did not however accept that the accounts should be presented to Parliament, with the Comptroller and Auditor General having access to their books and records. That, they felt, would be a step too far, still insisting on their status as 'a private estate' and being 'not funded by public monies', despite their tax exemptions – as apply to the Crown Estates – providing in effect an indirect public subsidy. As regards making their accounts 'clearer and more transparent', they felt that they had 'historically…volunteered disclosures that have gone beyond the minimum requirements' and thus saw no reason to do more.

Neither did they agree with the PAC recommendations to include any target and performance indicators, again asserting that the Duchy was a 'private landed estate' and any such information would be 'commercially sensitive'. However, in respect of the publication of additional information on the Duchy's 'charitable and other activities, and the principles that underline them', they seemed more than willing to comply. Not altogether surprising, given that the charitable efforts of the Prince of Wales are now so important in his public relations campaign. Referring to the Prince's annual review they lost no opportunity to put in a 'plug' for the Prince's charitable works and the amount of money raised.

Those representing the Duchy of Lancaster agreed that they should clarify the role of the Chancellor of the Duchy of Lancaster, an acknowledgement of the Chancellor having 'revocably delegated certain functions relating to the management of the Duchy to the Council'. They undertook to 'include a resume of the powers delegated to Council and those retained by the Chancellor over and above those delegated to Council for the efficient management of the Duchy and its assets'. Clarification of the Chancellor's role has, however, considerable political repercussions and is a matter for Parliament, not the Duchy, to decide.

The representatives also opposed the idea of the Comptroller and Auditor General having 'full access to the accounts of the Duchies' despite the requirement that they be presented to Parliament, and asserted the Duchy was 'not a public body and does not rely on any public funds'. The Duchy of Lancaster's representatives also agreed to provide more details about charitable donations. The charitable process is not as important an activity for the Queen in the way that it is for the heir to the throne. Whilst the Duchy does allocate funds to charity – mostly in respect of its rights under *Bona Vacantia* – the Queen does not need to 'sell' herself as a leading 'charitable entrepreneur' as the Prince of Wales does in order to maintain his popularity.

The Committee sought, within the extremely restricted period of time available, to address an exceedingly complex series of issues and one in which certain basic principles had not been adequately established from the outset. Without defining such first principles, it was hard to see that the process could be little more than an exploratory exercise in gentle persuasion of two bodies that regard themselves as being almost above the law, and certainly for most purposes above parliamentary scrutiny.

'THE CROWN', 'OWNERSHIP', AND 'TENURE'

English land law is based upon the mediaeval concept of feudal tenure, in which the only ultimate owner of any property in the country is the 'Crown'. Anyone owning freehold property does not 'own' it as such. Strictly speaking, it is 'held' in a form of tenure in which the 'Crown' retains ultimate ownership. Rather than the fixed term of years of a lease, it is held 'absolute and in perpetuity'. The 'Crown' of course, does not mean the person of the monarch as such, but the rather more nebulous 'Crown in Parliament', which has ultimate title to all property. People often confuse, perhaps not surprisingly, the notions of 'the Crown' – the abbreviated form of 'the Crown in Parliament' – with the idea of a 'crowned monarch'. The reigning monarch is for practical purposes little more than a cipher, now largely only symbolic of the power which now resides in the elected Parliament. It might perhaps make matters more honest if in this confusing clutter of fairy-tale terminology the word 'Crown' was replaced by the word 'State'.

The monarch does not 'own' State properties, Palaces, and so on, in an absolute sense, but rather as a cipher for the democratically elected

Parliament. This is not, of course, to forget that the monarch still possesses significant power through various royal prerogatives, though there is now greater acceptance of the need for some reform of these. The monarch also possesses the psychologically powerful title of Commander in Chief of the Armed Forces – with members of the military swearing an oath directly to the monarch rather than Parliament. This is a curious remnant of a non-democratic era, and says much in relation to notions of nationhood, citizenship and identity in the UK. In practice, most of the royal prerogative powers have been ceded to the Ministers of the Crown, principally the Prime Minister. Some specific real statutory power does still remain, notably within the Emergency Powers and Defence of the Realm Acts.

The fact that the rather abstract notion of the 'Crown' can appear to mean more than one thing also has powerful cultural overtones. The lavish ceremonial treatment of the monarch, with the highly symbolic 'crowning' of an individual, merely adds to the confusion. In the absence of a coherent, written constitutional settlement this is almost inevitable. Add to this a low level of constitutional awareness as a whole amongst the British public and it is easy to see how misunderstandings arise and are allowed to perpetuate.

Since Parliament is supreme, it is capable of disposing of the Duchies should it so wish. They are not, and cannot be, held 'above' Parliament in any sense. The investigation by the Public Accounts Committee in 2005 marked an assertion – although admittedly rather lacking in confidence at times – by Parliament of its position in this respect. Kevin Cahill has asserted that, as a result of the passing of the Human Rights Act any attempt to dispose of the Duchies would render Parliament liable to compensate the monarch and the heir to the throne in such a situation. This is unlikely. Were the current incomes to be replaced by defined salaries, since the incumbents do not have 'title' to the properties to lose, there could be no 'loss'. One cannot invoke the Human Rights Act simply because one's income has been reduced. Some might argue that no monarch would assent to such legislative changes. This might be true in theory, but in practice the Monarch would have no option but to bend to the will of an elected Parliament representing public opinion.

THE DUCHY OF LANCASTER

The profits (the Palace prefers the term 'surplus') of the Duchy of Lancaster constitute the Queen's 'official' income, in as far as such things are clearly set out in our unwritten constitution. This income is distinct from that obtained from her own personal sources – private estates and investments. As with the Duchy of Cornwall, the Duchy of Lancaster may be extended by the purchasing of additional property, but may not be disposed of, in whole or in part. The profits from the Duchy are paid to the monarch tax-free, but she may then offset expenses from that income against tax. The old Parliamentary allowances – salaries, in effect – paid to the 'working' royals, which the Queen reimbursed Parliament from 1993 – and from 2012 are entirely her responsibility, may fall into this category.

Having the income paid from the Duchy in this way certainly does in some way set at arm's length from a direct state payment – though no-one should be in any doubt as to the real source of the cash. Kevin Cahill makes plain the implications of this privileged arrangement:

> In this way the Duchy is the residue and epitome of all the tax dodges associated with the Crown and its unreformed hold on land in the United Kingdom. It is a little tax haven, but one that still, like all the best tax havens, milks its residents for their taxable revenue and then retains it, tax free, for the monarchy. It is also one of the best examples of formal administrative deceit, deceit aimed solely at maintaining the rational ignorance of the public and at concealing the irrational privileges of the Royal family[27].

Like the Duchy of Cornwall, the legal status of the Duchy of Lancaster is interesting. The official version, or at least that of the Duchy itself, is that it belongs to 'the Sovereign', although, again it cannot actually be sold off by the monarch, and logically it is Parliament which is ultimately in charge. Phillip Hall uncovered the existence of a second – and at the time 'secret' – volume of the official history of the Duchy; the Queen bases her title to the Duchy of Lancaster on her position as 'Duke of Lancaster'. Who actually grants that title? Logically, it is Parliament, as the monarch inherits the title of Duke of Lancaster on becoming monarch, once approved by the Privy Council – sitting as the Accession Council. As in the case of the title of the heir to the throne to the Duchy of Cornwall – it is possessed only in her 'official' and 'public' capacity. Were she to

3 'NICE LITTLE EARNERS': THE TWO DUCHIES

abdicate, the title of 'Duke of Lancaster' – and the Duchy income – would simply transfer to the succeeding monarch.

Kevin Cahill has proffered an alternative answer to the Duchy's ownership, albeit based on its own written material: 'Who owns the Duchy? The answer is no one. It owns itself. It is a body corporate that operates as a trust for the revenues that go to the Queen. This is, he maintains, reinforced by a note in the accounts, which says that the Duchy manages the land and investments in its ownership'[28]. However, whilst the Duchy may own these assets, somebody else in turn must own the Duchy. A fundamental principle of English law – as demonstrated by the concept of *Bona Vacantia* – is that no property can be 'ownerless'. So, Cahill's contention would seem to be fundamentally flawed. The reality is that it is 'the Crown', shorthand for the 'Crown in Parliament' – and for 'Crown' read 'State' – and not the Queen personally – who is the ultimate owner, a matter confirmed by the Crown Lands Act 1702. Thus Parliament, the real fount of power in our modern democracy, can resolve any matters relating to the Duchies whenever it wishes. All that is required is the will to do so.

Compared to the Prince of Wales's Duchy of Cornwall income, the Queen's Duchy of Lancaster income has generally occasioned less concern. Firstly, the Queen makes rather less money out of it. Secondly, she is the Queen, so the scale of her earnings is partly forgiven by virtue of the fact that she is the head of state. However, it is still curious that the release of these figures occasions little comment and analysis. Interestingly, the 2008 Civil List summary describes the Duchy of Lancaster income as being 'largely used by Her Majesty to meet official expenditure'. This is rather curious, as it is intended to provide an official independent personal income, so can this really be true? After all, if £40million was already being paid to cover the costs of doing the royal 'job' – and, by the way, what exactly did they mean by 'largely' – how much more could possibly be needed? If such claims are made, then at least they should be justified by detailed figures. If royal costs are spiralling so wildly, as it seems is being implied, this needs examining, but is it right for the Palace to use such unproven claims as a justification that they are somehow so 'hard done by' that they are having to dip into their own pocket? It would not be the first time this has happened – Prince Albert and

Queen Victoria were adept at financial whingeing, and pocketed a lot of Civil List money as a result.

One can only conclude that the British public has become so used to such large amounts that their capacity for surprise or concern has been dulled. The release dates for these annual accounts are also conveniently timed for the end of the Parliamentary year and the start of the holiday period when attention may be diverted elsewhere. Wimbledon tennis and other seasonal fixtures handily occur at this period, and other 'events' may also intervene. At the end of July 2007 the country's attention was focused on the clear-up operation after widespread flooding. Neither the Palace nor the Duchy of Lancaster made much of the fact that the Queen had enjoyed a pay rise of over £1million – over 10% – to a record level of £11.6million for the year. At a time of increasing concern at excessive payments for many corporate heads and the rich benefiting from the UK's lenient tax regime, most of the media failed to report it at all. A case of 'drowning' bad news, perhaps?

RURITANIAN REMNANTS
There is a point where the old world of the Duchies meets the modern political arena. Some public offices are just dismissed as little more than quaint remnants, historical legacies which remain as the innocent relics of ceremony and pageantry; and the position of the Chancellor of the Duchy of Lancaster is an example. The holder of this position is nominally the head of the Duchy's Governing Council yet is paid not by the Duchy but by the Government. The Chancellor is nominally appointed by the monarch but in reality by the Prime Minister. For a while the post was unfilled in 2006, with the government remarkably relaxed, when questioned, as to why this was so. The July 2007 Cabinet reshuffle saw the Minister of State for the Cabinet Office, Ed Miliband, assume the position of Chancellor as a secondary title. With the change of government, Lord Strathclyde took over as Chancellor in May 2010. Perhaps it will, in time, dwindle into obscurity.

Much of the unwritten British Constitution is testimony to such organic development and genuine ignorance even amongst the experts. The office of Lord Chancellor, with its inherent conflcts of interest, was reformed just a few years ago – bringing the UK at long last into line with cutting-edge eighteenth-century political thinking – by establishing the notion of the 'separation of powers'. An unfolding court case meant that the conflicts of interest inherent in the combined post would have meant that the Government would have certainly faced embarrassing problems in the event of an appeal against them on human rights grounds and the changes effectively pre-empted this from happening.

In 2003, when the Government finally agreed to announce what it believed to be its list of prerogative powers – a key element of our constitution – following parliamentary committee pressure, it admitted that it wasn't sure if that list contained them all. If the government itself has no idea what their powers are, who does? Perhaps the new Supreme Court will have to define those powers first. The formation of the Coalition government in 2010 also saved the UK from the potentially very controversial scenario of the Queen having to pick a leader in the event of a hung Parliament. To leave the decision in the aftermath of an uncertain election result to a hereditary monarch risked causing widespread concern by drawing the Queen into politics. With no written constitution to act as a guide, the Cabinet Office were navigating with a blank map. Pretty well everyone else uses the intelligent and eminently practical solution of having a written constitution – except the British (…and Saudi Arabia).

THE QUEEN'S DUCHY OF LANCASTER INCOME

2012	2011	2010	2009	2008	2007	2006	2005	2004
12.9	13.4	13.2	13.3	12.5	11.6	10.5	9.9	8.3

(£million)*

*This constitutes the Queen's official annual income which is taxable on a voluntary basis under the terms of the 1993 'Memorandum of Understanding'. It is paid into the 'Privy Purse' – a collective term for monies for the Queen's personal use which also derive from other sources. It is likely that the costs of the 'annuities' – annual incomes paid to leading members of the royal family – are reimbursed from this source before tax. The exception to the 1993 agreement reimbursements – and now set in statute by the Sovereign Grant Act 2012 – is the £359,000 annuity paid to the Duke of Edinburgh by Parliament each year and which is not required to be reimbursed by the Queen. The drop in income in 2012 to £12,870,000 (down from £13,280,000 in 2011) was attributed by the Duchy to a drop in their profits due principally to extensive property refurbishment costs to an office development – Wellington House in the Strand – and the Queen's Chapel in nearby Savoy Hill.

THE EFFECT OF FURTHER LORDS REFORM

Reform of the House of Lords – to date still unfinished business – could yet have a fundamental impact on the Duchies. As monarch, the Queen carries the title 'Duke of Lancaster' (Does this logically make Prince Philip 'the Duchess'?) and indeed there is a claim that the right to the income from the Duchy derives simply from the award of the title. Prince Charles holds the title of Duke of Cornwall only through his status as heir to the throne and thus possesses the right to the income only on that basis. Abolishing these titles could effectively sever the linkage between the incomes and the rights of the present recipient. Perhaps the whole tradition of titles – so dear to the British – could ultimately be abolished as part of the reform process initiated by Labour and still proceeding, at its customary glacial pace, under the coalition government in 2012.

The vote of the House of Commons in 2007 in support of a wholly elected Upper House is a clear pointer to a time when these anachronistic labels will have no further place in the constitution of this country. Tony Blair's achievement in abolishing the hereditary peers in the House of Lords is of perhaps greater historical significance than might at first appear. What remains is to abolish the titles which still form more than just a psychological 'link' with an undemocratic era.

THE FUTURE OF THE DUCHIES

What of the Duchies themselves? As Crown bodies they could simply be properly integrated into the Crown Estates, or retained with their profits separately 'ring-fenced' to provide a funding source for the monarch and heir, but with their management at arm's length from the beneficiaries. The exemption of the two Duchies from capital gains and corporation taxes is in fact entirely reasonable given that they are unincorporated Crown bodies. As such, they fall outside liability for such payments since the state cannot pay tax to itself. However, this position is anomalous, being particularly unfair to competing commercial bodies in that sector. This has naturally led to accusations that the Duchies thereby enjoy an unfair advantage, and one which in turn boosts their profits – which are then paid to the two lucky recipients, not the Treasury.

3 'NICE LITTLE EARNERS': THE TWO DUCHIES

IMMEDIATE CHANGES

The monarch and heir currently enjoy an enhanced benefit through the exemptions enjoyed by the Duchies themselves. In the absence of a wholesale change in the system of official remuneration for the monarch and heir, it is time for that remuneration to be amended to take account of those advantages. The fairest resolution would be for the net surpluses to first have deducted a notional tax equivalent to that paid by their commercial competitors before the remainder is then paid to the monarch and heir. Income tax would then be paid by the two recipients. Accusations of profiting unfairly through the Duchies tax-exempt status would thus be largely eliminated yet would leave unaltered the current tax positions of the Duchies themselves. This solution still fails to address the sheer scale of the amounts payable to the monarch and heir. Given that their official expenses are already met, they enjoy disproportionately and unnecessarily high official incomes.

It is time to decide whether, when increasing income inequality is an ever greater concern, those incomes should be reviewed and reduced to a more appropriate level. In May 2008 even the EU monetary affairs commissioner had decided that top pay and bonuses had become a 'social scourge'. By 2012 even Barclays Bank head Bob Diamond was coming in for criticism from shareholders over the scale of his remuneration, in a period of dissatisfaction that was becoming known as the 'Shareholder Spring' – and by the time of bank collusion in secretly rigging LIBOR interbank rates and his having to face a Commons committee he was acquiring genuine 'pariah' status . The levels of income now obtained from the Duchies for the respective recipients are grossly excessive, and the estates themselves enjoy privileges denied to competitors operating in the same commercial areas. The profits of the two bodies are now simply too crude a means of providing incomes for the monarch and heir. There is a clear potential conflict of interest in that the heir to the throne is not only the principal beneficiary from its income but also the head of the Duchy's ruling body – the Prince's Council. This is an undesirable situation in a public body and should be resolved at the earliest opportunity. A clear disconnection of the Duchies from their beneficiaries is logical and much-needed. As Crown bodies, the Duchies should simply be incorporated into the Crown Estates – or simply sold off.

HOW MUCH DO YOU PAY A QUEEN – OR AN HEIR TO THE THRONE?

The Duchies exist to meet the 'respective needs of the Households of the Queen and the Prince of Wales' – a decidedly vague directive. They are also intended to provide 'a degree of financial independence' from the Government of the day. They have, they maintain, a responsibility 'to generate as much income as is reasonably possible', subject to the requirements of 'sustainability, good management practice and,' in particular, balancing the interests of current and future beneficiaries'. There is no requirement to assess what might be a 'reasonable' level of personal income for a head of state or heir. Many might reasonably regard a gross annual income of over £18million for the heir to the throne and over £13million for the monarch as rather disproportionate.

After all, the expenses incurred in performance of their public duties are all met – they do not need to be rich to do their job. The fact that the heir receives more than the head of state seems, on a hierarchical basis alone, rather illogical. In absolute terms, the British monarch does incredibly well. For example, when compared with the United States of America. The US President is, of course, an executive head, rather than a largely ceremonial figure, so, in a sense, they could justifiably deserve more money than a non-executive head. They also serve only limited terms so their potential presidential earnings are thus limited. Since 2001, the President has received $400,000 per year – and their tax return is a public document. The British Prime Minister does not earn quite as much, but it is not so greatly dissimilar (£188,848 in 2007). US Presidential expenses are generally met by the Federal government. Even former US Presidents – often independently very wealthy and able to earn large amounts after their time in office – receive an official pension linked to comparable high-ranking US civil service and Cabinet levels of just $188,000 (2007).

Monarchs seem to traditionally do rather well, but the British monarchy is in a league of its own. A typical European monarch, the Belgian King, for example, receives an official allowance, equivalent to a salary, of £1.2million a year, while his heir gets just £533,000, both of which are

3 'NICE LITTLE EARNERS': THE TWO DUCHIES

then taxable. In a comparably large European nation with an elected non-executive head of state, Germany is notable. The President's annual earnings were – on 2007 budget estimates – just €199,000 (£133,330) before tax. Germany is exemplary in having a head of state with a modest profile and a correspondingly appropriate level of remuneration. It is a convention in democracies that public service should not, of its own, yield considerable personal financial benefit while performing those offices. Whilst politicians and Prime Ministers, for example, may sell their memoirs or give lectures once they have left office, that is ultimately a matter for the market. Quite why leading members of the British royal family should have an absolute right to get very rich, and to stay very rich, at public expense is curious and seldom questioned.

Treasury papers released in 2002 provide a clue as to the recent tolerance of the high level of the monarch's official earnings. In 1971, at the time of the dealings prior to the Civil List Act of 1972, the Duchy of Lancaster was providing the monarch with around £300,000 – the equivalent of a very much larger sum today, measurable in millions. This amount had been disregarded by ministers in calculating future royal needs only because, at the time, it was allegedly being used to fund part of the Civil List deficit which had arisen due to the ravages of inflation.

The Public Accounts Committee's hearing noted in 2005 that: 'Civil List legislation makes no provision for supporting the [heir's] official duties. They could have reminded themselves that within our unwritten constitution no 'duties' are actually specified at all. However, the following year Charles did receive £1,584,000 from the taxpayer in 'Grant-in-aid' to meet official expenses. Other expenses are claimed from his pre-tax Duchy income. It is an unsatisfactory state of affairs. The time has now come when a considered decision ought actually to be made about what would be an appropriate official income for the heir to the throne.

One could indeed ask whether the heir to the throne ought to be entitled to any special income or expense account provision at all? If so, then surely more strictly defined contractual terms should be demanded. A reasonable level of official salary might perhaps be calculated in relation to current remuneration in respect of the Prime Minister, Cabinet Ministers and senior civil servants, for example – together with a requirement to adhere to similar conditions regarding declarations of interests. The present position, whereby the heir is entitled to an open-ended multi-million pound income from a public body is bizarre. In return for this income, there are currently no specific requirements as to what the heir should actually do. If they are to fulfill an official role, then it should be as deputy head of state with defined duties.

Fixed allowances, voted directly from Parliament, would be the simplest and most straightforward solution, much in the manner of the 'annuity' which has been paid to the Duke of Edinburgh. For the heir to the throne, official duties should be rigorously defined with clear separation of his public office which would be directly state financed. As a condition of public office and money, declaration of interests as applies to Members of Parliament would encourage greater transparency and dispel concerns over conflicts between his public role and private life. Should the Prince be allowed to continue any commercial activities, however, he should reimburse the Duchy or the Exchequer for any benefit derived from the use of official titles and coats of arms as for instance has occurred through the 'Duchy Originals' business.

Only by instituting a more transparent system of remuneration for heir to the throne and the monarch, will we have a modern and accountable system that is acceptable for a twenty-first century democracy. Given that their official costs are already fully met by the taxpayer, their official incomes should not be of such a scale that public money is able to personally enrich the monarchy in the way that it does at present.

The entire monarchy could be financed from the Duchy incomes alone. The present combined figure of profits produced – just over £31million in 2012 – might be a convenient point for establishing a reduced and more appropriately scaled monarchy. This would, given the current quoted annual cost of around £40million, necessitate significant cost reductions – not including, of course, those presently undisclosed security costs! Such clear 'ring-fencing' could be established in a new constitutional settlement by an express clarification by statute of the Duchies position as part of the Crown Estates. This would make the Duchies properly accountable to Parliament and address a long overdue and much-needed rationalisation of the 1760 Civil List arrangements. This is another instance in which the new Sovereign Grant Act has fallen short in respect of properly addressing the overall scale of royal finances as a whole. There was a need to go back to first principles prior to drawing up any new legislation, and in this respect the government failed utterly.

3 'NICE LITTLE EARNERS': THE TWO DUCHIES

Without proper reform the monarch and heir to the throne continue to benefit excessively from the present arrangement, profiting disproportionately from public funds. Disquiet with high-level boardroom pay increases, but curiously few in the UK seem able to discern any problem with the huge amounts paid to the Queen and Prince Charles as official incomes. Or perhaps we should say 'official' incomes, given the nation's unwritten constitution. People are encouraged to think only in terms of the Civil List when it comes to royal funding, assuming that the money from the Duchies – if they think of it at all – is entirely 'private' and thus none of their concern. The style of presentation encourages this – the Civil List and Grant-in-aid's 'price of a loaf of bread per person' nonsense – coupled with a tradition of deferential public acceptance. As long as we continue to talk of 'Duchy surpluses' and other pseudo-fantastical historical terminology – at which so many of the population have a tendency to fall on one knee or bow – and refrain from asking searching questions – then the Windsor family will continue to benefit. Paying two people a combined total of over £31million a year as personal income out of state funds is a scandal.

4
Windsors' World: Life at the Taxpayers' Expense

Stop wasting my time
You know what I want
You know what I need
Or maybe you don't
Do I have to come right
Flat out and tell you everything?
Gimme some money
Gimme some money
Spinal Tap

The basis for the highly favoured financial status of the British royal family is the claimed need for a politically 'independent' income that is not only 'appropriate' but which also which conveys the necessary 'dignity' to the institution. There is definitely a big question as to whether dignity and wealth always necessarily go hand in hand. The monarch's and the heir to the throne's Duchy of Lancaster and Cornwall monies respectively provide a means of ensuring a largely 'independent' – but far from 'private' – income. Within the British constitution, however, the monarchy is an institution ultimately subordinate to Parliament so the notion of alleged 'independence' is preserved as a sop to royal pride. The generally deferential nature of Parliamentary scrutiny guarantees the monarch financial 'independence' in both public and private terms.

The Queen, as head of state, has a formal constitutional role. The same, however, cannot be said of the other members of the royal family who receive direct and indirect benefit from the taxpayer. The Prince of Wales is waiting for a job that will arise at some point in the future, but until then he has no constitutionally defined role – there is nothing that the he *must* do in return for his £17million plus a year from the Duchy of Cornwall. Of course, there is a degree of political and general public acceptability which accompanies the manner in which he spends his cash, but there are no rules. Other members of the Windsor family benefit similarly from the accident of birth; and similarly these benefits do not relate to any defined constitutional obligations. It is true that with the passing of the Sovereign Grant Act the Parliamentary allowances which they received in the past, and for which from 1993 the Queen had to reimburse Parliament, have now passed into history. These were, in effect, official salaries on a scale comparable to senior executives, accompanied by generous expenses. The expenses remain, paid in connection with duties which they effectively determine themselves and they also gain preferred access to prime state-owned property under especially favourable terms.

Despite all this, under our unwritten constitution they are not required to perform any specific duties. There are no contracts of employment, no specific attendance requirements and they need no qualifications. What they do is normally presented as the selfless performance of 'duties' – invariably the patronage of charitable causes, attendance at social functions, and so on – by a collection of miscellaneous so-called 'hard-working' royals. Despite the fact that they receive no official salaries as such, they are members of a very rich family which has been permitted by generations of public policy to gain and retain that wealth. One could argue that the Duchy of Lancaster income – by now around £13million a year – is grossly in excess of what is appropriate as an official income as such for merely one person, and is in reality is an effective 'umbrella' state subsidy paid via the Queen to be distributed amongst her family members. They then pick and choose what they would like to do as a justification for their social position and the financial benefit derived, on a level which matches their status in the royal hierarchy.

LIVING ON AN 'APPROPRIATE' AND 'INDEPENDENT' INCOME
In one respect in particular, members of the royal family enjoy a number of handy exceptions denied to others. Firstly, the Queen, the Heir to the Throne and the 'Consort of a former Sovereign', are exempt from inheritance tax. That's very handy – if you are close to one of these individuals, and being an immediate family member tends to put you pretty much at the head of the queue, then anything left to you has by inference been boosted by its tax-free status. Secondly, the royal family enjoys exemption from Freedom of Information legislation, so awkward questions are harder to ask with information being much harder – if not impossible – to obtain. Thirdly, unlike others in public positions, they are not required to declare their financial interests. This is despite the fact that they may be representing organisations – speaking as patrons, supporting causes, and so on, which have a commercial or other financial dimension. They are free from the normal processes of disclosure of interests which apply to politicians and civil servants yet their roles not infrequently involve situations in which conflicts could potentially arise.

The distinctions between their public roles and their private lives can be vague but little attempt is made to properly distinguish the two. There is no reason why the taxpayer should, directly or indirectly, fund favoured individuals in order to give them some purpose in life. The system of hereditary monarchy means funding an un-elected head of state, and one could argue that this is reasonable as long as it is generally accepted by the nation. However, it does not automatically follow that the remaining members of the family should be financed by the taxpayer at all, but especially not to the degree at present. As long as members of the royal family are subsidised by the state, they will do their best to find and perform such 'work' in an attempt to justify that cost. Little thought is given to whether such work really needs to be done at all, or whether it could be paid for by other bodies. A complex hierarchy of titles, roles and 'duties' provides a justification for this Ruritanian theatrical cast maintained by the taxpayer. Talent is not demanded, the players perform irrespective of their suitability for the task and receive financial benefits according to their place in the family hierarchy.

THE DUKE OF EDINBURGH
In all of this, one person has enjoyed a very privileged position – simply for *being married* to the Queen. The Duke of Edinburgh

continues to be paid directly by Parliament – £359,000 a year to be exact – and as we have seen, and despite this being ostensibly to meet costs of performing, once again unspecified, duties he appears to have put quite a bit aside to become a very wealthy man indeed. It was believed that, in the late 1940s, as the husband of the future Queen it would be impossible to have a career of his own and the government decided that the hard-pressed people of the UK should subsidise his lifestyle and bank account to accumulate some 'wealth'. This happy, unquestioning state of affairs persisted for decades, during which time the Duke's spare cash piled up. Those who remember the royal family's attempt to portray themselves as a 'normal' family in the BBC television 'fly on one's wall' documentary in the late 1960s may have even themselves forgotten that this followed a period – quite a long one, around a decade, in which rumours of the Duke's alleged infidelities had abounded. It is true that for a very long time, while Mrs Windsor was 'at home' being Queen, Prince Philip spent a lot of time and money enjoying himself both at home and abroad. This was before the invention of his eponymous Award Scheme – another case of the creation of a 'charity' shield with which to deflect possible criticism. Needless to say, the money for all of this fun came from the 'never had it so good' taxpayer. We may think that royal finances today come, if not exactly a microscope, then at least under a low-power magnifying glass, but in those halcyon days, scrutiny was relatively hands-off, with a more generally deferential culture prevailing.

As a former naval officer, the Duke could not resist the lure of the sea, and while 'ordinary' sailing yachts appealed, the royal 'yacht' *Britannia* appealed even more. He passed not just days, but weeks away on the lavish floating palace, with the taxpayer stoking cash into the boiler furnaces to propel the vessel from one sun-drenched destination to another. Even in the early 90s, the *Britannia* was still the luxury vantage-point from which the Duke could scan the yacht racing for the duration of Cowes Week on the Isle of Wight. This had been just one of his regular outings, little publicised, which had been going on for years. At a basic £70,000 (or its earlier equivalent) a day to run *Britannia*, Philip had done rather well since the 50s in having a handy floating 'home from home' on which to park his drinks and his binoculars.

4 WINDSORS' WORLD: LIFE AT THE TAXPAYERS' EXPENSE

THE PRINCE OF WALES – LIFE AS A ROYAL 'DISSIDENT'

In January 2006, the *Mail on Sunday* newspaper found itself in court in an action brought by the Prince of Wales. It was accused of divulging his private thoughts, thoughts which had been circulated to a circle of friends and admirers – including journalists. These 'limited edition' journals were his musings on a wide range of topics. Not surprisingly, extracts found their way into the pages of the *Mail on Sunday*. Few, however, were surprised by the rather familiar tone of the journals which echoed the Prince's favourite themes, and mourning for a 'lost' past when the world was a simpler and better place – and rather more respectful to princes.

The handover of Hong Kong to China in December 1997 gave the Prince a golden opportunity to lament the loss of empire. Although he should have known better, his bitter criticism of leading Chinese politicians as a group of 'old waxworks' was offensive and diplomatically inept in the extreme. No one, least of all the heir to the British throne, should have permitted himself to make such insulting remarks which could seriously embarrass an elected government and possibly compromise the nation's reputation.

On a previous occasion during an employment tribunal hearing, it was revealed that the Prince believed people, by implication both in his employment and elsewhere, should not seek to 'rise above their station'. His belief in a 'natural order' conveniently reinforces his access to great wealth and the prospect of becoming head of state solely by birthright. The Prince's career of self-promotion to justify his inherited title to a sceptical public was given priority after his divorce, and as heir to the throne, he was guaranteed access to a public platform from which to articulate his assorted 'renaissance man' views. To further enhance his popular appeal, his growing network of charities – based around his original Prince's Trust – provided a worthy set of causes with which to deflect criticism of his wealth and position. Added to this has been arranged a carefully crafted self-promotional 'manifesto' addressing numerous social and cultural issues which aim to enhance his public image. His promotional material, including a lavish website, appears full of worthy good intentions, but it also reveals a man whose self-importance seemingly knows no bounds – perhaps not so surprising for someone born to be king. As future monarch, he should by implication be a neutral constitutional figure who is 'above' politics. However, his numerous chosen crusading issues stray into what is a decidedly political arena, although he does not want to resign from the succession and subject himself to the democratic test by standing as an MP. That would mean giving up over £17million a year...

'MAKING A DIFFERENCE'
The Prince of Wales, according to his website, 'seeks, with the support of his wife, to do all he can to use his unique position to make a difference for the better both in the UK and internationally'. (www.princeofwales.gov.uk/personalprofiles/theprinceofwales) Previous emphasis promoting his role as that of 'Supporting the Queen', has been gradually downplayed in favour of the rather vague aim of 'making a difference'. To avoid the accusation that he is living a life of privilege at public expense he tries to convince an increasingly sceptical public that he is actually doing anything useful. However, to be honest, how many are going to check his website? – and his best policy to avoid contention has generally been to avoid publicity as far as possible. With a low profile, few questions are asked, and if they are, then one is effectively steered towards his charitable causes – and you can't argue with charity, can you?

Venturing ever further into the realms of glossy PR-speak, 'sustainability' has now become another favourite word with which to pepper most of his utterances. On April 2nd, 2012 he sent a video message to a United Nations New York conference on global sustainability entitled 'Happiness and Well-being: defining a new economic paradigm'. All very well-meaning, but don't forget that the UK taxpayer is funding the Prince to keep generating all this. Whilst on the one hand he has expressed a wish to represent 'stability and continuity', he also sees himself 'acting personally as a catalyst to achieve change, to generate debate'. However, genuine debate is not a favourite with Charles Windsor. He prefers the medium of the planned speech, in front of a selected, deferential audience – or indeed, as above, the video message. In short, he snipes from the sidelines, knowing that his tricky political status prohibits a proper debate. His position and wealth provide a platform, but also protect him from those who disagree. Although he could put principle before position, step down, and enter the democratic arena, he fails to do so. Accusations of 'interference' are met by his office with the claim that the Prince is 'always careful to avoid party political and politically contentious issues'. Many would disagree.

CAUSES AND CONCERNS

The various causes espoused by the Prince may be laudable in themselves, espousing environmental and heritage issues. Some, like the 'Mutton Renaissance Campaign', launched in 2004, risk sounding a trifle eccentric, but others, such as that supporting the Dalai Lama in the campaign for Tibetan freedom from China set him very firmly in political territory. His boycott of an official state banquet for the then visiting Chinese President, Jiang Zemin, represented a personal stance which is supposedly 'prohibited' by his position. As a condition of his status and wealth, he cannot be seen to indulge his personal whims. It is the price of the pact he 'signs' by agreeing to remain heir to the throne. He cannot have it both ways. In the opinion of a former PR advisor, the Prince actually sees himself as a 'dissident' against elected politicians who fail to do as he sees fit, and his failure to exert political influence seems to cause him a fair degree of angst. He has risked nothing, nor sacrificed anything for his beliefs. A dissident? Tell that to Chen Guangcheng...

Unlike the Prince of Wales himself, those he criticises are democratically elected, and his neutrality is an implicit condition of his position.

According to Liberal Democrat MP, Norman Baker; 'While I may often agree with what he says, I defend to the end our right not to hear him say it!' However, the Prince's uniquely privileged position gives him an opportunity to make statements which are guaranteed a wide audience yet which he is never prepared to discuss in open forum. They thus go unchallenged and, in fact, are treated by many with a degree of reverence simply as a consequence of who he is. Were he a true man of conviction, he could resign from the succession and stand for Parliament.

THE PRINCE: PROMOTING HIMSELF...

Many of Prince Charles' ideas accord with popular thinking, from the environment to organic food. He styles himself as a blend of agrarian eco-warrior and social benefactor. However, his own lifestyle reveals more than a few inconsistencies. This is a man who promotes restraint for the good of the environment yet who has several lavish homes, a fleet of cars, and who frequently travels by air – notably the fuel-inefficient helicopter – as well as the Royal Train. Trains carrying hundreds of passengers are good for the environment but one person and a handful of personal staff crossing the country in their own train uniquely misses the point.

His lavish website used to read more like the campaigning pages of a political party manifesto. With sections on 'Health', 'Education', 'Responsible Business', The Natural Environment', 'The Built Environment' and 'The Arts' (and an 'advertorial' section promoting his 'Duchy Originals' products range) he promoted himself as the next head of state in an almost absurdly inflated manner – almost in the manner of some North Korean 'Great Leader'. This must have become apparent even to his advisers, and it is interesting to see how the latest format of the website now offers a rather more sober and somewhat less ego-driven view of the man and his numerous causes.

Whilst politicians have up till now indulged his behaviour, they may be less tolerant in the future. Having railed against modern architecture in his notorious 'carbuncle' speech lamenting the extension to London's National Gallery, and being equally aghast at the proposal to build a Mies van der Rohe designed office block in the vicinity of St Paul's Cathedral in the City of London, the heir to the throne became famous as the champion of rather conservative, if not 'fogey-ish', architectural causes. If a design was not 'traditional' or essentially neo-Classical, then it was unlikely to get his seal of approval.

...AND INTERFERING: '...A SERIOUS POLITICAL ISSUE THAT MUST BE DEALT WITH AT THE HIGHEST LEVEL...'

The Prince provoked serious controversy in 2010 when it became known that he had brought his considerable influence to bear on the proposed redevelopment scheme for the former Chelsea Barracks site in London. The light and airy modern styled plans designed by world-famous architect Lord Rogers, did not meet with Charles' approval, and he favoured replacing it with a Quinlan Terry-designed pseudo-Wren-ish development designed to echo the nearby Royal Hospital. He sought to influence his personal (royal) friends, the ruling family of Qatar, owners of developers Qatari Diar who withdrew their planning application three months after a face to face meeting between Charles and the Emir of Qatar. Development co-partners the Candy Brothers sued for breach of contract. For High Court judge Justice Vos it raised 'a serious political issue that needed to be dealt with at the highest level', and noted that the Prince of Wales' position 'continued to impact' on the views of the officers and politicians (but primarily the latter) at Westminster City Council and the Greater London Assembly. Interference by a hereditary figure

– and the next head of state – in the democratic planning process is a serious matter indeed.

DUCHY DEVELOPMENTS
In reassuringly smooth and self-assured public relations language his charity, the Prince's Foundation for the Built Environment, makes the extravagant claim to be 'the only institution in the UK which specialises in providing consultancy and education services for large-scale urban development or regeneration projects'. Unfortunately for the Prince his efforts risk appearing hypocritical. As we have seen, there was decided embarrassment in 2005 when Duchy representatives were asked by the Public Accounts Committee about the existence of 'carbuncles' – examples of modern out-of-town retail 'sheds' and other business developments – within their large investment property portfolio. The Duchy's promotional material tends to focus upon picturesque stone-built rural buildings rather than the large commercial developments that are the backbone of its profitable portfolio.

Prince Charles even launched his very own architectural magazine, and not surprisingly, in the best royal tradition, it was lavish and heavily subsidised. Finding anyone prepared to buy it, however, was a problem. No more than an extravagant exercise in vanity publishing, it failed dismally. Keen to promote the architectural values in which he so strongly believed – and in the aftermath of his low public relations position following his separation from the Princess of Wales the previous year – the Prince now embarked upon a pet project of his own. In 1993 he oversaw the creation of a new village based upon his views of what should constitute an ideal and naturally ordered living environment. Poundbury, near Dorchester in Dorset, England, has given its name to a style of residential development – 'neo-Poundbury' – with its tightly clustered houses, narrow streets, a carefully contrived, rather 'jumbled' layout, frontages opening directly onto the street, with dwellings themselves styled largely in a neo-Georgian or New England fashion. The latter is no accident, with the Prince deriving much influence from Leon Krier, one of the architects responsible for the American-led 'New Urbanist' movement. Their aim was to counter the 'suburban sprawl' that characterised much housing development in the United States – and also in the UK – and sought to revive 'traditional' urban forms. Critics, however, accused the movement of being little more than 'standard suburbia with some bizarre touches'[1], little more than an exercise in nostalgia-driven pastiche. In April 2008 Government minister Hazel Blears attacked Poundbury as owing more to 'self-aggrandisement' than concern for its residents[2]. By spring, 2008, there were plans for another, grander 'neo-market town' in Wiltshire.

'WHERE AM I?' – 'IN THE VILLAGE...'

As a concept, Poundbury is far from original – witness Sir Clough Williams-Ellis' specially constructed village of Portmeirion in North Wales, perhaps best known as the setting for the cult 60s TV series The Prisoner. The resemblance of the Prince's development to the fictional location is perhaps closer than many might wish to admit. Writing about the TV series' location, years before the Prince's development, writer Robert Fairclough's words seem eerily prescient: 'Behind a picturesque veneer lies an environment obsessed with control – administered by a "Number 2" who is unaccountable and with little more than a theatrical pretence to participation by its residents'. There is an uncanny symbolic similarity to a renaissance man 'trapped' in the obligations of an hereditary system: 'Who is Number 2? : alternating between good-natured bonhomie and threats, this Number 2 relishes crossing intellectual swords.... He accepts his fate as one of the Village's "lifers", but equally believes in the pioneering spirit of the community'[3].

Visually, however, Poundbury is rather more mundane than 'The Village' – and less picturesque too. Devoid of its 'false perspectives and deceptive sense of scale' – and without the more dramatic scenery. However the participation of its residents, the almost ominous note of 'remote control' and 'other-worldly' atmosphere would probably be familiar to that of 'Number 6' in The Prisoner. A woman, criticising facilities in Poundbury, commented that: 'We have a playground across from us and it's not big enough. And it's in the wrong place. Mrs Hart mentioned this to the Duchy people and she says there are now "rumours" that it will move'. 'Prince Charles does take an interest in our views', said another resident – 'When my husband died, he sent me a note'[4].

Poundbury is a village where everyone is supposed to be on their best behaviour, and just a little too tidy, as if poised for 'the Prince' to arrive at any moment. Despite its positive points, it is not quite the 'real' world. It is perhaps no coincidence that the set for the Jim Carey film 'The

> Truman Show', in which the protagonist is trapped unwittingly in a TV reality-show town was itself shot in a 'New-Urbanist' development. A rather contrived environment created to convey a sense of 'instant history', Poundbury reinforces the oft-repeated affirmation of the Prince of Wales' belief in the concept of a 'natural order', where discreet control is the pervasive norm. There could be a sense that it is Charles' very own 'Petit Trianon', but it is definitely for others, not the Prince himself. He prefers the detached privacy of genuinely historic Highgrove and his Scottish castles, a great many miles away – metaphorically and in reality – from his 'ideal' model living environment. Be seeing you...

WHOSE GOOD CAUSE?

There seems no limit to the talents of the heir to the throne – from pseudo-rustic purveyor of organic nibbles to rockin' promoter of the 2004 Urban Music festival at London's Earl's Court. Perhaps one should not be harsh – it is difficult to challenge the 'motherhood and apple-pie' good intentions of his many and varied charitable causes. However, there is a very real sense that the Prince is straying into both political and quasi-commercial territory whilst simultaneously fufilling a public role and all the while being paid by the state. From acting as a ' platform of emerging talent' with both the 2004 festival and the Prince's Trust's many 'Party in the Park' fundraisers, he is able to use both influence and money not merely to promote the causes themselves but also to develop a far wider and more co-ordinated campaign of self-promotion through them.

While the good intentions and higher motives of these campaigns are laudable, there is a large question mark over the use of the Duchy – a publicly owned asset – being used as a promotional vehicle and to subsidise his numerous activities. With a large staff effectively paid for by the Duchy he has a distinct and some might say unfair competitive advantage for his causes. Most of all, it is the use of the royal 'brand' being used to promote an intensely personal agenda which causes concern. It is as much about what is good for the long term interests of one man in a uniquely privileged position as about the causes themselves. The time has come when the Prince of Wales ought to make a fundamental choice; either to devote his life, as Charles Windsor, to his many and varied causes and to operate his charities as truly independent entities devoid of any hint of public subsidy, or to accept that there is a quite serious incompatibility between his personal campaigning, commercial activities and the position of monarch to which he one day hopes to succeed. What appears to be becoming established is the emergence of the Prince's charitable empire – as an adjunct of the Duchy – becoming an hereditary asset to be passed on to the next generation as a handy counter to accusations of royal privilege.

THE GOOD LIFE
Commenting on the Prince's Duchy income, one Public Accounts Committee member, Alan Williams, speaking in 2005, felt that the level of these earnings might cause envy amongst the less privileged: 'Can you not understand that an average of £6million a year for 14 years makes it look to the public as if the Prince is winning the Lottery every year?'[5]. By 2011 the Prince's annual Duchy income had risen to over £17million. Whilst it may be expensive just 'being' a royal heir – even if such expenses are tax-deductible – and state Grants-in-aid cover other costs – there seems little real challenge to the scale and remit of his 'role'. As a result it has expanded in scope, with the tax-payer picking up the tab, to suit the pretensions of the incumbent. The money is given with little accountability and no definition of the Prince's duties in return for this money. There would appear to be little real differentiation in terms of time spent by the Prince in performing his 'official' duties and his very extensive personal charitable causes, and his private life. Royal 'value for money' is never examined rationally. The tax-payer contributes the costs of maintaining his palace in the capital – £461,000 – and the £1,485,000 travel costs incurred in performing his constitutionally undefined role (2006-07), for example.

The Prince's home, Highgrove House, is surrounded by extensive private gardens, but even the bill for maintaining these is regarded as largely tax-deductible in view of the many events held there by the Prince to which members of the public are invited. A total staff of 158.9 'full-time equivalent' staff (2010/11), up from a mere 142 in 2006, attend to his every need – from lawn-mowing to toothpaste-squeezing – in order to support his official and charitable efforts, as well as his private life. For a glimpse of Charles' life on Planet Highgrove in May 2012, curious royal fans could treat themselves to lunch and a guided tour of the gardens at a cost of £149. If you're struggling a little in the recession, then you can settle for afternoon tea and a tour for a bargain £119. All remaining profits, naturally, go to the Prince's many charities.

The total cost of the Prince's staff, both 'personal' and 'official', amounts to staggering £6.5million. By 2010/11 this figure had leapt to £9,444,000, with just £1,080,000 being spent on travel). No wonder he is able to 'do' so much. However, his private secretary, Sir Michael Peat, in his smooth accompaniment to the Prince's annual accounts in 2006 described the staffing level overall as 'lean'. But 'lean' compared to what, exactly? His fifteen million pounds-plus gross annual income was then – and still is – quite a lot of money, and even the Prince of Wales has probably got pretty much all he needs. An 'operating surplus' of £2,003,000 remained, but this was whisked away in 'payments and transfers' to arrive at a less grand figure of just £136,000. Having too much left over might prompt the Public Accounts Committee to have another good look at whether one man really needs quite as much as we allow him to have.

CHARITY BEGINS AT HIGHGROVE

As the saying goes, charity begins at home, but for the Duchy – and the Prince – it seems to end up there as well. In 2007 the Duchy gave £153,000 to charity, including £75,000 to the Duchy of Cornwall Benevolent Fund, while £104,000 went to 'a variety of charities, mainly operating in the southwest of England'. No further details, but was he basically subsidising his own charities with state-originated funding? We may never know. In 2008, £215,000 was donated, with £130,000 going to the Duchy's Benevolent Fund. All these would have been augmented by the taxpayer through tax relief on charitable donations. If those charities were not entirely unconnected with the Prince himself, then money would seem to be being paid direct from a state asset – the Prince's Duchy earnings – direct to his favourite charities – all to benefit the Prince's 'charitable entrepreneur' image. It truly confirms his belief in a 'virtuous circle', but for whose benefit exactly?

By contrast, his eldest son William seems to have sought to live a somewhat lower-key – and cost – lifestyle. Since his marriage to Kate Middleton, they have managed with minimal help at their Anglesey home, and expect to occupy a relatively modest apartment in Kensington Palace. Whether this sets a longer-term trend is hard to say at this stage, but William and Kate may well adopt a rather more modest approach to life once he, most probably, steps down from his flying career in the not too distant future. By his 30th birthday in June 2012, William was expected to inherit £10million from his late mother's estate, so whatever happens, life won't be too tough – except perhaps by his father's standards. And an apartment in a royal Palace is still, of course, an apartment in a royal Palace, even if, in the author's experience, some of these are usually rather modest, bordering in some cases on the terminally dull. Still, it's all about location, location, location...

It will remain to be seen how Prince Charles manages with the retirement of his key financial adviser, Sir Michael Peat who has, it is generally accepted, acted as a restraining hand on the Prince's tendency to overspend and enjoy a lavish and generally indulgent lifestyle on what is ultimately public money. William may understand what his father seems not to do, that the ultimate survival of the Windsor dynasty may rest with an ability to both understand and to show restraint on a scale they seem to have not hitherto really understood.

PRINCE ANDREW: THE GRAND MIDDLE-AGED DUKE OF YORK

For years, as 'Special Representative for International Trade and Investment', the Queen's 'favourite' son, Prince Andrew, the Duke of York, travelled between the world's more exotic locations in the course of supposedly promoting the country's economy, at a cost to the taxpayer of £779,469 in 2007-08 for the bigger trips alone. This curious position would seem to have come into existence purely to give the Prince something to do following his retirement from the Navy, and one which could blend his love of flying, travel in general and meeting people in an atmosphere of social conviviality where he would be the centre of attention. Was it paid? No. Were there generous expenses to cover all this jet-setting? Yes. However, when questions started to be asked about this curious role, it became apparent that nobody seemed to be actually in charge of this high-end sales rep. As the *Daily Mail* elicited from a UKTI spokesperson: '[His] role is independent of UK Trade and Investment and is neither a paid position nor a formal UKTI Board appointment'[6]. Andrew was 'appointed' by the then Prime Minister Tony Blair in 2001, but without any contract or term of office. He was not answerable to ministers, and decided his own itinerary, which was managed by his own staff at Buckingham Palace.

Pressing 'official' engagements have included a crucially important 'driving-in' ceremony in September 2005 at the Royal and Ancient Golf Club at St Andrews in Scotland, following which he returned to RAF

Northolt, all at a cost of £11,555 in travel expenses alone. Whether public funds ought to be used for a trip to a Scottish golf club is highly questionable. If an exclusive organisation such as the 'Royal and Ancient' wants the Duke of York to turn up and speak then it really ought to be a private arrangement – although it ought possibly to include a fee payable to the Exchequer for the 'hire' of one of their royals which cost the taxpayer so much to maintain. Given the Duke's 'Special International Representative' title, domestic golfing appointments would appear to fall outside his normal job remit, as Scotland is still part of the United Kingdom. Yet the taxpayer still pays for such trips. The Duke, labelled 'Air Miles Andy' by the tabloids, is a keen golfer. The fact that many of his official trips seem to have 'meshed' in an almost uncanny fashion with golf tournaments both national and international is evident to any reader of *The Times* 'Court Circular'. In May 2005, a number of officially but intriguingly listed 'other engagements' were combined with a trip to Portrush Golf Club near Belfast from RAF Northolt which cost the taxpayer £3,401. There is no record of a return trip, though were the return leg to have cost less than £2,500 then this would fall below the disclosure limit. Add 'security' and other extras, and golf becomes an expensive hobby – for the taxpayer.

Andrew's curious – and effectively, as it turned out, self-appointed – role as the UK's 'Special Trade Representative, continued to give cause for concern. By 2011, patience with him was wearing very thin. Allegations of rudeness to foreign dignitaries were mounting, coupled with a reputation for crass and tactless behaviour in general. The former ambassador to Italy, Yugoslavia and Ireland, Sir Ivor Roberts revealed how he'd been responsible for clearing up the mess caused by a man who was spoken of by UK diplomatic staff in the Gulf as 'HBH': 'His Buffoon Highness'. He also has a reputation for contentious comments with a political dimension – such as being critical of anti-fraud investigators seeking to probe a UK arms deal with Saudi Arabia. His choice of friends – apart from the ongoing embarrassment of his continuing relationship with his ex-wife – has been highlighted by very poor judgement, including convicted US billionaire child sex offender Jeffrey Epstein. Being pictured in the close company of one of the girls involved didn't exactly help the Duke's reputation. To this can be added his friendship with convicted Libyan gun smuggler Tarek Kaituni[7].

The amassed wealth of the royal family has considerable 'trickle-down' effect to its immediate members. Gifts or 'transfers' of money and property, or concessions to occupy state-owned Crown Estate property, enable members of the Windsor family, with apparently insufficient means of financial support, to live lives of luxury. Andrew Windsor is a retired naval officer, who after many years of distinguished service – including a period on active duty in the Falklands – now lives at Windsor Royal Lodge. His naval pension is relatively modest – though anyone with a public sector pension is indeed privileged – yet he occupies a large, lavish thirty-room property, complete with seven staff cottages – all recently refurbished at great expense and set within 40 hectares of grounds within Windsor Great Park. He secured a 7-year renewable lease on the Lodge for a price of £1million, together with an agreement to refurbish it at an agreed cost of £7.5million.

These were considerable sums for the 'Special Representative' – an unpaid post, though it had a very generous expense account, which since 2004-5 was been funded by the government. Should he choose to vacate the Royal Lodge within the next 25 years – he has the option to renew the 7-year lease – then he will be refunded part of this cost on a sliding scale. The lease can only be assigned to his widow, despite the divorce, and her two daughters – or, conveniently, a trust arranged for their benefit – otherwise it reverts to the Crown Estate. The property was previously occupied by his grandmother the Queen Mother, following the royal tradition of keeping such luxury state property in the family[8].

The 2001 Royal Rich Report speculated that, given a known trust fund set up when the Duke of York was born was estimated at the time to be worth around £1million, it might have been expected to be worth around £7million by 2001. Assuming that it had not been eroded as a result of his marriage to Sarah Ferguson this would yield a reasonable income. He also receives an annual £249,000 Parliamentary 'allowance' paid for out of the Civil List but which is now reimbursed by his mother. His annual income is substantial, but probably not *that* great – and taxed, too. Yet he was somehow able to afford £8.5million of building work on his new home. Furthermore the lease prohibits selling it on at a profit in the future. Andrew was keen to move his ex-wife out of their old home at Sunninghill – not a Crown Estate property – and sell it, presumably to cover costs of the work at Royal Lodge. Until then, the Queen who had paid for Sunninghill in the first place, has been most likely supporting him. What would they do without that Duchy of Lancaster money?

Indeed, Sunninghill remained unsold for five years until its sale to Kazakh business tycoon Timur Kulibayev – another friend – for £15million in 2008. The Duke has visited Kazakhstan on a number of occasions, both in an official and private capacity in recent years, and the fact that the property was sold for £3million above its guide price prompted worries as to whether there was, as Ian Davidson MP commented, 'anything else involved in the deal'. The lack of proper transparency surrounding Andrew's role as 'Special Representative for Trade and Investment' – and then to be involved in such a transaction with someone well connected to Kazakhstan's ruling and business elite is one which raises profound concerns. Little wonder that it prompted allegations that he might have exploited his official position for personal gain, though Buckingham Palace was quick to issue a denial[9]. The Duke appears to have considerable investments. However, unlike Members of Parliament, Cabinet Ministers and senior civil servants, he is under no obligation to disclose whether any of these are invested in companies where there might be a conflict of interest in relation to his official duties.

Andrew's closeness to his ex-wife was also getting ever more embarrassing. Her reputation as a slow-motion financial car crash is legendary, with her almost constantly teetering on the verge of bankruptcy. She has acquired traditional royal spendthrift habits, but since her divorce has lacked the necessary matching income, thus requiring endless financial bail-outs from friends – and no doubt the Duke himself. This was bad enough, but then in 2010 came more bad news – a press 'sting' in which she was filmed offering access to her ex-husband for cash. With alleged debts of around £5million she certainly needed the money, but who exactly would be interested in paying her asking price of £500,000 to meet 'HBH'? Campaign group 'Republic' had lodged a formal complaint with UK's Department for Trade and Investment in respect of various allegations regarding the Duke. The fact that it was in effect a 'self-appointment' made it rather tricky for the department to handle, what with the usual deference bestowed upon royal personages in our unwritten constitutional system. Nobody appeared to want to take responsibility for someone who was costing the taxpayer (and still does) a fortune in travel expenses. The Coalition government's Business Secretary, Vince Cable, remarked that the Duke of York '…would have to judge his own position', but added that there would be 'conversations' about the Duke's future role. It was all adding up to a picture of a man who whose mixture of monster ego, rudeness and poor judgement was perhaps not so perfectly suited to represent the UK on the world stage as its 'Special Trade Representative' after all. He was quietly dropped – or perhaps persuaded to drop himself – from the role in July 2011.

He now travels the globe representing his mother, the Queen – and by definition the country. If he wasn't up to the task of representing the nation in respect of its trade, why should the nation be subsidising him to represent it more generally? By May 2012 he was standing in for his mother on a tour of India, where he could be seen strutting around in a white colonial uniform reminiscent of Lord Curzon in the dying days of Empire – with more gold braid than Libyan dictator Colonel Gaddafi in his heyday.

His entourage travel around the globe with him, in the manner of an extravagant rock star, including a valet carrying the Prince's treasured ironing board, which itself must have racked up a fair number of air-miles of its own. On May 14th 2012 the *Daily Mail* revealed that how, when offered accommodation in a very tasteful Lutyens bungalow in the British Embassy grounds for the duration of the tour, he turned it down in favour of the 4,425sq. foot Maharaja Suite in Delhi's Leela Palace Hotel – at a cost of over £3,000 to the UK taxpayer. Don't forget that the taxpayer is also forking out rather a lot to keep its remnants of 'Raj'-era luxury infrastructure empty just in case roving royals deign to drop in occasionally. The tour also encompassed several other destinations across the sub-continent, each demanding stopovers in hotels of suitable grandeur. Strutting about in the full-white 'n gold braid uniform of an Honorary Rear Admiral (he actually reached the rank of Commander whilst actually serving), he manages to live a life of ultra-regal opulence but now without the pretence of being a 'Special Trade representative'. Plus ca change…

THE ROYAL 'OCCUPY' MOVEMENT…
As the Queen's grandchildren come of age, a whole new burden is placed upon the long-suffering taxpayer. Whilst Mrs Anne Laurence – a.k.a. the 'Princess Royal' – has decided to eschew royal titles for her children, it did not prevent her daughter Zara Phillips from benefiting from around £400,000 of taxpayers' cash to pay for the cost of policing her wedding to rugby player Mike Tindall. Edward and Sophie's children are still young, but as they become older and start to enter the

world of 'celebrity' royals, no doubt the public will have to start helping out their parents in paying for a lifestyle commensurate with their perceived status.

Princesses Beatrice and Eugenie – well known for their dubious taste in headwear – do their bit in helping to drain the public coffers simply for being the offspring of the Duke of York. It was reported (*Daily Mail* 30/6/09) that Beatrice's flat in St James' Palace had been refurbished for a not exactly budget price of £300,000 so as to provide an acceptable base while she was a London student. The Duke has seemingly expected a greater role for his daughters – not unlike himself, in fact – and with it all the accompanying expectations of expenses and enhanced security.

William, as likely future King, naturally has a security detail, though it is relatively low key, and his brother Harry, also currently in the employ of the armed forces, operates under this existing umbrella. The competence of such experts is, however, less than reassuring. While on the Sandringham estate, the royal brothers' shooting party was evidently dangerously close to a mystery gunman who shot a protected hen harrier. Accompanying protection officers were unable to identify – in fact they hadn't even noticed – the armed interloper. Not infrequent trips to Kensington night-club Bouji's have required accompanying protection officers to protect Harry from the paparazzi – and vice versa. Perhaps more controversially, whilst Harry has laudably pursued an army career, including active service in Afghanistan, there are those who assert that this service of itself can impose heightened risks to his colleagues on account of his being such a high value target to the enemy.

Basically, with or without a high-profile role, junior royals, however disingenuously, seem to generate cost to the taxpayer. High or low profile, they are, like it or not, a security problem, imposing a cost on the public simply by being who they are. It is an almost unavoidable effect of simply having a royal family, but is exacerbated by the seeming willingness of the authorities to agree to pay up. A rather more clear-cut situation, with a clear expectation for those beyond the position of monarch and heir to the throne being expected to fund their own security might begin to address the problem.

DECLARATIONS OF INTEREST

From parish councillors to Members of Parliament, there are strict rules on declarations of personal interest which must be followed. Curiously, the other members of the legislature, those who occupy seats in the House of Lords, are required only to register interests on a voluntary basis. No doubt the presumption would seem to be that the further up the social hierarchy one travels, the more trustworthy one must automatically become. By the time one has reached the heights of royalty, there is absolute trust. Members of the royal family, though they may be appearing at official functions, and speaking in support of a wide variety of organisations, are not required to declare interests – notably investments held in companies and other organisations. Whilst the Duke of York acted as the UK's 'Special Representative for Trade and Investment', there was no requirement to disclose the fact that he might have been – or someone on his behalf – buying, selling or holding shares in a company that he may have been promoting at one of the many events he attended across the globe. Where members of the Royal family seek to justify their state-subsidised positions by becoming involved in the business world, the potential for conflicts of interest will always arise.

The Earl of Wessex was briefly 'famous' for his less than successful 'career' as a television producer, with his attempts to cash in on his royal connections with programmes, rather predictably, about royalty. Despite the generosity of wealthy backers, financial success eluded him and his company, Ardent Productions, was eventually forced to close. His wife, already established before their marriage in a public relations career, also had to give up her business interests following a News of the World expose which revealed her willingness to exploit her royal connections. There was a potential conflict of interest when, not long after her marriage to the Queen's youngest son, the couple embarked on a royal tour of the USA. There were concerns that the publicly funded trip might also have valuable PR potential for the couple's then respective business interests.

The Prince of Wales's venture into the commercial world, through his 'Duchy Originals' brand – though now distanced following its 2009 takeover by Waitrose Plc – also raised fundamental questions of potential conflicts of interest for someone with a uniquely high profile who also benefits from public money of many millions of pounds a year. His official website used to carry a 'pack-shot' of one of the Prince's 'Duchy' products – which themselves carry his official coat of arms, and a title which goes with the public position of heir to the throne, on the packaging – and accompanying information on the company and its products. One would have been unlikely to find a comparably blatant advertorial 'sales pitch' for a product on any other government website.

THE EARL AND COUNTESS OF WESSEX: LIFE AT BAGSHOT PARK

Following Edward and Sophie Wessex's failed attempt to mix public roles with private enterprise they were persuaded to pursue a more traditional 'working' royal role. Dropping their business careers they reverted to old-style ways, augmenting the nation's meet-and-greet team without which the *Times* Court Social listings would look rather thin. Unless one is an avid reader of this tide table of the nation's cultural backwaters, or actually involved with one of the organizations with which Edward and his spouse are scheduled to share a few fleeting minutes, then one could be forgiven for having forgotten their very existence. However, a visitor to the southern part of Windsor Great Park would be treated to a glimpse of the physically impressive Mansion House, Bagshot Park – the Wessex's quite ludicrously extravagant fifty-seven room residence into which they moved in 1998.

The Crown Estates had long searched for potential tenants for the stately pile, but following what was termed a 'discreet marketing campaign', there were just two offers; to use the property as either a conference centre or a hotel. Both were rejected for failing to 'meet the statutory obligation to maintain the character of a Royal Park' and the fact that the hotel 'would have involved additional land occupied by others and potentially more complex planning considerations'. Neither option met the Crown Estate's preference of residential use. What could they do with such a high-maintenance property fit only for the most select of clients?

Happily, they were contacted by young media entrepreneur (at the time) Edward Windsor, who was looking to start a family and desperate for a home with a room quota big enough for his self-image. His Royal Highness had, it seems, 'expressed an interest' in the property. In due course, following 'discussions', the property was his, on a fifty-year lease, for an initial annual rental of £5,000 – a virtual 'peppercorn' rent. Following agreed refurbishment this was to rise to £90,000 per year thereafter, subject to a 15 year review. Edward's share of the restoration costs was to come to an estimated £580,000, with the taxpayer dipping into their Crown Estate pocket for £1.6million, having already paid £1.8million through the Ministry of Defence budget for dilapidations from the property's previous occupants, the Army Chaplains Department. As with all builders' estimates, the costs increased somewhat, and Edward – or someone who could actually afford to pay them – faced an eventual bill of some £1,380,000. Included in the lease too, was Sunningdale Lodge, a mere 'bijou' in comparison. Quite why a couple with one child – although a second has since arrived – needed yet another property in addition to one the size of a large hotel is rather baffling. Perhaps it was simply easier for the Crown Estates than looking for other – non-royal – tenants capable of passing the stringent acceptability criteria.

Such grandeur, however, had to be paid for. Fortunately the lease permitted the subletting of the stable block, and by a happy coincidence, much of the annual rental for the entire sprawling mansion was met by a small commercial firm willing to rent those stables. The rent to be paid was over half the amount that the Earl would be paying – and not the initial 'peppercorn' sum – for his entire house. The enterprise in question was of course Edward's own Ardent Productions. The Earl was lucky to be able to sub-let for commercial purposes. Would other fledgling businesses have been allowed to set up in a Royal Park? However, the company, despite everything in its favour, from the best contacts and no shortage of backers, never managed to shed its image of a hobby project for a spoilt rich kid. Totally reliant on family connections for ideas, most of its projects focused on the British monarchy. Despite funding from rich notables – reputed to include KwikFit car exhaust tycoon Tom Farmer, DFS furniture superstores owner Lord Kirkham, and the Sultan of Brunei – Ardent couldn't actually afford to pay the rent. Not only that, it was also revealed, embarrassingly, to have been an Ardent film crew that had breached the media agreement not to film Edward's nephew William whilst he was studying at Edinburgh University. The rest of the family were, in true royal tradition, far from amused, and the public relations damage, combined with the 'News of the World's 'fake Sheikh' revelations, was considerable. Both Edward and Sophie were forced to give up their respective business interests and with them the rent not being paid on Bagshot Park by Ardent. Edward took over fronting the Duke of Edinburgh's Award Scheme from his father. No doubt mummy has to help out with the rent these days...

4 WINDSORS' WORLD: LIFE AT THE TAXPAYERS' EXPENSE

PRINCESS ALEXANDRA: PARK AND RIDE
Thatched House Lodge in Richmond Park is currently occupied by HRH Princess Alexandra on a 150-year lease, originally purchased by her late husband Mr Angus Ogilvy. Set amid the rolling acres of the Royal Park with its wandering herds of deer, it is an enviable location conveniently close to the metropolis. The lease on the Lodge now runs from 1994, and was purchased for £670,000, with an annual rental of £1,000 initially, rising by a further £1,000 every twenty-five years, to a maximum of £6,000 in the final twenty-five year period. Once again, the right to occupy such a unique property at a rental that wouldn't secure you a West End lock-up garage these days seems to rest primarily on being the Queen's cousin. In slightly more modest circumstances, but no less enviable surroundings, Princess Alexandra's daughter, Marina Ogilvy, benefits from a modest little cottage in Windsor Great Park, which is rented on an assured short hold tenancy at market value.

VERY AFFORDABLE HOUSING
Enquiries by MPs Ian Davidson and Alan Williams in January 2005, culminating in their report later that year detailed the 'procedures in letting Crown properties to members of the Royal Family'[10]. The means by which these properties are allocated is, we are assured, in a manner 'consistent with the procedures'. However, it is rather curious that such procedures mean that leading members of the royal family seem to have an unerring ability to find themselves at the head of the queue when tenants are sought for these fine residences. On the one hand, the Crown Estate maintains that it 'does not have any special procedures when negotiating agreements with the Royal Family', yet emphasises its 'discreet and targeted approach to letting unusual, high value residential properties'. The market for such properties is, admittedly, always going to be restricted. Both Windsor Royal Lodge and Mansion House, Bagshot Park, have a Grade 2 listing status, which may restrict possible alterations. The select super-rich few in the market for such 'homes' are probably confined largely to a handful of 'resident non-domiciles': corporate tycoons, oil sheikhs and Russian oligarchs. However, they may find that some of their plans do not find favour with the local planning authorities.

The reality is that there are few who can either afford, or indeed actually want, such properties in their present form. However, it is clear that, in practice, those who are not royal might as well not apply. Not surprisingly, too, 'security' is a handy excuse for being choosy. Whether this means a potential threat to their royal neighbours or the prospective tenants themselves was not explored in any detail by Williams' and Davidson's report. The royal family already cost the taxpayer at least £100million a year to protect. Moreover, much of Windsor Great Park is accessible to the public, so it might be thought that any threat is likely to come from visitors rather than permanent residents.

The reality is that 'security considerations' can be a convenient 'catch-all' term by which to avoid the more difficult issue of actually deciding what should be done with these properties. In the 'people like us' stakes – a crucial requirement in terms of acceptability to inhabit such Crown property – it would seem that being royal is the main criteria for leasing a residence in a Royal Park. Though most members of the extended Windsor family are not poor, even they would, on the face of it, struggle to maintain such properties. The fact that, unaided, Edward and Sophie Wessex would not have been able to consider moving into such a property as Bagshot Park is indicative of two significant facts. Firstly, their status as son and daughter-in-law of the monarch gives them primary eligibility to get to top of the Crown property housing queue. Secondly, without the colossal dedicated income provided exclusively to the Queen by the Duchy of Lancaster – state property itself – the largesse which keeps the Earl and Countess of Wessex in the manner to which they are accustomed would have to cease.

Theoretically, Royal Lodge and Bagshot Park still retain the status of 'grace and favour' residences, and this was the previous basis upon which they were occupied. The fact is that it would now be politically unacceptable for them to be occupied in this way both now and in the future. Whilst market level rental charges are now imposed, access is still both restricted to a most favoured few and in any case fails to address what should be the long-term future for these publicly owned properties.

'I WANT THAT ONE PLEASE, MUMMY...'

The Queen Mother died in the spring of 2002. Her former residence, Clarence House, occupies a prime site at the side of the Mall just a few hundred metres from Buckingham Palace. No sooner had nineteen removal trucks shifted the nation's favourite grandmother's few possessions out of the shabby old property than it was announced that a new resident would be moving in once renovation works had been completed. Not exactly a 'tenant' – as there is no formal lease – the new 'Occupier' was to be none other than HRH the Prince of Wales, who was finding it hard to manage in the cramped confines of nearby St James' Palace. Naturally, the taxpayer would foot the refurbishment costs, save for some of the decorations[11].

The Prince has his choice of homes. In addition to Clarence House – a State property maintained at public expense – and Highgrove House, his extravagant 'tied cottage' which he rents, for tax reasons, to avoid incurring 'benefit in kind' liability, he also uses Birkhall, on the Queen's Balmoral estate, and yet another Scottish property, the Castle of Mey, formerly owned by the Queen Mother, now by a family trust. All this means that Charles can claim, in a rather disingenuous fashion, that he owns no property. Further properties may be needed to cater for the next generation. Part of the Harewood Estate, near Ross on Wye, some 900 acres, was acquired by the Duchy of Cornwall in 2000 with plans to build a £3million 'manor' house, a possible new residence for Charles' son William or perhaps Harry. More recently came the news in 2007 that Charles had purchased a Welsh farmhouse in Carmarthenshire. Though likely to have in reality to have been paid for by the Duchy of Cornwall, it was variously described as a potential 'buy to let' for tourists, an organic farm for Charles to cultivate, an occasional weekend retreat, or a Welsh base enabling his son William, as future Prince of Wales, to 'bond' with the Principality.

'CRISIS: WHAT HOUSING CRISIS?'

In respect of their 'official' residences, the situation whereby the royal family still retain first, second and third choice in the allocation process of royal properties – the game of royal 'musical chairs', whether they are Royal Palaces or Crown Estate properties – is quite impossible to justify. The process of accountability, where it appears to exist at all, is profoundly inadequate. Indeed, the very idea that anyone should be entitled to access such properties on the basis of no more than a blood relationship to the nation's head of state, is bizarre. As with so much of our unwritten constitution, especially that involving the monarchy, it is a blend of precedent and generous helpings of deference. Government ministers, over-awed by their induction process and with so much else to do, are reluctant to embark on challenging the institution. They are likely to find themselves exposed to high-profile media vilification. Remember, for example, the late Mo Mowlam's tame suggestion that the monarch might consider having a more modest, modern, official residence. The resulting tabloid furore was little short of absurd, but not surprising given the general attitude toward even tentative mention of royal reform.

GETTING ONE'S FOOT IN THE DOOR
So exactly what process enabled the heir to the throne to demand such prime real estate? The Prince of Wales's move from St James' Palace to his late grandmother's residence prompted Norman Baker MP, to ask precisely that question of the then Secretary of State for Culture, Media and Sport, in July 2003[12]. The answer was suitably unrevealing as to the administrative minutiae: 'The Occupied Palaces are owned by the Queen as Sovereign on behalf of the nation. How the properties are used in fulfilling the requirements and functions of the Head of State is a matter for Her Majesty the Queen although proposals are discussed with this Department wherever appropriate'.

Appropriate for whom? It should be remembered that a property such as Clarence House, if deemed 'Occupied' – that is, with a senior royal living in it – is maintained by the taxpayer through the quaintly termed 'Grant-in-aid' (soon to be replaced by the 'Sovereign Grant') paid to the Royal Household. If it is 'Unoccupied' then Historic Royal Palaces, an independent charity, maintains it. Whilst it gets no government funding as such it is able to generate income through visitor admissions and various grants in order to maintain such heritage attractions as Hampton Court. In practice, royal properties are not left empty for long unless Historic Royal Palaces can generate a healthy visitor income from them. Clarence House was then swiftly 're-Occupied', ensuring that the taxpayer stepped in as soon as possible to start paying the bills. The claim that the Queen 'owns' these buildings 'on behalf of the nation' cannot disguise the reality. These are State properties, not 'hers'. The State pays when the monarch occupies them and even when not occupied they are ultimately still its responsibility. Although the new Sovereign Grant Act does contain an express clause ensuring 'responsibility' for the maintenance of the royal palaces, it would appear that this relates to ensuring that they spend the element of the new Sovereign Grant designed to replace the property Grant-in-aid specifically on repair and maintenance of the Palaces.

The 'ownership' in this case relates to the Queen's official status as monarch, not as an private individual, and as such real decisions relating to the properties ultimately rest with Parliament. The Prince of Wales's ability to 'Occupy' a palace – given that he is not the monarch, would seem to rest on the same vague basis as his right to choose whether to pay tax *as if he were the monarch* – that 'peculiar' title again.

However, it seems that when a leading member of the Windsor family takes a fancy to one of these desirable state-owned residences the democratic process, for practical purposes, does not intrude at all. In the same vein, the 2008 report on 'Grant-in-aid' for the royal palaces announced that 'Apartment Eight' at Kensington Palace – apparently empty for 'many years' – was being refurbished at a cost of £500,000 to the taxpayer in order to be let to four of the Prince of Wales's charities. The rent was to amortise those costs over a seven year period, but again it seemed that members of the royal family were picking and choosing what to do with State property – primarily for their own convenience – with little regard for alternative uses and with no proper publicly accountable authorisation process.

Apparently, if Prince Charles wanted Clarence House, and the Queen was happy, then he was in. It is a Royal Palace after all. However, the picture is not that simple. The Queen occupies Royal Palaces in her official capacity as monarch. Just because she is Queen should not mean that she can assign state property as she wishes. She does not 'own' it in a personal capacity. Parliament's approval in such an important case should be obligatory. In comparison the Crown Estate process appears to be somewhat more transparent, although members of the royal family seem to have an unerring knack of getting through the door in front of anyone else. An alternative use for Clarence House was apparently never considered after it had been vacated. With a Royal Collection bursting at the seams with art treasures 'held for the nation', it would make an ideal Central London gallery venue for some of this valuable resource. The Queen Mother had paid no rent for Clarence House for fifty years, yet the public had to pay the greater part of the renovation costs of £3.2million required to put the building into an acceptable state of repair after she had vacated it. Charles Windsor was to contribute £1.6million towards 'soft furnishings, including carpets, light fittings and curtains' but only £78,000, inclusive of VAT towards the cost of decorations – this presumably to counter accusations that public money was being spent on rooms exclusively for the use of his then girlfriend, Camilla Parker-Bowles and her family[13].

KEEPING IT IN THE FAMILY

Further down the royal housing ladder, others still continue to benefit from direct and indirect taxpayer support. In December 2005, a Parliamentary question sought to ascertain who could actually be regarded as 'working' members. Harriet Harman's answer listed the following: 'as having undertaken official duties and functions on Her Majesty's behalf: The Duke of Edinburgh, The Prince of Wales and The Duchess of Cornwall, The Princess Royal, The Duke of York, The Earl and Countess of Wessex, The Duke and Duchess of Gloucester, The Duke and Duchess of Kent and Princess Alexandra'[14]. Those described in the Minister's response are the current lucky 'cast list' of royal performers for whom the taxpayer is required to contribute in return for their 'official duties'.

A PRINCESS CALLED MICHAEL

Keen observers will have spotted the absence in that list of Prince and Princess Michael of Kent. Whilst the Prince, the Queen's cousin, cannot succeed to the throne as he married a Catholic, and is not thus an official 'working royal', the two have benefited greatly from their position as 'hangers-on by appointment' to the Windsor clan. Shortly after their marriage, the Queen 'gave' them the use of a large apartment at Kensington Palace – a state asset – for which they paid nothing for around fifteen years. In 1994 they were required to contribute just £69 per week as a 'service charge'. Following, not surprisingly, a torrent of public complaints in respect of this bargain deal, the Queen was forced to yield to considerable pressure and in 2002 agreed to pay rent of £120,000 a year 'in recognition of the Royal engagements and work for various charities which Prince and Princess Michael of Kent have undertaken at their own expense, and without any public funding'[15].

It seems a bit odd that the Kents have lived a 'royal' lifestyle – and in a royal palace – for which they assumed the public would pay. Being excluded from the succession might logically be regarded as being the dividing line for eligibility. However, a 'grey' area developed over the years where they traded largely on their royal connections, an arrangement tolerated in return for their largely 'unofficial' royal roles.

4 WINDSORS' WORLD: LIFE AT THE TAXPAYERS' EXPENSE

A News of the World reporter found the Princess available for £25,000 – to open a Dubai shopping mall.

The difference between 'official' and 'unofficial' can be sometimes difficult to discern, but rests essentially on the whim of the monarch. Nonetheless, potentially large amounts of public money that may be paid out as expenses are at stake – not to mention getting access to prime state-owned London property. The Kents' cosy arrangement for their Kensington Palace apartment was originally designed to last until 2009, but following injudicious remarks relating to other members of the royal family recorded by an undercover press reporter, the Queen was reported to have brought forward their eviction date to 2007, but in 2012 they were still there. To help subsidise their future life in the real world, they have had to sell their country residence, Nether Lypiatt Manor in Gloucester, for £5.75million in May 2006[16]. They would have found London rents rather high by now, but have been saved by the generosity of £13million-a-year-plus Duchy of Lancaster-backed Mrs Elizabeth Windsor, who relented in her decision to kick them out of 'KP', and now coughs up £100,000 a year to keep them in their London pad. Thoughtfully, despite the fact that they don't perform any official royal 'duties', the UK taxpayer stumps up around £250,000 a year for police protection officers for the happy couple. But of course it's 'security' so it's a secret and we can't officially be told the actual cost...

Their 'royal' lifestyle has long been a bit of a struggle as, unfortunately, they both suffer from delusions of grandeur, combined with an expensive taste in art and antiques, but without that crucially necessary accompanying ingredient – money. Self-confessed blaggers, who would, in the Princess's own words, 'go anywhere for a hot meal', the Kents have also been the recipients of cash from a number of less than completely transparent sources, including from UK-exiled Russian oligarch Boris Berezovsky[17]. Imperial Russian Czar Nicholas II look-alike Prince Michael's rather opaque business links have long been a matter of concern and speculation, as the Kents manage to 'live it large' – despite their personal operating company Cantium running up losses – whilst simultaneously pleading poverty. They live in state property, get state protection, yet they have no official role – no-one has ever asked them to perform one – and there is no reason why they should. Yet they hang around, imposing themselves on the nation, A few proper declarations of financial interests from these 'shadow' royals wouldn't go amiss...

'THE BEST HOUSING BENEFIT SCHEME IN EUROPE'...

The reason for Norman Baker's original Parliamentary question was to ascertain quite how HRH the Prince of Wales, already handsomely catered for, with extensive apartments in St James' Palace was so easily able to acquire Clarence House as his London *pied a terre*. It followed the Queen Mother's death with no public application process involved and the move seemed remarkably seamless. No wonder Alan Williams MP once described the Windsors' living arrangements as 'the best housing benefit scheme in Europe'. Somehow, with apparently no formal application procedure or public scrutiny, a man with no defined constitutional role other than merely being the next in line to the throne at some indeterminate point in the future, and already in receipt of an official multi-million pound income, was able to appropriate a palatial building restored and maintained at public expense.

'Working' members of the royal family, for which the only qualification is either birth or marriage into the Windsor clan – there simply for being *who* they are – are clearly indulged by the taxpayer in their housing arrangements. Ian Davidson and Alan Williams' 2005 report noted that 'The Crown Estate does not have any special procedures when negotiating agreements with the Royal Family' and a demonstrably lightweight 'authorisation process' applies in respect of Royal Palaces. A 'discreet and targeted approach to letting' permits members of the Windsor family to enjoy luxury housing at the taxpayer's expense.

A slightly cynical subject might perhaps describe the present royal housing process as follows: 'The taxpayers are merely mugs and suckers who pay to provide the Windsor family with a stock of prime real estate from which they can pick and choose pretty much as they wish, subject to the barest minimum of official interference. Once in, they can line the walls with priceless works of art from the 'Royal Collection' that the Queen insists are not really 'hers', but 'ours' and which she is merely 'holding for the nation'. Politicians have no real desire to get mixed up in the entire grubby business and are generally happy to let them get on with it. And if the royals want to move in, the taxpayer will help pay for the builders to fix the place up'. What a bargain...

The heir to the throne pays no rent for Clarence House, and neither does he seem to pay tax on it as a benefit in kind. Is such a palatial dwelling for the Prince of Wales really necessary, and what sort of example does it set? 'Minor royals' get a slightly less favourable deal in that they have to pay what are adjudged to be 'market' rates for their leases on Crown (State) properties. However, the Queen is a very rich woman and is ably assisted by that most chivalrous of individuals, the taxpayer. Her income from the Duchy of Lancaster provides her with many millions of pounds a year to spend at her own discretion which enables her to help her struggling offspring and relatives keep a roof over their heads.

5
Charity and Royal 'Brand' Ownership

We do lot for charridy, mate!
'Smashie' and 'Nicey' (Harry Enfield and Paul Whitehouse)

A CHANGING WORLD

Throughout the first half of the twentieth century, Britain had been remarkably uncritical of its monarchy. Two world wars, with their focus on the need for national unity and the celebratory mood engendered by the Coronation in 1953 in the post-war period had eclipsed the critics. Writer and commentator Malcolm Muggeridge challenged the monarchy on principle in the late 1950s, but this was a viewpoint rarely raised, and the situation remained largely so for the next three decades. Republicans such as MP Willie Hamilton had sought to make the case for an alternative but were on the whole regarded as lone voices, sidelined by political parties as mildly eccentric. This was a convenient way to isolate a view which although held privately by many sat well outside the political agenda.

By the early 1990s this situation was beginning to change. General discontent with the workings of the British constitution had gained momentum in the late 1980s, and a growing number of people were beginning to question the hitherto seemingly unassailable position of the Windsor family as providers of the country's heads of state. From the time the Queen had bemoaned her 'annus horribilis' of 1992, events were beginning to unravel the monarchy's previously almost untouchable position. High profile divorces – important where family integrity forms the basis of a state institution – and a greater questioning of the very point of principle underpinning the institution, began to erode its foundations.

The monarchy now has to justify its position actively. They now have to compete in a celebrity culture for the attention and affection of the public. However, the monarchy has climbed a steep learning curve, gradually became more adept at both defending, and increasingly, promoting itself. Monarchy has to a great extent become a branch of the new celebrity culture, and as such now has to compete for attention with those famous not simply for who they are, but also for what they have achieved.

Charitable works have evolved as key justification for their existence, constituting a significant part of their 'official' work. Their position as 'patrons' reflects their elevated position in the social and cultural hierarchy and as such they form the focus of social events, derived ultimately from no other than their birth. 'Invitation' to be a patron is in reality a formality, a steady progression into the charitable field – there is no election process. These days, it is possible to watch the seamless progression by royal family members, such as Prince Harry and his brother, with their involvement in charities ranging from the disabled to African wildlife conservation. The causes espoused are all very worthy, and very hard to criticise. Indeed, if it were on a questionnaire, it would be all but impossible to tick the 'disagree' box. In this way, royal family members slide into public life, any criticism effectively negated in the public eye by their 'charitable works'.

'SELLING' THE NEXT MONARCH

Defending an hereditary institution in the context of an otherwise increasingly democratic nation is difficult. Indeed, on the basis of simple logic, it is impossible to justify. Further still, Prince Charles, the monarchy's next and only candidate was, by the early 1990s, a less tha appealing product to sell to a sceptical public. Unpopular in the aftermath of his separation and subsequent divorce from the Princess of Wales, the Prince would clearly

5 CHARITY AND ROYAL 'BRAND' OWNERSHIP

have to work hard to rebuild himself in the public's esteem. The 'worst-case scenario' would be to change the order of the succession. By the early 1990s, for Prince Charles and his advisors the position was clear. He needed to make himself acceptable to the public as a whole and in a way that would be straightforward to justify and difficult to criticise.

But where to start? The Prince of Wales is a difficult candidate. His personal record of marital infidelity was a particular problem given his future role as Supreme Governor of the Church of England. Perceptions of eccentricity and politically contentious outspokenness, and a reputation for an absurdly expensive lifestyle – with criticism on that last front coming not least from his own mother – was never going to make him easy to promote. The solution was to come from an area in which the Prince already had a record of involvement – charity. The Prince's Trust had been set up to provide a worthwhile focus for a man who, at the time in 1976, had no family or job. Having just left the Navy after a brief period of service, he decided to put his £7,400 severance pay towards founding the Prince's Trust. From now on his charitable role would be crucial, and counter to hitherto accepted practice, he would have to shout about it.

DOING IT FOR CHARITY

To avoid the accusation of being a pampered drone, worthwhile causes were used to provide a focus in Charles' life, and there is little doubt that he has taken that role very seriously. However, even by the late 1990s a more serious 'makeover' was necessary. There was a prevailingly negative public perception regarding the Prince's conduct toward his late ex-wife, Diana, and his relationship with his long-term mistress, Camilla Parker-Bowles.

The British royal family has a long history of involvement in the charity field. In the days before proper institutionalised social welfare provisions this was an important role. Monarchy and government were closely integrated, so the provision of charity by the monarch was appropriate. With time, there was less integration, but the monarchy remained as patron of social causes, reinforcing its position at the apex of society, and in turn able to validate the generosity of those progressively further down the social order. Embedded at the top of a beneficent social pyramid, the royals did not look entirely favourably on what they saw as a usurpation of 'their' role with the founding of the welfare state.

Since Charles' public 'rehabilitation', charitable events – and the charities themselves – would increase in number, get bigger, be more high-profile, and with significantly increased turnover. No longer was Charles Windsor a mere 'patron', now he was being promoted as a 'charitable entrepreneur'. This approach has sought to increase his acceptability through promotion of a 'soft' monarchy, accentuating charitable and environmental aspects, and down-playing the 'hard' aspects – the unaccountable prerogative and legislated emergency powers – and the public source of his income. Any valid criticism of the Prince's activities is countered by the 'but he does so much for charity' response. It is superficially appealing but disingenuous.

THE 'CHARITABLE ENTREPRENEUR'
The Prince's website used to proudly trumpet this new description, blending this with work done over the past 30 years. Using contemporary corporate-speak, the Prince was described as having been 'prescient in identifying charitable need and setting up and driving forward charities to meet it'. In this work, 'his sixteen core charities represent, as a group, the largest multi-cause charitable enterprise in the UK'. The website used effusive language to praise 'the Prince's longterm and innovative perspective', and his work to 'address areas of previously unmet need'. Under the website's 'Promoting and Protecting' banner, the message was definitely that of the beneficent potentate. The 2007 Duchy of Cornwall Annual Review referred to the 'Inspirational leadership from His Royal Highness the Prince of Wales'. Further effusive compliments – including obsequious reviews for the book 'Radical Prince', itself little more than an uncritical showcase for his many pet causes – bordered upon the absurd: 'In an age when leaders have forgotten how to lead [he is] an inspiration to the entire world', and a 'contemporary visionary'. To a rational observer, the content was starting to look as if the Prince was operating in something of a self-delusionary bubble reminiscent of a North Korean 'Great Leader', and it is notable that this ego-driven nonsense seems to have been finally replaced by a somewhat more restrained tone.

There is another concern. Are Charles' charities getting an extra helping hand from the taxpayer, a hidden subsidy that can give them an edge over other competing charities? As the reader will have noted in Chapter 2, Charles is a big train enthusiast – especially the Royal Train. Remember the trip on November 4th 2010 – just one of many of his train journeys? costing the taxpayer nearly £19,000. It included stop-offs to attend various functions for his Prince's Trust charities. Why was the taxpayer funding all this, so Charles' own charities could get a specific boost? Other charities' functions don't have access to taxpayer funded ceremonial travel in a special train which may also add that special royal touch. It forms, in effect, a state subsidy to certain favoured charities – the Princes' own charities. Perhaps the Prince's Trust ought to have paid a large slice of that train travel bill...

KING GONG

The absurdity of the Prince of Wales bedecked with a chest full of personalised family-awarded medals make the comparison with undemocratic 'banana republic' leaders more than a little apt. For the 150th anniversary ceremony for Victoria Cross recipients held in June 2006, it was instructive to note that while he was standing alongside veterans with medals awarded for bravery and courage under fire – people who had actually risked their lives on the battlefield – the Prince wore five medals: his 'Queen's Service Order' medal, awarded in 1983; the 'Coronation Medal', which he was given in 1953 as a child for attending his mother's Coronation ceremony; the 'Silver Jubilee Medal', awarded in 1977, presumably for turning up to Mum's Jubilee; the 'Canadian Forces Decoration' awarded in 1991 and the 'New Zealand Commemorative Medal' ('One went to New Zealand and, er, all one got was this medal..') given to him in 1990.

All these 'gongs' may look impressive – or absurdly kitsch. They are all for show, no more than post-Imperial 'bling'. The British may have laughed at Ugandan despot Idi Amin in the 1970s with his ludicrous array of self-awarded medals – many of them replicas of accepted British orders. But what, in truth, is the difference between a caricature 'tin-pot dictator' and the Prince's empty awards – and unearned military ranks that promote him year by year?

TRYING TOO HARD?

There is a real danger that the Prince's good works now risk appearing almost too worthy – not to say rather tasteless – given the self-righteous trumpeting tone of the accolades. While much of the work, in itself, is worthy, to talk of 'unmet need' in areas of social welfare and health, in particular, is to enter very political territory. Support for young people wishing to set up their own small businesses is a laudable aim, but it has a distinctly political dimension. For someone who is increasing his level of involvement in matters of state for his eventual accession to the throne, this is a contentious matter, there is risk of conflict between everyday government policy and the monarch's political neutrality.

Charles is not merely competing for celebrity status in a world where all those in public life – politicians, business leaders, 'celebrities' and so on – must fight for media attention on a daily basis; he is actually fighting what is in effect a long-term election campaign. The Prince's website used to read more like a party manifesto, with its emphasis on his endeavours in the areas of 'health', 'education', 'responsible business', 'the natural environment', 'the built environment', and 'the arts'. To this impressive list was added his commercial 'Duchy Originals' brand. It all rather looked like a one-man political party that also sold organic food. It must have seemed too much to his advisers, and the new version is markedly more modest and reasonable – and Waitrose now run Duchy Originals.

'CAMPAIGNING FOR KING'

Prince Charles has made no secret of his personal views on a wide variety of issues, from architecture, farming, and health, and this has led him into conflict with a wide variety of people, from politicians to professional specialists in those fields. There is a high degree of hypocrisy too. Protesting his environmental credentials can seem a little rich coming from a man who regularly travels by helicopter or a gas-guzzling Bentley. His statements might be dismissed purely as personal opinions, but when an opinionated layman is, through his influential position, able to gain an unprecedented degree of coverage simply by being the son of a head of state, then there is cause for concern.

What other reason could possibly explain the somewhat strange event that took place on May 23rd 2006, when the Prince addressed a meeting of health ministers at the World Health Organisation Assembly in Geneva. He urged every country on the globe – surely a sign of a zealousness verging on megalomania – to adopt complementary therapies alongside conventional treatments. Whilst one may perhaps agree in principle with what some 'alternative' therapies may have to offer, would any other unqualified layman have been allowed to air his personal opinions to such a professional group? His pronouncements on medical matters had already drawn sharp criticism from the medical profession. The Visiting Professor of Medical Humanities at University College, London made it very clear in an open letter to the Prince, published in the British Medical Journal in 2004, that: 'The power of my authority comes with a knowledge built on 40 years of study and 25 years of active involvement in cancer research...Your power and authority rest on an accident of birth'.

A similar dispute occurred in the case of Professor Edzard Ernst of Exeter University, who had become concerned with the validity of a report which had come to his attention. He was concerned at the influence of the 'alternative' therapy lobby – of which the Prince is a significant and influential promoter through the work of some of his charities. A Channel Four documentary of the affair in March 2007 resulted in a letter to the University's Vice-Chancellor from the Prince's Private Secretary which had the potential to enmesh Professor Ernst in career-threatening disciplinary proceedings. Ernst had branded the alternative therapy report 'outrageous and deeply flawed', whilst Clarence House accused him of a 'serious breach of confidentiality' in having approached the media[1]. Ernst – the UK's first professor of complementary medicind later raised the matter again in respect of the Prince's 'Duchy Originals' range of 'detox' health products, condemning the claims made for the luxury products as 'outright quackery', and being 'implausible, unproven and dangerous'. (http://news.bbc.co.uk/1/hi/health/7934568.stm)

The Prince would seem to prefer exerting influence but not in the form of open public debate. Prominent businessman and former politician Lord Haskins has stated that many public figures have viewed Prince Charles as a 'lobbyist': 'They think they have to give a 'disproportionate' amount of time listening to his point of view and they know he is trying to use his position to influence policy'[2].

'GIVIN' IN THE USA' – CHUCK'S BIG HIT

Prince Charles has made great efforts to maximise his income for his charities, but in order to do so he has had to look beyond the shores of his own future kingdom. And where better to do this than the United

States of America. Though the Prince's visit at the end of October 2005 was intended to boost the British tourist industry – that perennial excuse for a royal visit – it would also be an excellent opportunity to ingratiate himself with many of America's socially aspirant rich – and get them to bankroll his many and varied charities. Such people are, in the words of American author Kitty Kelley, willing to 'pay any amount of money to rub up against royalty'[3].

It had been twenty years since Charles had brought his young wife, Diana, the Princess of Wales; and now he was to introduce Camilla, her status recently changed from mistress to spouse, to American high society. Along with an official trip, and a chance to 'sell' Camilla to the States, was an opportunity to pursue up his own private agenda, promoting his charity work. Here was the perfect moment, paid for by the British taxpayer, to pursue the charitable aims which are so important for 'selling' Charles to an often skeptical British public. In her article Kelley explained how money raised by regally-struck rich Americans, each paying a minimum of $100,000, was channelled through a US-based arm of his UK charities, set up in1997. In return for giving donors would be invited to dinner at his country residences at Highgrove and in Scotland.

Kitty Kelley's investigations also revealed the extent of money donated to the Prince of Wales Foundation in Washington DC. In 2003 more than $6million had been raised (£3.4million), most of which had gone in expenses, leaving just $1.4million for 'good causes'. By 2006, further concerns about the Prince's US-based charitable arm had surfaced. The Foundation's executive director, Robert Higdon, earned £310,000 in the same year as the charity itself gave out just £325,018 of its £1milllion income. British diplomats were concerned that the charity risked becoming 'an embarrassment' with its lavish parties and dinners[4].

ROOM AT THE TOP TABLE
Charles is famous for his Highgrove House parties where diners from around the world pay handsomely to support the Prince's good causes. In addition, there are the charity polo matches, Highland flings at Balmoral and other events which constitute the greater part of his fund-raising activities. For a rich donor, being seen with the Prince of Wales is worth a lot more than just the warm glow that comes from knowing that some of one's money is going to a good cause. This is the

apex of high-end 'schmoozing', a world where a generous donation is the admission ticket to the British royal circle; its myriad business and social links making it a superlative networking event with enormous potential rewards. By March, 2003 allegations of a 'cash for access' culture surrounding the Prince of Wales's charitable fundraising events tarnished the gloss. The social kudos and networking potential of events such as these has a value of which even already high achievers are keen to take advantage.

Despite a UK court sentence '*in absentia*' (as well as US legal proceedings pending) Turkish businessman Czem Uzan – whose family had faced accusations of fraud and racketeering – had attended dinners between 2000 and 2001 in return for £400,000 in donations. Had this sum been suggested as being about the right amount for someone in Uzan's position, and had the Prince's charity staff, impressed at the scale of their potential donor's generosity, simply neglected to investigate his background? It was an embarrassing incident for Clarence House, but from the point of view of any donor, being seen with British royalty provides social and business validation amongst one's peers. The Prince's choice of corporate donors was sometimes no better. It was reported in 2002 that the collapsed Enron Corporation – a byword for corporate corruption – had donated a total of £800,000 during the 1990s[5].

The 'charitable entrepreneur' label implies risk and personal skill. Contrary to the image, conveyed by this description, Prince Charles has risked nothing. State money, his Duchy of Cornwall income, has grown considerably over the years, and underpins his privileged position. From 'just' £7.47million in 2001, the Duchy is now providing him well over double that – over £17million in 2011 – thanks to a more sophisticated investment strategy and uniquely favourable tax status. Here is a ready-made state-backed infrastructure, exclusively for his own use, with which to promote his favourite cause – his acceptability as future King. His charity work is used to brush aside all criticisms. Examined more closely, however, the amounts donated by the very rich are disproportionately low both to their own wealth but chiefly to the amount of praise showered on Charles for taking the money. All this connects to broader concerns about the taxation of the very rich. The 2012 Budget was accompanied by controversy that the rich – and super-rich – in the UK were able to benefit from very low overall tax rates as a result of diverting income through tax-efficient charitable institutions.

'CASH FOR ACCESS'

Any criticism of wealthy individuals is invariably immediately countered by a declaration of their charitable good works. Whilst the Prince of Wales may, in the wealth stakes, pale in comparison with the Swedish packaging billionaire Dr Hans Rausing, a resident in the UK for tax purposes since 1982 – having taken advantage of non-domicile resident status – there is a similarity between the two in using charity as a justification for wealth.

It was only through Parliamentary questions in April 2006 that Member of Parliament Norman Baker was able to elicit the fact that in January of that year that Dr Rausing (Senior) – the beneficiary, with his immediate family of an income of some £4million a week and paying very little UK tax indeed – was now the recipient of an honourary knighthood for having been, in the words of the then Foreign Secretary, Jack Straw, 'one of the most significant private philanthropists in the UK', having paid £146million to charity in the last 12 years. This was in exchange for living in a country which had he been properly taxed on his enormous wealth, might have seen a lot more of his money. It is not known if the generous 'Sir' Hans was a donor to any of the Prince's many charities, but the rich, famous, and others have queued up to give money in return for a place at the Highgrove dining table with all its networking benefits and social kudos.

Following the 2012 Budget, the whole question of the super-rich using charitable donations to minimise their tax bills became – and remains – a hotly debated subject. A restriction upon non-domicile tax status has also appeared, but for the very rich its imposition of a £30,000 per annum payment was unlikely to deter those for whom that equated to the cost of their children's nanny – or her car...

FLAUNTING IT

The Prince's charities brought in 'around £109million' in the year 2004-5, a figure which he claims to having assisted 'directly or indirectly' – whatever that means, precisely – in raising. The 'charitable entrepreneur' has nevertheless deflected attention from the fact that his considerable wealth – not to mention his attention-gaining status – is both inherited and relies on unique access to the profits of what is really public property. Never mind that key components in the traditional definition of 'entrepreneurship' are those of competition and financial risk, something of which the Prince does not have a very extensive knowledge. The defence of his inherited position becomes ever more difficult, and the simple assumption that he will inherit the throne without the need for a high level of public approval cannot be taken for granted. His complex 'umbrella' of charitable works is now the main means available to him to justify himself and the money he receives.

Lucy Kellaway, writing in the *Financial Times*, has summed up the position well, pointing out that 'millionaires are generous while the middle classes can't afford to be'. She has devised a simple test to ascertain the worthiness of a donor's claims – Firstly, 'it must hurt a bit; [for] to give something you wouldn't miss doesn't count', and secondly, 'you mustn't make a song and dance about it, or else it isn't generosity either; it's publicity'[6]. Judged by the Kellaway test, the Prince of Wales doesn't do too well. His own donations are relatively meagre, as he gets others to donate and then basks in the reflected glory.

As a 'charitable entrepreneur', his role is as facilitator rather than donor. There is no great sense that a man with a multi-million pound annual income is actually dipping into his own pocket. Indeed, the taxpayer backs the infrastructure, any cost to the Prince himself can be put down as expenses and offset against tax. His rich donors as well have complex motives for their generosity. As for the 'song and dance' aspect, just look at his promotional material, he shouts loudly about what he does and it deflects criticism. One thing is certain, without his protective 'charity shield', defending his privileged position would be a lot harder than it is at present.

Being an 'entrepreneur' however, even if one stretches the concept to include a state-subsidised monarch in waiting, carries implicit risks. Charles' glossy architectural magazine, as we have seen, failed to find any buyers, and even the luxury food and goods brand 'Duchy Originals' hit hard times, having to be rescued by leading supermarket chain Waitrose. But no matter, when you have millions of pounds of taxpayers' cash heading your way, year on year, what's the problem? You just get your valet to dust you off, and head on to the next of your many ongoing projects…

GOOD CAUSES FOR CONCERN

The Prince of Wales's status as a 'charitable entrepreneur' is now a key component in his campaign of self-promotion as the next Head of State – greatly assisted by the unique advantage conveyed by the income provided exclusively to him as heir to the throne by the Duchy of Cornwall. For many years now, this state-subsidised promotional campaign has been pivotal in establishing his acceptability for both his present position and his future role. Charities enjoying royal patronage are clearly placed at a comparative advantage, with the guarantee of high profile and implied validation. From the royal perspective, charitable involvement reinforces the image of a benevolent institution in a superior social and cultural position, which benefits the royal family as much as the charity in question.

This however, contrasts fundamentally with modern state-based welfare in which support is exchanged in return for payment of tax and carries with it less notion of 'compliance' with a recognised cultural behavior pattern. Rather than the modern 'contractual' nature of the transaction, the notion of 'benevolence' confers on the recipient an implied social 'inferiority', which should have no place in a modern society. Whilst it establishes, as Jeremy Paxman has pointed out, a 'symbolic engagement with the lives of the people'[7], this can be a convenient way of justifying the royal family's innate privilege through giving – or, more usually, facilitating giving by others rather than themselves.

There is increasing concern at the rise of Britain's 'super-rich'; they are able to avoid tax on their disproportionately huge incomes yet simultaneously seem to offset this by donations to charity. In Britain's cultural hierarchy, the royal family is a key component in this high-turnover 'industry'. These big donors give a large amount, but compared with a fair contribution through taxation, this is a bargain. In a *Guardian* interview, Jean Shaoul, professor of public accountability at Manchester Business School, argued; 'At a time of ever-increasing polarisation of society, some people feel compelled to offer a few crumbs to the public. It's a down-payment towards the dismantling of social insurance which could benefit a few individuals and big corporations'[8]. Writing in the same paper, Polly Toynbee felt that 'Donors with their hefty cheques can cause serious trouble for good charities doing difficult, skilled work', and raised concern that those used to absolute control in their business lives would find it hard to relinquish such involvement when putting their cash into charitable causes, leading perhaps to undue influence.

The royal family – and the Prince of Wales in particular – are now more than ever before heavily involved in the charitable sphere, and their arbitrarily directed favours can actually cost the taxpayer money in pursuit of favourite royal causes. The Prince, for example, can promote and support key charities that assist his own favoured agenda which then can gain a hefty contribution boost in gift aid from the taxpayer. For someone who is supposed to pursue a neutral public role as future head of state, this should raise considerable concern[9].

Whilst charitable work is now regarded as a justification for the monarchy in its own right, the money raised may not greatly exceed the annual cost of the institution itself. Reducing the annual cost of the UK monarchy by £100milllion a year and giving the amount saved each year directly to charity could be a simple solution, with the allocation spread by a democratic process. If the monarchy were removed entirely, does anyone seriously imagine that charitable giving would in any case suddenly dry up? Moreover, charities upon which royals bestow their patronage are not necessarily the best or most effective. Take for example the 'Wooden Spoon' charity, with the Princess Royal as patron, which in 2007 came in the bottom 5% of 1,400 charities examined by charity watchdog 'Intelligent Giving'. A mere £1.7million out of a total of £4.4million raised actually went to charitable causes, with the rest spent on its lavish loss-making social events which often boost the royal image as much as the charity itself[10]. On that basis, the public pays to support the monarchy, then pays yet more through charitable donations which helps indirectly to boost the royals' popularity so that they don't question exactly what this extended family is doing for its money, and so on.

THE 'CHARITABLE' BRAND
It can even be argued that the Prince's numerous charities have also become a 'brand' in their own right. Espousing a broad range of his favourite causes, the money is raised as much through the highly recognisable image of the royal family itself as through the Prince's personal efforts. For that reason, the part played by the public title used in that branding should be recognised as the public asset it really is. The state contribution played by the Duchy of Cornwall money and infrastructure – as well as the funding which the supports the monarchy more generally – is crucial, and the essential contribution of the publicly owned elements ought to be contractually defined. The 'Prince' part of the 'Prince's Trust' brand, for example, is of very significant value indeed, and very much a 'public' asset. The Prince himself needs to understand the distinction, it isn't just him personally who keeps the show on the road.

PROMOTING THE ROYAL BRAND – COMMERCIALISING THE MONARCHY

Neither personal skill nor qualifications are necessary to be the heir to the throne. However, effective PR is necessary to remain acceptable in the public eye and to justify a privileged existence. Charitable work is fine, but on its own it lacks a commercial dimension, and the latter is a key means by which to divert accusations of 'failing to pay one's way'. An interest in environmental matters has helped. This right-on blend has been a PR winner, and with the ready-made Duchy infrastructure the Prince has not actually had to do that much. The art was delegation, not difficult for a man who had delegated even the tedious daily squeezing of a toothpaste tube for the greater part of his life. The Duchy of Cornwall afforded the nucleus of an administration system around which the expanding charitable structures could be constructed.

A man who could afford a diverse, multi-faceted lifestyle, the Prince had developed a keen interest in the principles of organic farming, and, possessing a large property portfolio that included many agricultural estates, was easily able to take this interest further. Investment capital was not a problem – not only did he have the money, but he had the farms too. Organic farming led to the development of an outlet for the output, when the Prince first began to market organic biscuits made from cereals produced on his own farm under the 'Duchy Originals' label. The magic words were 'added value'. Here was a way of marketing either his own products or those marketed under the distinctive brand which could take advantage of the Windsor family's own global image – big enough to rival even celebrity duo David and Victoria Beckham.

Why not use the Duchy's coat of arms, or the Prince's 'feathers' insignia – surely nobody would notice these were official titles – on the packaging? One could even plug the product on the Prince's official government website. Blatantly, it was commercial – and thus seeking to counter the spoilt royal 'drone' image – adding value not merely in financial terms but also to the Prince's pseudo-entrepreneurial kudos. Operating under the umbrella of the Duchy of Cornwall estate, the growing brand was assisted by the fact that – thanks to its unique legal status – the Duchy is exempt from the need to pay corporation and capital gains tax.

Thanks to all these competitive advantages, Charles could easily afford to 'generously' donate Duchy Originals' profits to charity – that would avoid accusations of profiteering. He could use the brand to reinforce his reputation for environmental concern. Being the heir to the throne he would be guaranteed an audience at the highest level, 'value' would be added in more ways than one, with the taxpayer ultimately backing the whole edifice. What a winner.

Well, it was until 2008. The economic downturn rather reduced the number of consumers who were prepared to pay extra for Duchy products in order to boost the glow of the Prince's charitable halo. Organic, high margin products were severely hit by the recession and Duchy products could increasingly to be found regularly marked down in price to get them off the shelves. In 2008 Duchy Originals' turnover slumped from £4.06million the previous year to £2.2million – turning an operating profit of £57,000 into an overall £3.3million loss. This left nothing for Charles' charities for two years in a row. Facing embarrassing financial meltdown, Duchy Originals was effectively taken over by supermarket chain Waitrose, part of the John Lewis retail group, who bought a majority stake in the business in September 2009.

The Duchy Originals website and its products now bear the accompanying Waitrose name – the Duchy Originals website history rather glosses over the whole 'takeover' business with exceptional economy, emphasising merely a 'partnership' that one could be forgiven for thinking happened spontaneously for no other apparent reason. The Prince appears on the site as a bucolic tweeded figure singing the praises of the product range and its underlying philosophy.' But do taxpayers get a cut for their heir to the throne's endorsement appearances which help boost Duchy Original's profits – which still go to support the Prince's charities…? Waitrose happily end up with a brand that's endorsed by the heir to the throne, is branded with a coat of arms available only to the heir to the throne, giving them a top of the range brand with royal kudos. Never knowingly undersold? No wonder…

SELLING ORGANIC FOOD OR THE ORGANIC PRINCE?

The very worthy 'Invest in Fish South West', was launched in 2004, a three-year project designed to promote the fishing industry based in south-west England. It was supported by the World Wild Life Fund UK, who campaigned for sustainable fishing practices, the National

Federation of Fishermen's Organisations, and Marks and Spencer, a leading food retailer. A keynote speaker at the event was one Charles Windsor, and one expense account journey on the royal train for that year stood out. Royal travel on public duty is reimbursed by the taxpayer, and the taxpayer, it was revealed, had footed the bill for that one trip to the tune of £44,908 in order that the Prince, who famously dislikes early appointments, could arrive in Plymouth first thing in the morning having spent a restful night's sleep on the journey from Aberdeen, not far from his Highland retreat. The journey lasted from April 26th to the 28th 2004, a journey time even the Victorians would have been hard pressed to have made as drawn-out as it was. The princely business entrepreneur could doze peacefully to his next conveniently timed appointment. It was definitely a lesson in mixing business with pleasure at public expense.

Once at his destination, the purpose of the journey might at first seem to be entirely worthy – to promote a regional fishing industry in the face of tough foreign competition and to protect endangered fish stocks. However, despite the usual protestations of impartiality that the monarchy normally employ when addressing matters with a political and commercial dimension, here was a man who takes every opportunity to promote his own particular beliefs and principles at a trade gathering. Coincidentally, it was a trade which was allied closely to his favourite causes regarding naturally produced foodstuffs and environmental concerns. Whilst the meeting had a social dimension, it was without a doubt first and foremost a trade event, and the Prince would be espousing his own beliefs on a subject in which he had a significant degree of personal commercial involvement as an organic producer himself and through his related 'Duchy Originals' brands. Were these purely royal duties that the taxpayer was being asked to finance, or was this something with a predominantly commercial dimension for which the promoting trade body ought to have been paying?. A travel expense claim for a shade under £45,000 is big even for a commercial entity, but with the event being construed as 'public', the taxpayer conveniently paid up, the Prince deemed to be performing royal duties.

'DUCHY ORIGINALS' – WHOSE BRAND IS IT ANYWAY?

The Prince of Wales increased the scale and profile of his 'Duchy Originals' brand, from its modest origins within the protected confines of the Duchy of Cornwall. Although now owned by Waitrose plc, after Duchy Originals hit hard times, it still benefits by association and connections to the Duchy of Cornwall, and the Prince of Wales himself. Though there is now a little more 'distance' than before – although the Prince was never actually a Duchy Originals director as such – when an heir to the throne becomes involved in a business venture which is closely intertwined with the Duchy itself, together with the promotion of aims which are combined in his official role, business interests and personal life, a considerable degree of convenient confusion can result. Was the Prince promoting organic foods, his own charities, his assorted pet causes, or the monarchy in general? Even his supporters sometimes get a little confused. In a keynote address Lord Watson of Richmond, seemed a little confused when he stated: 'Witness how he has turned the Duchy of Cornwall into a CSR [Corporate and Social Responsibility] 'brand' available in all best supermarkets'[11].

But what exactly is the Duchy 'brand', who really owns it, and should the Prince of Wales be entitled to display his official 'public' title and logo as a marketing tool? The Prince of Wales may be the Duke of Cornwall, and he may be entitled to the income from the profits of the estate, but that does not automatically mean that he can do exactly as he wishes with it. Firstly, he can't sell it. It is, ultimately, a public asset, and as such that fact would suggest that some of the things which the Prince seems to take for granted are not necessarily quite as straightforward as he might like to think. Shoppers will note that 'Duchy Originals' products feature the distinctive 'feathers' logo of the Prince of Wales, as well as the shield emblem of the Duchy of Cornwall itself. These logos have been licensed to Duchy Originals Ltd. Both symbols convey the up-market credentials of the royal 'brand', with its accompanying resonance of quality, heritage and implied validation.

It is highly questionable whether the Duchy itself, as, ultimately, a public asset, or the Prince, really ought to have the right to assign its coat of arms in this way for commercial purposes to a limited company. If anyone has that right it is logically Parliament itself. After all, the Prince has the right to the Duchy income, but that does not necessarily mean that he – or even the Duchy Council, its ruling body for day to day purposes – has the right to convey title in its coat of arms, even on a temporary basis. One could argue that the right to assign use of these logos rests firmly with 'the Crown' and thus Parliament's approval needs to be sought.

TRADE MARK NO. 2379665

"Duchy', 'Duchy Originals' and the arms of the Duchy of Cornwall are', assiduous readers of packaging small-print will notice, 'registered trademarks of Duchy Originals Ltd'[12]. And who seems able to grant this lucrative perk? – none other than the 'Possessor of the Duchy of Cornwall'. Official documentation avoids naming names. Ostensibly, this would seem to be none other than HRH Prince of Wales himself, but it is here we descend into the world of royal 'front' companies – in this case 'Choughs Nominees Ltd', handily registered just across the road from Buckingham Palace, and clients of royal solicitors Farrer and Co. It is 'Choughs Nominees' – the chough, a member of the crow family, is the main emblem on the Duchy coat of arms, by the way – who are actually listed as proprietors of Trade Mark No. 2379665. The next renewal date date is in 2014, but it is to be hoped that next time around some serious questions will be asked about this commercial use of public assets.

The right to bestow a very considerable trading advantage with what is ultimately a public asset should be challenged. The UK Patent Office defines such assignment as 'the legal transfer of ownership of a trademark from one person, or organisation, to another'. However, in this case, does the Prince – who does not own the Duchy but is merely entitled to an income from it whilst he is heir to the throne – actually have the right to do this at all? He is head of the Duchy's ruling council, but this highlights a profound conflict of interest.

'Possession' is defined as 'to have as property, to own', and specifically relates to notions of 'ownership'. As we have already seen, the case for any claim by an heir to the throne to actually 'own' the Duchy is, at best, extremely tenuous. The actual 'possessor' of the Duchy would seem to be the State itself – overseen and regulated by Parliament. As a result, the right of 'Choughs Nominees' to actually assign such branding assets as logos would seem to be rather doubtful indeed.

The titles of 'Prince of Wales' and 'Duke of Cornwall' are official 'public' – 'Crown' – titles, not possessed in a private capacity but bestowed by the Queen in her public role as head of state. Mrs

5 CHARITY AND ROYAL 'BRAND' OWNERSHIP

Elizabeth Windsor can't make Charles Windsor the Prince of Wales – and thus, as heir, the Duke of Cornwall – she can only do so in her official capacity as Queen, although such a power may be in her 'personal' gift. It is still personal to her only as monarch. As such, those titles are in fact public property, and any commercial use of them, or their official symbols should, if they are used at all, be for the public benefit, not that of the Prince personally – or of Waitrose Plc. who now control the 'Duchy Originals' brand. Indeed, one could argue that in fact the Prince and the supermarket chain should be reimbursing the taxpayer for the 'hire' of these official emblems when used in a promotional capacity on commercial products.

The Duchy is a Crown body, and as such should be obliged to seek best value for the use of such State assets. Were the Duchy not to make an appropriate market-rate charge for such use of its emblem then it could be accused of not maximising its commercial potential, and the Exchequer should be benefitting from this.

YOU'VE SEEN THE FILM, NOW BUY THE BISCUITS...
At the time of the Queen's visit to the US in May 2007, it became known that Charles was anxious for his 'Duchy Originals' brand to capitalise on the success of the British film *The Queen*, starring Helen Mirren. Film merchandising is fine, but when the business tie-in concerned is so closely linked to the heir to the British throne, it is another matter entirely. There is a fundamental issues at stake relating to a potential conflict of interest in relation to the Prince's status as heir to the throne. With his company then enjoying more successful results – turning over £53million in 2006-7 – Charles looked set to cash in both financially and in PR terms on the basis of his mother's official position. The fact that any residual money goes – rather vaguely, no actual charities are explicitly named – 'to charity', does not of itself excuse the fact that this is a form of commercial exploitation of Crown (State) assets.

In August 2005 'Scottish Business in the Community', proudly announced the Prince of Wales' involvement in a new campaign:

> On 2nd August 2005, SBC President, HRH Prince Charles, launched his North Highland Initiative at the Castle of Mey in Caithness. In the first instance the Initiative will market beef, lamb and mutton from the North Highlands but will be widened to include other foods, as well as helping to promote tourism and the area's historic buildings. A new company,

North Highland Products Ltd., has been established to market and sell a range of Mey Selections, endorsed by Prince Charles[13].

The promotion of tourism, heritage and local businesses comes within the monarchy's more general remit, and can, on the face of it, only be a good thing for the area concerned. However, the campaign related closely to the Prince's then food business interests, and given its location, likely to buy and sell products from animals raised on the royal family's own property at the Castle of Mey. Are North Highland Products likely to be reimbursing the taxpayer for the 'hire' of the Prince in his capacity as heir to the throne, with all the value of the 'royal' brand image when he endorses those products?

This is the commercialisation of the monarchy, given that the heir to the throne likes to be taxed – and treated generally – as if he were the monarch – and as the monarchy is ultimately 'owned' by the nation through Parliament, should the taxpayer not be able to make a charge for such 'hiring-out'? At the very least, such promotion should, on the same basis as of any local councillor, Member of Parliament, Government Minister or civil servant, be subject to identical requirements of disclosure of interests by the Prince – or indeed any other member of the royal family.

A WORD FROM OUR SPONSORS

Guests at Highgrove have an opportunity to view Charles' exotic Islamic-style tiled garden provided courtesy of the Spanish tile producers Porcelanosa. The company was already a supplier to the Duchy. In May 2001 Charles agreed to open the company's new factory there – a classic case of celebrity endorsement. This followed their agreement to construct the original version of the garden as the focus of the Prince's Foundation Charity exhibit at the Chelsea Flower Show[14].

This came at an opportune time for the company as they were then planning a high-profile launch campaign in the UK. Having had his Chelsea show-piece built, Charles liked it so much that he arranged to have it transferred, in improved form, to Highgrove House. Porcelanosa donated, transported and reconstructed the garden, complete with trees, plants and ornate water-features at an estimated cost well in excess of £100,000.

Later that year, in August, Charles held an event at Highgrove to thank the company for their generosity and hard work. Happily for them, the guest list comprised interior designers, contractors, property developers Berkeley homes, Miller Homes, and celebrities including Claudia Schiffer. Just hours before the start, Charles fell off a polo pony, and was duly kept in hospital overnight. Missing the event, he sent his speech to his son William, who, with his brother Harry, stood in for him.

The evening went well, and garden sponsors Porcelanosa got the publicity they had wanted so much, having arranged for one of 'Hello' magazine's photographers to be in attendance. The presence of supermodels and the Windsor family's photogenic younger generation may have dominated much of the popular media, but the real scandal was the blatant commercialisation of the relationship between a publicity-seeking contractor – later awarded a Royal Warrant – and the heir to the throne.

CASH FOR GIFTS

In March 2003, an internal inquiry into allegations of misconduct within the Prince of Wales' Household – the rather bizarre juxtaposition of allegations of male rape and a culture of the unchecked sale of official gifts for private gain – reported its findings. Set up in the wake of royal butler Paul Burrell's trial fiasco, the inquiry, by Sir Michael Peat and Sir Edmund Lawson QC, was criticised from the outset. The chief member of the Prince's staff was investigating the Prince's staff. It was regarded as unlikely to be properly impartial and would thus face allegations of 'whitewash'. In respect of the 'below stairs' gifts culture, however, the inquiry exposed a system that operated almost unchecked.

Only a brief three-year period was examined, and revealed that 'a lack of adequate records made it difficult to identify whether or not official gifts have been sold, exchanged or given away'. However, although no specific evidence was found that Household employees corruptly accepted bribes or improper payments from suppliers or aspiring Royal Warrant Holders, it was admitted that 'a range of gifts and entertainment from Royal Warrant Holders and other suppliers' had been accepted. Despite a requirement in their terms of employment not to 'accept presents from firms or tradesmen', the inquiry admitted that 'this term was not enforced and the practice of accepting presents and entertainment was with the knowledge and implicit approval of senior management'. In one case gifts and entertainment amounted, in aggregate, to 'several thousand pounds'.

Michael Fawcett, a member of the staff close to the Prince himself, was singled out in the report. Whilst the investigation acknowledged that it had 'not produced any evidence of financial impropriety on his part', it did concede that Fawcett 'did infringe the internal rules relating to gifts from suppliers…'. Fawcett left his post under pressure, but would continue to provide services to his former employer as an 'outside contractor'. His name came up again during the course of the investigation into the Duchies of Cornwall and Lancaster by the Public Accounts Committee in November 2005; Ian Davidson MP questioned the sale of Duchy property – a house lived in by Mr Fawcett in Hampton Hill, Surrey – at what he alleged was below market price[15].

ROYAL WARRANTS

A somewhat 'grey' area of the relationship between the monarchy and the commercial world has been allowed to develop to a point where a proper system of accountability and control is required. Possession of the 'Royal Warrant' has for many generations been a means of displaying cachet and validation upon commercial organisations in a society which reflects a cultural outlook that still acknowledges the status of a monarchy able to 'bestow' favours. Those who contract with the monarchy can be rewarded with a form of official endorsement that still carries much weight in promotional terms. Is it not just a form of advertising? Not exactly.

Commercial competition means that suppliers in specialist areas may have much to lose if they are not prepared to concede what are sometimes extremely tough contractual terms to the royal households. In return for this they may be rewarded with an official endorsement which carries much weight both within their own commercial sphere and in the world outside. The bargains driven are hard – the author has experienced this at first hand[16].

Businesses large and small may be pitted against each other, encouraged to reduce prices well below cost to the stage where they are little more than gifts. Isn't that just business? No, because this is not a normal business to business relationship. It is a relationship between businesses which may be under not only considerable competitive pressure,

5 CHARITY AND ROYAL 'BRAND' OWNERSHIP

but cultural pressure too, to concede to individuals – warrants are granted by the separate members of the institution itself – who sit at the top of the constitutional and social hierarchy of the nation, and thus may enjoy favoured financial and fiscal status. What exists could be regarded as little more than a culture of institutionalized bribery. Even assuming a company is graciously awarded 'Royal Warrant holder' status, it must, as a condition of acceptance of the Warrant, join an organisation in which regalia and evidence of membership have to be bought. No pay, no warrant. Warrant-holding status is not merely evidence of having supplied the Royal Household, but is a 'privilege' granted on a discretionary basis, and one for which the Palace charges. Not merely does this public institution use its considerable leverage to extract deals that businesses may find difficult to refuse, but, worst of all, there is no requirement for the details of such deals to be disclosed.

The Warrant-Holder's Association operates like an exclusive club, with crests and decals of differing levels of ostentation available – at a price. It doesn't come cheap, but perhaps if you are Bentley Cars – who presented the Queen with a custom-built limousine in 2002 worth at least £1million – that is not a high price to pay. As with conflicts of interest in relation to the performance of their royal duties in general, the entire process would perhaps be better if there was proper transparency, with the administration of the Warrant process being completely independent, rather than run by the Royal Household itself[17].

There are signs, however, that the lure of the royal warrant may not be as strong as it was once felt to be. Food brands like Walkers, Heinz, Jacobs and Sharwoods have dropped the royal insignia from many of their products. The increasingly globalised standardisation of product names and packaging is part of the reason, and, revealed in a survey by brand design agency Coley Porter Bell, the sheer number awarded may have served to devalue them – plus the fact that only 13% of consumers polled felt that royal seals made a difference anyway. ('How the royal warrant has lost its shine for British brands' – *Daily Mail* – 20/1/11)

PAYING FOR THE PRIVILEGE

The 'Crown' – in essence the notion of the nation's power centre – in a modern parliamentary democracy is, in effect, the property of the nation, and any official positions and titles held are the property of the nation too. Any use of royal titles, for example, when not in the express performance of an official duty, should require a payment to be made by the title-holders to the public purse. A strict appreciation of the true value of the royal 'brand' – and an individual 'royal' to the State – makes the differentiation of 'public' and 'private' roles in respect of members of the royal family vital.

The use by the Princess Royal of an official helicopter in April 2004 to fly from her home and back to present awards at a Pony Club meeting in Hertfordshire is a case in point. At £4,710, the flight was, of course, only part of the total. It excludes, for example, administration, insurance and security costs. Preliminary organisation and the attendance of royal protection officers could easily double that cost to at least £10,000. Yet this was not really a public occasion at all but a small private function, and if they wanted a celebrity guest, the club could have met the attendant costs themselves. Should the 'Princess Royal' have been able to hire herself out as a public figure for a private event, and should the taxpayer have had to pay the overheads?

A culture of secrecy and deference means that an institution such as the Duchy of Cornwall is scarcely regulated at all. In consequence, it has become possible for it to be utilised as a broad platform with which the heir to the throne has been able to generate personal wealth and from which to promote himself to the public as an acceptable successor to the position of head of state of the nation – one which he would in any case automatically inherit. Irrespective of the motives and probity of the Prince's charitable donors, beyond an ostensibly respectable facade lies a less visible world where transparency is not high on the agenda. Whilst Zara Philips may be the face of a Land Rover advertising campaign, and her brother's wedding was sponsored by *Hello* magazine, the heir to the throne opened up 'Highgrove', a shop to sell organic produce and items from his 'Duchy Originals' and 'Duchy Collections' ranges. Even the prospect of a chain of outlets was not entirely discounted[18]. On June 22nd, 2008 the website www.business.times.online.co.uk was announcing that there were plans to launch 'Duchy Originals' in both the USA and India, as part of a five year plan to boost annual turnover from £50million to £200million. These elaborate plans melted away as the failing economy took its toll on his premium product brand and it was taken over by Waitrose, but 'HRH' still acts as the 'face' of the brand, featuring on the Duchy Originals' website.

The Prince of Wales's forays into the commercial sphere have raised new areas of concern with relation to the use of the royal 'brand' by individual members. At the end of June 2008, just ahead of the annual Duchy of Cornwall accounts being announced, plans were revealed for the Prince of Wales to launch a £1billion property fund in conjunction with Credit Suisse. Intended to fund 'sustainable developments', a third of the fund was to be owned by the Prince's charities. As ever, it seemed, Prince Charles would 'not have a formal role' – a handy legal get-out – but was nonetheless most definitely the 'driving force' behind this project. This would take his charities, and their brand-enhancing potential, onto an altogether new level[19]. Whilst Duchy Originals may have since come to grief, be rescued by a supermarket chain, and scale back some of their more ambitious plans, it remains possible for royal family members to endorse and effectively run – even if they keep off the board as an actual director – commercial enterprises, and charities with a significant commercial dimension, relatively free of proper controls and not even obliged to disclose those interests. With the marriage of Prince William and Catherine Middleton, a further commercial strand has appeared. The Middleton family run a successful mail-order business; 'Party Pieces', selling party goods. This now includes royal themed products, from flags and party hats, as well as china teapots, mugs, and so on. With the 2012 Diamond Jubilee, yet another irresistible commercial opportunity presented itself, and the Middletons have thus cashed in on their own daughter's wedding – and beyond. No doubt they will be looking forward to the day their son-in-law William becomes King...

The royal brand is the property of the nation as a whole, not a commercial plaything for members of the royal family. Leading members of the royal family enjoy a privileged existence, and do so at the expense of the taxpayer. Despite the defence that they work hard in return for this indulgence, there is no real sign that they are actually overworked. Indeed, one suspects that they are more than happy with the arrangement. If the workload was really that onerous, it is unlikely they would continue to do it. The processes of accountability are weak and infrequent. Whilst the present Queen has generally been able to deflect, or at least to pre-empt criticism, and to avoid conspicuous displays of wealth, the heir to the throne has been rather less successful and would seem to want the best of both worlds.

6
The Royal Collection: 'Held' for the Nation

Art for arts sake,
Money for God's sake...
10cc

Dynasties collect treasure. Whether liberal or tyrannical, monarchical or totalitarian, none seem able to resist the compulsion to acquire material goods in all forms. Rare treasure, art, gold and jewels – all have an especial allure to the rich and powerful. The desire to accumulate treasure stems from the desire to accumulate wealth, both for financial security and as an expression of their power and status. Enemies were conquered and their assets acquired, the ultimate cultural evocation of the eminence of the victor over the vanquished.

Originally, such an accumulation of treasured assets was an integral part of the day-to-day holding of accessible public financial resources. Gold plate might be melted down for coinage, and the distinction between the monarch's treasure and the funds available to perform the functions of government were effectively indistinguishable. Over time, in the United Kingdom, the monarch's art collection has acquired the status of a national cultural resource, whilst the latter, the public wealth of the nation, has become 'the Treasury', in effect the nation's collective bank account. The Treasury, headed by the Chancellor of the Exchequer, though not forgetting the contribution of the First Lord of the Treasury – the original, official title of the Prime Minister – is accountable to Parliament on a day to day basis.

THE ROYAL COLLECTION
The wealth accumulated by generations of British monarchs as works of art has become an enduring symbol of monarchical grandeur although the institution is now subordinate to an elected Parliament. The nation itself, on behalf of the people, has also acquired art and artefacts via purchase or donation. Museums and art galleries have been established so that the British public can appreciate their own treasures. In the past, visitors have paid to enter national public museums and galleries but they are now admitted free of charge, the costs of maintaining these treasures being met by general taxation. Private collections, often held by charitably constituted bodies, similarly exhibit their works, for which the visitor, not unreasonably, is required to pay.

Visitors to the 'Queen's Gallery' – an annexe of Buckingham Palace – must pay to visit what are described as 'the Queen's pictures'. But do they belong to her personally? Not exactly. One might assume that the art displayed in this modest collection is the property of the monarch herself. They would be wrong, for what the visitor pays to see in the Queen's Gallery is but the tiny tip of an artistic iceberg – the 'Royal Collection'. They belong to the monarch through their official position only. The decorative and symbolic process of the accumulation of 'treasures', in the form of art, jewellery and other items has been permitted to continue in the form of this Royal Collection. In this sense the monarch still maintains a far more ancient tradition in holding a large resource in their official, public capacity as the Head of State.

WHAT EXACTLY IS THE ROYAL COLLECTION?

The Royal Collection is the result of the accumulation of works of art over a period of approximately three and a half centuries by British monarchy. These works have been bought by, or donated or bequeathed to the monarch in their official capacity. It is an absolutely enormous and probably unrivalled collection ranging from paintings and sculpture to

6 THE ROYAL COLLECTION: 'HELD' FOR THE NATION

jewellery and tapestries, and with a value estimated by Robin Simon, art critic and acknowledged expert on the Collection, as amounting to some £12.7billion in 2011[1]. This vast collection of paintings, sculpture and other treasures is held by the Queen in her official capacity as monarch. As such, it is a public collection, the property of the state.

Given the rise in art values since 2001, the total valuation of the Collection now is likely to be very considerably higher. In terms of sheer quantity, the figure of approximately 7,000 paintings, 500,000 prints and 30,000 watercolours and drawings, not to mention sculptures, photographs, documents and other treasures gives some idea of the scale. It includes the famous Crown Jewels, held at the Tower of London and described as 'priceless' by the Historic Royal Palaces Trust. This collection, reserved for use on state occasions, comprises tens of thousands of jewels including the colossal 105.6 carat 'Koh-I-Noor' diamond – the UK's ownership of which is disputed by some – and another crown which alone contains some 6,000 diamonds.

The Collection is held 'in trust' for the nation, meaning that it is not the exclusive property of the monarch personally but held as such in their official capacity and then transferred 'in trust for her successors and the Nation'[2]. The 1993 Memorandum of Understanding set out the official position and administrative details in respect of what it termed the 'new arrangements' for royal finances. This had followed the Windsor Castle fire and the ensuing pressure to review the taxation position of the monarch and the heir to the throne. In this agreement the Royal Trustees defined the Royal Collection as being 'held by the Queen as Sovereign and [passing] from one Sovereign to the next. The Collection cannot be sold to generate private income or capital for the use of the Queen '. It's a pity that what actually constitutes the Collection wasn't accurately defined at the time.

On exactly that point, the then Chancellor of the Exchequer, Gordon Brown, responding to a parliamentary question in 2000, asserted that 'there is a computerised inventory of the Royal Collection'[3]. This was actually an evasive reply in itself, as the actual question had asked 'if an inventory exists to distinguish assets held by the Queen a) as Sovereign and b) as individual'. Given that, as will be explained later, there is no statutorily defined date from which items are, or are not included, the comprehensive nature of Mr Brown's 'inventory' is probably not to be relied upon.

WHO OWNS THE COLLECTION?

The matter of actual ownership of the Collection is avoided in official documents. It is invariably recorded as simply being 'held' by the Queen, and this rather nebulous phraseology is reflected in both the legal niceties and the style and process of its management. Speculation of the Queen's personal wealth is frequently marked by misunderstanding and ignorance as to ownership of items that fall within the aegis of the Collection. Items which are demonstrably in the public domain – jewellery used only for State functions, for example – are sometimes deemed as 'the Queen's' in a simplistic attempt to inflate the her wealth as much as possible by those speculating as to how much she may be worth.

As in other areas which ought to define clearly the modern relationship between the monarchy and the state, a distinct reluctance to call a spade a spade prevails. This is in part attributable to the absence of a written constitution, but no less likely is due to deference. This mindset harks back to a distinctly pre-democratic era and can thus perpetuate the erroneous notion that the Collection is 'the Queen's' rather than that of the nation. In the words of Robin Simon, '…few people can tell you, in this age of highly skilled politicians, lawyers, accountants and civil servants, or are willing to say, who really owns the Royal Collection. It all depends on whom you listened to last'[4].

The matter has been examined in the past by the House of Commons Public Accounts Committee who raised the question of ownership (in relation to the Historic Royal Palaces Trust) in their 2000 Report. There had been concern over money received from ticket admissions to Buckingham Palace. These admissions were suggested by the Royal Household as a means of paying for repairs to Windsor Castle – for which the public had refused to pay. However, the Committee discovered that with the repair bills all met, continuing revenue from admissions were being diverted to the Royal Collection through a unilateral decision by the Palace.

Whilst no-one could criticise the eminently laudable principle of maintaining the Collection, the practice itself was rather more questionable. The Royal Household argued that 'no approval had been needed because the income belonged to the Queen'[5]. However, if the assets from which the income derived – both palaces and art – were only 'held' by the Queen 'for the nation', on what basis did they think that automatically entitled her to benefit from the income on the basis of a purely temporary agreement? The truth is that this takes us into the notoriously complex and shady area of prerogative powers exercised by government ministers, as had been the case with the 1993 Memorandum of Understanding. These financial arrangements were seen by the Royal Household as their justification for retaining the money – and making agreements which were effectively beyond Parliament's remit in terms of proper accountability.

'OWNERSHIP' AND 'UNDERSTANDINGS'

At this point, mention must be made of the different types of 'ownership' which are involved in the complex sphere of property which occupies the strange netherworld where the monarch, the royal family, the state – in its guise of 'the Crown', and the government meets. Philip Hall, the author of *Royal Fortune*, referring to the statement by Lord Cobbold to a Select Committee undertaking a review of royal finance in 1971, defined a total of eight areas in which the monarch's wealth is held, and considers the Royal Collection to fall into the third category, that which is 'Inalienable by Custom'[6]. It must be remembered that there are no absolute definitions incorporated into statute law in this respect. These definitions are essentially little more than opinions or interpretations of what is 'understood' to be the true position. Hall also refers to 'a significant amount of royal opportunism' which does little to help matters, other than to its own advantage. It is deeply worrying that the ownership of billions of pounds worth of art seems to rest on such a flimsy basis[7].

The Collection was defined by Cobbold 'as covering all pictures and works of art purchased or acquired by all Sovereigns up to the death of Queen Victoria, and also certain property acquired [since]'. This, by the way, is as being distinct from the second category, that of 'Legally Inalienable Property', which is taken essentially to comprise the Royal Palaces and the Crown Jewels. The Palaces and Crown Jewels are not saleable. The former Hall cites as being so based on the judgement of the Treasury Solicitor. The latter, it seems, were so categorized merely in the opinion of Lord Cobbold. It is somewhat curious that one set of decorative items, the Crown Jewels, which some might allege as having a deeper symbolic status – not to mention being worth rather a lot – fall into such a vague category. While the Collection is merely 'inalienable' – in practice not to be disposed of by the monarch – this is deemed to be only by 'custom', Hall quotes

Cobbold's statement that this arrangement is based on little more than 'an understanding'.

Lord Cobbold preferred to obfuscate the real issues by saying he did not want to 'presume to deal with the legal technicalities'. This can more likely be read as simply that successive governments have persisted in allowing a vague notion of 'ownership' to persist simply in order to avoid any kind of showdown with the monarchy, who thereby as a result seem to get the best of all worlds. The Queen gets to keep the Collection, choose what goes in it, administer it, restrict access, and obtains all the kudos from possessing it.

JUMPING THROUGH LOOPHOLES

As a result of the various confusions, what appears to be little more than an informal agreement permits the Collection to be kept inalienable only 'by custom'. Curiously, too, why the distinction between items in the Collection acquired before the death of Queen Victoria, and those acquired after? Also, why the use of that curious, and legally extremely loose, and perhaps extraordinarily convenient, term – 'certain property'?

Why does that date have such magic significance? It would seem that there is no logical rationale whatsoever. However, it means that anything purchased or 'acquired' after January 22nd, 1901 by the monarch in their official capacity can be incorporated into the Royal Collection. Not only that, but it seems that inclusion is on a discretionary basis, and one which is decided only by the Royal Household itself. If monarchy is, as its proponents insist, all about 'continuity', why then devise seemingly arbitrary 'cut-off dates' around which hang important distinctions of ownership? After all, each monarch simply performs a successive walk-on part in the ongoing dynastic performance. If eligibility for inclusion in the Collection is itself less than certain, then it is hard to see how one can accurately ascertain what it definitively contains. Nothing special, apart from the demise of one of many monarchs, happened on that day in 1901. Given the important 'watershed' dates for the modern monarchy, why not 1688, for instance, or 1760?

'Acquired', is also an interesting term. It means in effect whatever the Royal Household which oversees the Collection wishes it to mean. By the same token, if the definition of what is in the Collection – 'acquired after

6 THE ROYAL COLLECTION: 'HELD' FOR THE NATION

1901' – permits unlimited discretion, what is to prevent 'transfers' of items 'acquired' after 1901?, with that 'discretion' residing, so it seems, at what is ultimately the whim of the monarch. It would seem that this gives the Royal Household virtually unlimited leeway in moving items into or out of the Collection acquired by it in the last century. Ostensibly, this would appear to give the monarch the opportunity to dispose of such items, having first 'transferred' them out of the Collection.

Given the high values which artworks have now acquired, this freedom would have strong tax implications for items which would fall outside, for instance, the scope of the 1993 Memorandum of Understanding involving 'transfers' – not just bequests, for example – between the Sovereign and their successor, the heir to the throne and the 'Consort of a former Sovereign'. There is no evidence that any such transfer or transaction has, in fact, occurred, but the way in which the Collection is constituted would seem to allow this were a monarch so minded.

Robin Simon, writing in the Royal Rich Report in 2001, refers to the fact that the Royal Collection itself had, at the time of his article, in effect redefined the 'post-1901' parameter, by instead using the date of the death of the present Queen's father, King George VI, as the crucial benchmark. He notes, firstly, that there is no evidence for any such change in 'any Parliamentary proceedings', but also that the Collection 'does not include acquisitions by the Queen Mother during his reign, unless she has already nominated an item or they ultimately appear as such in her will'. As George VI's widow, the Queen Mother was uniquely placed to take advantage – and one she could pass on through the 1993 Memorandum of Understanding to her daughter the Queen, free of any tax liability – of her ability to acquire works of art that would have then had 'discretionary' status. Did, for instance, her known collection of rare French Impressionist paintings, now worth many tens – if not hundreds – of millions of pounds each belongs to the Collection or not? 'Discretion' as to whether such pictures fall within the remit of a Royal Collection, and are thus 'held' for the nation – or whether they are merely 'private' – would appear to rest entirely with the monarch.

The fact that the Queen Mother's will, and those of other leading royals, are 'uniquely' permitted to remain private means that any such 'transfers' as permitted by the 1993 Memorandum of Understanding may remain secret. This leaves the opportunity for a considerable amount of less than transparent practice to occur. A will is normally a public document, but a 'convention' has been established that the

> contents of royal wills remain secret. In 2008, legal proceedings were under way to legally challenge this 'tradition' to ensure that all royal wills are like those of all other citizens – 'public' documents and thus available for inspection[8]. Unfortunately, the challenge failed.

As Phillip Hall pointed out in his book 'Royal Fortune', monarchs from Queen Victoria to George VI made very considerable savings out of Civil List payments which they were able to divert for their own personal use, acquiring or improving real estate. Therefore, the public ought not unreasonably, to be permitted a say in what happens to these properties. The Balmoral and Sandringham estates were acquired in this way. This ability to retain money for official 'expenses' and divert it to more personal collections of everything from fine art to valuable stamps has greatly assisted in pursuing private obsessions.

Perhaps King George VI's vast stamp collection was helped in some small way by the million pounds he obtained from *Bona Vacantia* income from the intestate residents of the Duchy of Lancaster who died in action during the Second World War. One thing is certain, these and other assets were not necessarily acquired with money that had derived purely from private earnings, but rather by lenient practices which would not be tolerated today.

IT'S 'OURS', BUT HOW MUCH CAN WE ACTUALLY SEE?

How much of the Royal Collection is actually accessible to the public? Sadly – or perhaps disgracefully, depending upon one's particular viewpoint, not much. Although an inventory exists, its integrity is somewhat questionable as there seems to be some doubt as to the exact qualification for inclusion within it in the first place. In other words, only the Palace really knows what it has, and though they publish a list, does it really include everything? Why is the Collection run in this way? There are two basic reasons for this. Firstly, this is the way that things have always been done, and the Palace has a reputation for sticking to tradition, especially when it is in its own interest. Secondly, even the Palace may not know, or at least would probably find it more convenient not to know.

As so often in history, we have been here before. Following the trial and execution of Charles I, and the founding of the Commonwealth, the new regime had to decide what to do with the works of art that it had inherited from the late monarch and his predecessors[9]. A process of cataloguing the collection was succeeded by the sale and distribution of the assets as the new regime deemed appropriate. This was far from in any way plundering the assets. Charles I had, in the best monarchical tradition, spendthrift habits, and the Commonwealth used the proceeds from these sales to help defray some of the horrendous debts which they had inherited. At that time, the distinction between the 'public' and 'private' personae of the monarch – until an was Act passed in 1800 in respect of real estate, at least – was even harder to ascertain than at present, and distinguishing between acquisitions and gifts made by and to the monarch in whichever capacity was not easy.

THE TIP OF THE ICEBERG

The contents of the Queen's Gallery, for example, the Royal Collection's primary central London visitor resource, represents a miniscule fraction of the Collection as a whole. Very limited numbers of works from the Collection as a whole are loaned to other museums and galleries for outside exhibition. How many exactly? Well, the Collection's Annual report for 2004-05 proudly refers to fact that '20 pictures were lent to exhibitions in the United Kingdom and abroad', while '40 works of art were lent to 17 exhibitions' at home and abroad. Just 53 drawings and watercolours, 2 prints and 1 solitary pastel were loaned to 15 exhibitions – just 5 of which were in the UK – out of around 7,000 paintings, 500,000 prints and 30,000 drawings and watercolours, let alone sculptures, photographs, etc.[10]. That hardly sounds like the height of generosity. It would also appear to be in a broader cultural sense a serious under-use of such a unique and extensive resource. A more generous and imaginative lending policy could also make the collection a more economically self-sustaining entity.

Unlike for instance, the National Gallery, the Tate galleries and the V&A, entrance to the Queen's Gallery is not free. There is an unresolved distinction between items available for view in national public galleries and those which, despite their 'for the nation' status within the Royal Collection means that the public must pay to see them. The Palace might well protest that they must make their own arrangements to maintain and administer the Royal Collection, but why not simply merge it with the nation's collection as a whole to form a unified State Collection? It would absolve the Palace of an onerous responsibility and rationalise what is an obvious anomaly.

The prevailing deferential culture does not encourage openness and accountability, and management is left to the Royal Household itself. On a day to day – or decade to decade basis, more likely – intervention is rare. As in the matter of the authorisation process for the allocation of royal palaces – the use of Clarence House by the Prince of Wales, for example – the administration system would, for practical purposes, seem to be rather 'hands-off'. We can at least hope that the passing of the 2012 Sovereign Grant Act will help to improve royal accountability in Parliament, and with it the running of the Royal Collection. Despite these being ultimately public resources funded directly or indirectly by the taxpayer, the government appears to be content to allow the Royal Household to run matters relatively undisturbed. Nor does the fact that items within the Collection are available for borrowing by other members of the immediate royal family – not just the official head of state – convey the impression of an extremely valuable state asset under regular and rigorous scrutiny. They are treated for practical purposes as if they were a private collection for the Queen to lend as she wishes. They may not, of course, be sold, but if a painting is to find its way into a room in a royal residence, and the resident becomes rather attached to it, it's as good as theirs until they die.

For example, In June 2006, a large collection of items, described as the property of the Queen's late sister, Princess Margaret, were auctioned by Christies in order to raise money to pay off inheritance tax liabilities. Concern was raised at the time that not all the items should really have been sold. For example, a chair used by the late Queen Mary at one of the Coronation ceremonies was sold, yet it is debatable whether it was originally commissioned and paid for privately. Incidentally, given Queen Mary's reputation for 'acquiring' items she fancied, it is highly unlikely that she would have bought it anyway. Items used for 'official' purposes would, more than likely, have been claimed on expenses. In such a case, its title might then be regarded as remaining with 'the Crown'. Some items had been donated as presents to the Princess by Commonwealth countries. The question arises as to whether these gifts were given to the Princess in respect of her status as an 'official' personage, or in a 'private' capacity. If given in respect of her 'public', not 'private' capacity, then the title in those gifts would be vested in the Crown and they would strictly form part of the Royal Collection and not be saleable. Alternatively, any money realised would go to the Royal Collection. An appraisal may have

6 THE ROYAL COLLECTION: 'HELD' FOR THE NATION

taken place, but this is not an area that is subject to an open, public process, despite all such Royal Collection items supposedly being 'held on behalf of the nation'.

In July 2006, it transpired that some of the late Princess Margaret's items had, in fact, been bought by Historic Royal Palaces Trust (which administers the 'Unoccupied' Royal Palaces), to go on public display in Kensington Palace. Princess Margaret's children had been keen to realise the maximum possible for her possessions to meet inheritance tax liabilities, and were happy to see these items go under the hammer at Christies. (Coincidentally, the Princess's son, Viscount Linley, as a director of Christies, might possibly have benefited indirectly in that capacity through the company's commission on the sales in question. Unlike MPs there are no requirements for declarations of interests in respect of royal family members). Viscount Linley and his sister, Lady Sarah Chatto, needed just £3million to placate the taxman, but in the end realised some £13.6million. How fortunate that Historic Royal Palaces Trust which maintains those royal properties not supported by 'Grant-in-aid' was able to step in and help to boost the wealth of Princess Margaret's children[11]. The Trust was keen to emphasise that there had been no consultation between Historic Royal Palaces and the children before the sale. This is not to suggest there was any improper practice, but the lack of proper transparency and the often blurred distinction between the public and private roles of members of the royal family is a profoundly undesirable situation.

YESTERDAY'S PAPERS – THE ROYAL ARCHIVES

Another resource of vital national significance, the Royal Archives, is also held by the Royal Household under similar conditions to the Royal Collection. Held and administered internally, it is, for practical purposes, under the private control of the monarch despite relating to matters involving the monarch or her predecessors in their public capacity. Access is at the discretion of the monarch rather than a neutral independent authority as is the process of what is held or otherwise disposed of. Thus the 'weeding' of such archives is possible without necessarily complying with the standards demanded of the National Archives. The Royal Archives certainly contains documents of crucial national significance given the inevitable 'overlap' between the public and private lives of monarchs and leading members of the royal family. Can items be sold off, for instance? There are no rules, only precedent, and Phillip Hall's opinion that the contents are inalienable 'in practice' is not at all reassuring.

By having such control, the monarch is in effect able to restrict access to those who are guaranteed to be sympathetic to the royals. In this way, the royal 'version' of history can be maintained on an indefinite basis. As a repository for documents which refer to the monarch's official – and public – duties, we have an absolute right to know what they contain, from papers relating to the Hess affair, the death of the Duke of Kent during the Second World War, and Sir Anthony Blunt, to name but a few. Papers relating to the late Duke of Windsor, for example, are securely held, preventing a properly objective assessment of the royal family's role in the years immediately preceding the outbreak of the Second World War[12].

The proof of the Queen's political 'neutrality' – or otherwise – throughout her reign, and possible knowledge of the less admirable and undemocratic events of the late 1960s and 1970s, may also sit within the Archives. Lord Louis Mountbatten's assertion that the Queen had become 'concerned' at the complaints about the elected government led by Harold Wilson has been cited as the possible justification for his alleged involvement in coup plans in that period. If that is so, was the Queen herself aware of such plots? And was this situation complicated by the Windsor family ties? The possession of such a resource conveys the ability of the monarchy to, in effect, 'rewrite' history, by choosing to conveniently suppress details which might not reflect so favourably upon the conduct of a family who are entrusted with the job of providing the nation's heads of state. It is possible that the Royal Archives contain valuable evidence in this respect, and in a democracy we, the people, have a right to know. After all, it is we who pay for this institution.

'Openness' is not a concept which comes easily to the British system of governance, and the monarchy benefits from this situation. The inventory and management of the Royal Collection is another symptom of this lack of openness which is exploited by the Palace and contributes to the 'mystique' of royalty. This mystique is a powerful cultural weapon, defined by Robin Simon as 'a vital element in the propaganda that surrounds the Monarchy in an aura of splendour'. In a real democracy it would be obvious for the State to have full control of an asset which it owns, a next step in opening our secretive constitution. Instead of a presumption of public accessibility and collective ownership, the tone of presentation of that small proportion of cultural treasures open to view is that of grudging beneficence:

> When one enters the galleries at the palace of Holyroodhouse or Buckingham Palace, one is made to feel that one is there on sufferance, by the Queen's dispensation. In some essential way, we are made to feel we have no right to be there. It is partly the entrance fee and the liveried staff, but also the way that the collection is sold to the public not on the claims of great art that it contains, but on that great art's connection with the monarchy[13].

The Royal Collection is symptomatic of the current attitude of the Palace toward the people of this nation. It is secretive, distant, and redolent of a pre-democratic era. It is also particularly reluctant to share any of the works of art it holds with other galleries and institutions. It is 'notorious for its unwillingness to lend', with a curator – anxious to remain anonymous – revealing to journalist Charlotte Higgins that 'sometimes you are told you can't have [an item] because the Queen will miss it'[14]. So, the Queen would miss it? Yet we are told she takes such pride in her role as 'custodian' for what is ours – as citizens – by right.

'BY GRACIOUS PERMISSION…'

Whilst the public good, '…in trust for…the Nation', is unfailingly invoked whenever the matter of ownership is raised – and quickly deflected – the tone in which objects in the Collection are displayed leaves one in little doubt who the Palace thinks the Collection really belongs to. Pictures are fawningly credited as being displayed '…by gracious permission of Her Majesty…'. Not only that, but the terms under which the very small part of the Collection open to public view is made available, are quite different from national institutions. In the National Gallery, they are displayed free of charge, and public money enables care of a collection of paintings held by and for the nation to be made accessible to as many people as possible.

> The Royal Collection has now grown to such a scale that to expect the Royal Collection Trust to raise and administer funds for its upkeep as it does at present is simply no longer tenable or indeed desirable. The present situation merely plays into the Palace's hands. The total income generated by the Royal Collection amounted to a total of £22,591,000 in 2004-05, for example, a figure that includes admissions and sales made at the various royal palaces, but probably represents a considerable under-utilisation of the Collection as a whole. The fact that the Royal Library received just 160 enquiries and was visited by just 11 researchers in 2004-5, with a total of 290 visitors, while only 75 researchers visited the Royal Archives in the same period, suggests that the resources are similarly under-utilised or, more likely, that the admissions criteria are perhaps too stringent and over-selective. The implication is that one is admitted to the Archives on the understanding that one is not going to look for anything that would reflect negatively upon the monarchy – nor that one might even be shown it in the first place.

A VERY BRITISH 'MUDDLE'

Following the demise of the Commonwealth in 1660, Charles II set to work 'reassembling' both his late father's art collection wherever possible and accumulating one of his own. Since that time, British monarchs have sought to augment this collection both in their private capacity and in their official position as Heads of State. This has created a very British 'muddle'. In centuries past there was no real differentiation between the public and private 'personae' of the monarch. As we have seen earlier, not until 1800 was it established by statute that a monarch could own land personally, and separate from their official role. However, there has not really been as yet any equivalent legislation to cover other material possessions. While making the monarch accountable to Parliament avoided absolute monarchy, the difference between the notion of what were the 'public' and 'private' elements of the monarch meant that it was, and still is, often difficult to separate the two. The methods of acquisition over the years mean that in some cases there may not exist a clear proof of the circumstances, and date, of acquisition and therefore proof of title to the works in question.

6 THE ROYAL COLLECTION: 'HELD' FOR THE NATION

INCREASING ART VALUES

Great art has not merely become more sought after and 'collectable' simply for aesthetic reasons, but increasingly for investment purposes. It is now worth more than ever before. As a hedge against fluctuations in the value of currencies or other investments, art has performed exceptionally well. In May 2012, a version of Edvard Munch's painting, 'The Scream' sold for £74million ($120million), making it the most expensive painting in the world. Sought after not merely by collectors for aesthetic reasons alone, art is now a key component of the investment portfolios of 'super-rich' private investors, corporations and investment funds. With vast sums of money from across the globe chasing prized works of art, in particular from the emerging markets of the Far East and Latin America, values have soared. The intrinsic worth of a single item may now easily be worth tens of millions of pounds – or more. The provenance of a work of art that once belonged to a British monarch, for example, might well boost the perceived value of that item by a very considerable additional amount were it to find its way onto the open market.

The Royal Collection is not, of course, a resource to be valued for its financial worth alone. It is the property of the nation and a significant element in its cultural heritage. However, any dispute as to ultimate ownership – occasioned, for instance, in the event of a republic being established in Britain – would bring this matter to a head. A former royal facing a life without the proceeds of a Duchy to insulate them from financial reality could be amply cushioned by the proceeds of just one or two works by a major artist. The crucial question is whose property would provide the cushion, the monarchy's property – or the nation's?

As long as the Royal Collection stays where it is, many may be quite happy to let the situation remain as it is. A few works on show, the rest safe in vaults somewhere, or hanging inside royal residences for the personal aesthetic pleasure of those who reside there. A visitor to the areas of Buckingham Palace not frequented by the public in the short time during which parts of the Palace are opened to the paying public would be intrigued by the works of art which might hang along even a relatively mundane corridor. To question whether such unseen items are really the property of Mrs Elizabeth Windsor, or are instead being 'held' for a grateful public – who will probably never be able to see them goes to the heart of the matter.

The right of the people of the nation to have access to the entire Royal Collection should be asserted at the earliest opportunity. For the time being, however, 'the collection remains, in large part, as inaccessible to the general populace as [in the time] of Charles I'[15]. The Royal Collection is ours, and it is time that we were able to see it, all of it, on our terms, not at the monarch's 'pleasure'. A logical wholesale re-evaluation of the terms upon which the nation's cultural heritage is held and administered is now required. The Government itself holds a very considerable resource in the shape of the Government Art Collection, with works of art held by it being allocated to public buildings, government offices and British embassies abroad. This collection, combined with the works held by the National Gallery and the Royal Collection could be merged to form a new unified State Collection administered on a consistent basis. Such a restructuring could provide an opportunity for a new system of administration and maintenance, ensuring the widest possible access for a resource which belongs to the people of this nation.

7
Looking to the Future

Speak of next year and the devil laughs
Japanese proverb

In June 2012 the Queen announced that she had been 'touched deeply' and 'humbled' by the scale of the celebrations to mark her Diamond Jubilee. Sixty years on the throne is a rarity, not seen since her predecessor Queen Victoria. The monarchy would appear to enjoy at present a reasonably consistent and high level of support. It is also worth noting that whilst hundreds of thousands may have lined the Thames on June 3rd to watch the royal flotilla, and many organized their various celebratory events across the country, a great many did not. St Pancras was busy with tens of thousands queueing to board the Eurostar – and in airports too – keen to escape the celebrations. A superficial conclusion drawn from viewing the mainstream media's schedule-filling coverage of the Jubilee celebrations might be to assume that virtually every loyal subject – save for a tiny dissenting few – was standing in the rain, tiny Union flag in hand – cheering on their monarch.

So was the whole country celebrating? It is hard to tell. The fact must be accepted that those visibly cheering or celebrating were by definition a self-selecting audience. Save for republican protesters, all others were there because they wanted to be there to cheer – or at least catch a glimpse of – the Queen. Those who did not want to would, not surprisingly, have stayed away. There were also the many tourists – there to witness an event which to their eyes, who, as outsiders, might more easily be persuaded was one of a nation in its entirety celebrating its monarch's sixtieth year on the throne. Beyond those who made the effort to actually attend the events in London itself were those who watched the proceedings on television or online. In addition, one can add the vast numbers who attended local community events – the popularly acclaimed street-parties, beacon-lightings, and so on. But were all those attending fully paid-up monarchists? Doubtless the greater majority, but it is more than likely that there were many partners, neighbours and friends who were prepared to bite their lip, force a smile for the Queen and join in with those keener on the event than they were. Those of a more overt republican persuasion may find it hard to understand those who whilst holding a critical view of the monarchy may still be reluctant to air their true views as a result of strong social pressures.

Fear of 'rocking the boat' can still exist, even in 2012. Pressure from family members, work colleagues – possibly more so if in a senior position – and others, can mean that many lack the self-confidence to remain seated while everyone else stands for the national anthem. That latter practice has increasingly disappeared from everyday life, but large-scale events like the Jubilee or a royal wedding can still exercise a degree of pressure upon many to conform.

What does this tell us about monarchist – and republican – sentiment in 2012? It is true that republicans campaigned visibly, and were also accorded a higher profile than ever before. This has been part of a gradual development in the last two decades or so. It is noticeable that the BBC at least acknowledged the existence of views of the monarchy that were contrary to the perceived predominant norm. Those with long-term experience of republican campaigning note with satisfaction the loss of the taboo of openly challenging the monarchy in the early 1990s. This state of affairs, however, was not achieved easily. Since then, more reasoned discussion has become accepted in the media. That said, Britain remains a monarchist nation. When polled, a large majority support the monarchy, and the numbers have remained reasonably steady in recent years.

7 LOOKING TO THE FUTURE

It is a now a decade and a half since the death of Diana, Princess of Wales, a point at which it was by no means impossible that we might have witnessed the very demise of the monarchy. It is easy to forget that the pressure came then, ironically, from monarchists, not republicans. Since then, the Prince of Wales has sought to rehabilitate a poor public image, married his former mistress, and enjoys a limited degree of popular support. Prince William married Kate Middleton in 2011 and both enjoy a high level of popularity. So does William's brother, Harry. The Queen now has a greatly diminished workload and a lower public profile, but increasing her appearance levels for the 2012 Diamond Jubilee, for example. The Duke of York stood in for her on a tour of India in May 2012, for instance, and the Duke of Edinburgh, now over ninety, has not surprisingly reduced his workload, and was unable through ill-health to appear at all of the Jubilee celebrations.

Support for the monarchy remains high, though more likely to a large extent by default. For many, it is easier to 'go with the flow' than to actively dissent. After all, this is a monarchist nation. We have a monarchy, it represents the status quo. Most people in the country can remember only the present Queen as monarch. Acceptance is easier than dissent, especially in a nation in which reminders of monarchy are everywhere, hard wired into our institutions and in our cultural infrastructure. In the 1980s, the monarchy enjoyed high popular support, and this picture remained until the early 1990s, when the public learnt that the Queen paid virtually no tax. Following the Windsor fire, royal popularity slumped, and the Windsors struggled to regain popular support, whilst Diana, Princess of Wales' ratings soared. The greatest criticism of the Queen for her perceived lack of sympathy at the time of Diana's death came from the monarchist camp and might have led to the very down fall of the institution itself. Even monarchists can be fickle.

Huge royal events aside, when by definition the most loyal supporters will be out in force and the rest will find something else to do out of sight of the crowds and the cameras, perhaps the less many of the public see of the royal family; the more they are likely to tolerate them. In the case of the Queen, acceptance through her long-term presence, assisted in no small part by her age, which of itself is likely to elicit sympathy and tend to dilute any antipathy. Time, however, will tell whether the present levels of support are maintained. It is probably best to regard it merely as conditional upon presenting a image which is unchallenged by broader circumstances.

An innate conservatism helps the monarchy's continued acceptance, and is also assisted by a high level of tolerance. The public may object to overpaid bankers, but they refuse to countenance, for instance, any suggestion to reduce the heir to the throne's £17million a year income. There is almost a sense of wilful denial. 'But it's different…', '…he does so much for charity…', '…he's royal…', and so on. The Duchy incomes are scarcely seen as 'incomes', but as something else. Many may not realise that the Queen receives over £13million a year as an income from the state. Again, because she is the Queen, many feel the need for her to get a lot of money, and would not challenge this situation, unless an event of significance – like that in 1992 – presented itself. Even then, there might be considerable reluctance to even doubt their own beliefs.

UNCERTAIN ECONOMIC TIMES
The retention of a highly rich and highly rewarded monarchy will become increasingly harder to sustain as this country experiences the difficult economic climate affecting not merely Europe but the world. 'Great Britain' is far from immune from the continuing threats to the world financial system. The 'fog in Channel…Europe cut off' attitude will not save Britain. Banks – even British ones – are exposed to the toxic fall-out from the effects of a quarter of a century of financial deregulation on both sides of the Atlantic. Indeed, the City of London is at the very heart of the business of the financial alchemy which is still in the process of unravelling. British consumers hold far more unsecured credit card debt than all of those in the rest of Europe combined. Our housing market remains highly inflated – asset prices boosted by the inflow of money from across the globe who see the UK as a safe haven. It is 'safe' also because their money is welcomed, with fewer questions asked, and because – unlike Europe for example – we are reluctant to impose a financial transaction tax on an errant financial community. No-one should dare to assume that things will remain no worse than they are at present, let alone improve significantly. Banks have received billions of public money, to the extent that the government effectively owns some of our high-street banks, yet they resist pressure to lend to parts of our economy, not least small and medium sized businesses. Dissatisfaction levels are high, both with

banks and with politicians – neither of whom appear to have any real answers. The former are loathed, the latter discredited. The Government of the day may struggle, but neither are the Opposition seen as having the answers.

Serious unfolding economic problems will do little to help the British monarchy's cause in the long term. Growing inequality in the UK, worsening housing problems, and widespread youth unemployment do not bode well for a privileged and lavishly funded royal family. It is possible that Prince William has perceived that the Windsors may need to change fundamentally to survive – hence his present penchant for a low-key lifestyle – but his father continues to happily bask in his £17million a year income state-funded luxury. A glimpse of the potential dangers inherent in all this – an almost Marie Antoinette moment – was evident on December 9th 2010 when the Prince of Wales and his wife were caught up in part of the West End anti-tuition fee riots that night. Thousands of protesters were in London that day, with accompanying violent outbursts, and it was in the midst of this that Charles, ignoring police advice, insisted on making his way to a evening at the London Palladium theatre in a very conspicuous Rolls-Royce limousine. Scarcely less ostentatious than a gilded pumpkin-shaped pantomime horse-drawn coach, the car was attacked and the royal couple were put in genuine fear for their safety.

ANOTHER BIG FAT WINDSOR WEDDING...

The marriage of Prince William and Catherine Middleton in 2011 did see an undeniably high level of popular interest, though the institutionalised hard-wired element of state-sponsored festivity made it hard to avoid. An officially imposed public holiday meant that those who were less than enthused by the whole business could at least get away from those who actually wanted to celebrate the event – but for many it was an unwanted day off work, possibly without pay. Estimates of the cost to the nation of taking a day off have naturally varied, but it is widely accepted, as a raw subdivision of annual national GDP figures, to be a minimum of £2.5 billion a day, rising to as much as £5billion. The key juxtaposition of the royal wedding with other Bank holidays in the Easter period, however, with many companies forced to shut down production for a longer period than they would have wanted may have led the total loss to amount to as much as £30billion according to some estimates. Policing the 2011 royal wedding, according to a *Daily Mail* article, cost around £20million due to the heavy cost of overtime, while the government's Department of Culture Media and Sport put the figure at £10million – rather more than the £7.4million it cost to police the G20 protests in London in 2009. An inquiry to the Ministry of Defence (See Appendix) by a Mr Tony Flury elicited a response claiming that the 'marginal' cost to the MoD – including flypasts etc amounted to just £77,818. That doesn't seem a lot. Ring up a big events company for an estimate – or ask a film production company how much it would cost to actually put on a comparable Cecil B de Mille scaled extravaganza. The Home Office was responsible for security, not the MoD, and of course the cost of that is a secret we can't possibly be told…

…AND PUT OUT MORE JUBILEE FLAGS…

Monarchists may delight in the way in which Britain can put on a grand pageant. We may be great at 'pomp and circumstance', but sadly it may be one of the few remaining things we are actually any good at. The wedding may have provided a claimed £2billion boost to tourism, and a rise in the sales of alcohol and Chinese-made plastic flags, but the Confederation of British Industry estimated that the day itself cost the country £5billion, at a time when the economy could least afford to take the day off. A 'feel-good' factor perhaps, but when an economy is in serious recession it all smacks rather of self-delusion. June 2012, with the Queen's Diamond Jubilee celebrations featuring not one but two Bank holidays on June 4th and 5th, merely boosts the expense to a seriously struggling economy. By May 2012 the government, in the face of the nation's gloomier than expected economic performance, was itself conceding that the summer Bank holidays, including the extra royal 'celebrations', and the London Olympics, could knock as much as half a percentage point off the UK's predicted economic growth figures. Also, contrary to much popular belief, the nature of many employment contracts means that these extra Bank holidays can cost employees a day's pay. Many do not realise this, so the monarchy 'treating' the populace to yet another day off can impose a very heavy cost to those who can least afford to celebrate – and often don't know until some time after they have cleared up the flags and empty bottles and returned to work.

7 LOOKING TO THE FUTURE

THE IMPACT OF THE SOVEREIGN GRANT ACT

As Mao Zedong once said of the impact of the French revolution, it is too early to tell. The new Sovereign Grant Act will take effect from 2013. To what degree this new legislation will really affect the degree of funding for the monarchy – and with it public perception – naturally remains to be seen. Described by *Daily Mail* journalist Geoffrey Levy as the 'bombshell that nobody noticed', the announcement was slipped into Chancellor George Osborne's first Budget speech. Already, however, we can see that the new Sovereign Grant payments are rising significantly, given that the 2013 and 2014 figures are already set as they are based upon the Crown Estates profits for two years back.

Whilst the Act institutes a degree of accountability, it in some ways harks back to the pre-1760 arrangement, giving the monarchy access to a Sovereign Support Grant based on a 15% share of the profits of the £6.6billion Crown Estates property empire. As we have already seen, the Crown Estates do not 'belong' to the monarch – other than in the most tenuous titular sense – and certainly not in any way in a personal capacity, but one could be forgiven for thinking that that is the way that the royal family would like to see it. In no small part, the Prince of Wales' campaigning for a better deal – he would have liked the entire £200million plus annual Estates profits! – may have paid off. However, Parliament retains the upper hand, and can should it so wish, vary the percentage up – but also down. The monarchy benefits, for example, from the sale of offshore wind-farm licences granted by the Crown Estates – no wonder Charles is such a fan, not only on purely environmental grounds, but also from the licences granted for offshore aggregate extraction, something that many have blamed for increased rates of coastal erosion on England's east coast.

To argue as some have done that the new arrangement frees the monarchy from Parliamentary review is incorrect. Accountability would appear to be improved – a government minister will now be answerable in Parliament on matters pertaining to the monarchy. Some elements of the 1993 Memorandum of Understanding – the most recent document affecting some royal financial arrangements, but a non-statutory informal one – are now given statutory force. It is a start. However, the monarch and heir to the throne still pay their taxes on a voluntary basis – but are still exempt from inheritance tax. That remains a scandal.

Parliament may now possess improved statutory means to reign in a wayward monarch where it hurts most – in the wallet. But in truth, that has always been the case. What really matters is if they actually decide to exercise the power over the monarchy which they have always had. Parliament has the power, what it needs is the will to enforce that power should it be deemed necessary. Should Charles, as King, overstep his neutral remit, and intervene in a politically contentious fashion, parliamentary sanction could be swift and severe. The monarchy can take nothing for granted. In reality, the notion that the old system of ten-yearly review of royal finance was any better is way off the mark. In practice, debate was very limited indeed and of low profile, accompanied by the custom of general debate in the media being a generally taboo subject until the early 1990s. Parliamentary debate was generally shunted into the background and afforded little debating time. In practice, the monarchy will have to tread carefully, for in worsening economic times any sense that they are doing rather too well at public expense could yet engender a high degree of criticism.

PUBLIC OPINION

The monarchy would appear to be safe – for the present. On the basis of annual polls taken since 1993, support for the institution has averaged around 69-72%, with republicans polling around 18-20%. True to form, a Guardian-ICM poll in May 2012 reported that 69% believed that Britain would be 'worse off' without the monarchy, an admittedly rather vague question. 22% believed we'd be better off, and 9% didn't know. One could argue that the track record of the country hasn't been so great while the present Queen has been head of state, so how much worse could things be? The performance of successive governments has rather more bearing on the nation's level of success, but in our system people are apt to attribute also god-like powers to monarchs when in fact for most practical purposes a non-executive, largely ceremonial, hereditary head of state who has been in the position for six decades rather smacks more of institutionalised 'presenteeism'.

All that aside, polling shows us that there have been slight fluctuations but the overall picture is fairly consistent. Support for the Queen remains high, supporting the idea that she has been 'doing a good job' and with an overwhelming number assuming the monarchy will still be around in ten years. Talk of twenty years, however, and the doubts

7 LOOKING TO THE FUTURE

start to creep in. By then, it is obvious to any respondent that the Queen is unlikely to be around. In general, questions really revolve around an unchanging situation – the continuing presence of an existing monarch – in which the electorate have no power anyway to make any change to what is just a constitutional fait accompli – they aren't able to vote out a monarch. It is also noticeable that – perhaps it is not totally unexpected given the the fact that the British are so used to always having a monarch around – that when asked to imagine a president, who is likely to serve only one, or no more than two, five year terms, they think of the president as if they were simply another monarch. The idea that they would be voted in for just a few years, then to leave and replaced by someone else, never seems to be envisaged. The association of monarchical 'perpetuity' is transferred to a president, despite the reality of the transience of their position. Classic political 'hate figures' – eg. Tony Blair, are used by critics of a republican system, yet the reality is that he, for example, is so universally loathed that he would never be elected, assuming that he would dare to stand, and also there seems to be the worry that even if he did stand, he would be elected 'for ever' – (in the manner of a monarch).

Once you get around to the matter of the succession, however, then things start to look a little less clear cut. The May 2012 poll noted that when the Queen dies or abdicates 48% felt the throne should go to William – and only 39% sticking with Charles, the next in line, and 10% believed it would be an appropriate time to move to a republican system.

These figures all match past polling fairly consistently, which, taken together, convey a good general view of public sentiment. Doubt as to the monarchy's ability to survive in the longer term is demonstrated by past polling showing around half of monarchists who doubt the monarchy will still be around in twenty years time. Most people believe that the Queen should not retire, but it remains to be seen if future illness or infirmity will affect this view. This highlights a disconnect between much public sentiment and realism. For an institution that depends upon death to secure the promotion of the next officeholder, it would seem that these views simply reflect a form of procrastination and a reluctance to face facts.

The public are also very fickle. A Sunday Times-YouGov poll on June 10th 2012 attempted to measure popular feeling in the aftermath of the Jubilee. Two weeks before the Jubilee, 44% would have preferred William to become King in preference to his father, Charles, with only 38% backing the latter. A week after the event, however, the figures were exactly reversed. Beforehand, 47% deemed Prince Philip to be an 'asset' to the royal family, but a week after the Jubilee – and his mid-ceremony hospitalisation – the figure had risen to 58%, and those in favour of a monarchy rose to 75% after the celebrations.

A clear thread has appeared in polling for some time showing a division of monarchist support into two camps; William versus Charles. This isn't the traditional form of monarchist succession, for it shows a degree of uncertainty with the basic monarchical principle, that the next in line gets in. Instead, it shows a desire to keep the royal show on the road by backing the least worse candidate from a rather odd single family. It is a curious 'halfway house' between monarchy and republicanism, and far from convincing other than as a one-off stop-gap measure, perhaps only suitable as a transitionary step from one system to another. Polls have suggested that Prince Charles is felt by only a fraction over a half of the population as likely to be a 'good King'- whatever that rather fairy-tale description is really intended to convey. With a similar number opposed to his wife being called 'Queen', Clarence House has pre-empted further disappointing ratings in future by announcing that the Duchess of Cornwall would apparently prefer to known as 'Princess Consort'[1]. In the opinion of constitutional expert Robert Blackburn, 'whatever title a husband or wife of the head of state is given is purely titular and ceremonial' ('King and Country: Monarchy and the future King Charles III') That was a while ago, it is likely that, when the time comes, the mainstream media will still announce her as 'Queen Camilla'. Given the largely unwritten nature of our constitution, this reflects the ad hoc manner in which the monarchy has made constant 'adjustments' and invented titles to suit the occasion and expediency. 'Tradition' in respect of the monarchy is an extremely flexible concept.

SUCCESSION: THE ULTIMATE STRESS POINT

Successions are the ultimate stress points for any dynasty. Like a general election for a democratic government, they are the test of public acceptance. The problem for the British monarchy is that it is now so out of step with the present age – and the manner of supine acceptance of hereditary succession which is unlikely to be tolerated as in the past – that any adjustment could severely test its very existence. The present Queen represents a monarchy of publicly funded privilege and great wealth far from the everyday realities of the vast majority of the population. Yet the carefully honed public image which portrays a woman of simple and restrained tastes is plainly at variance with the reality of the situation. Her grandson, William, and his wife are keen to portray an image of their lifestyle as simple and unpretentious. Whilst this may be relatively easy whilst pursuing an RAF career and living in Anglesey largely out of the public eye, it remains to be seen how things play out in the longer term. The plain veneer conceals a rich interior. Meanwhile, through this period, rising inequality in British society, strikingly evident since the beginning of the 1960s[2] has been worsening in the final decade of the 20th century, and beyond[3]. The gap between rich and poor is widening, and much of the perceived prosperity is founded upon highly inflated asset values and unprecedented levels of consumer debt. The severe economic downturn could yet prove critical indeed for the monarchy, as it did in the early 1990s.

Britain is also a fundamentally different society from that of the 1950s, and a much more diverse nation. Consequently, the very notion of allegiance becomes a very much more complex one than it was over half a century ago. Ethnic diversity, as well as the globalisation of communications media, means that the horizons of the ordinary citizen extend much further than in the past. The simple, traditional notion of loyalty to 'Queen and country' no longer exists. Used to choice in every other facet of life, will the British tolerate being simply presented with their next head of state, no questions asked? With increased population mobility, citizenship itself has almost become a consumer product – especially for the rich who are able to 'fast-track' their citizenship applications to get into the UK. Within this climate, the 'New Elizabethan' monarchy draws to its close. The Queen, embodiment of the past, ages perceptibly, reduces her official commitments, and prepares her eldest son for the changeover.

SUCCESSION BY STEALTH: 'A SORT OF REGENCY'

The Queen's noticeable absence from the country's VE Day ceremony in the spring of 2005 was evidence of a reduction in the ageing monarch's workload. The Prince of Wales appeared on her behalf. This was one of the first major events to signify the gradual retirement from her duties. In January 2006 an announcement of a planned reduction of the Queen's duties in favour of Prince Charles appeared in the media as the Queen approached her eightieth birthday[4]. However, this reduction in duties is less compatible with the role and responsibilities of a head of state. *The Sunday Mirror* reported a 'royal insider' as saying:

> This isn't an abdication, but it involves *a sort of regency*. We will have a monarch on the throne in good health but who only comes out for state occasions like the opening of Parliament and Trooping the Colour, and a second-in-command who runs the shop and will do investitures, foreign trips, and everything else. [Author's italics]

A second-hand statement from a Palace courtier sufficed to gloss over the responsibilities of a head of state who exercises critical reserve prerogative and statutory powers – and very considerable influence, both in the social and cultural heirarchy, and as Commander-in-Chief of the armed forces.

There was another reason: the need by the Palace to boost the less than high esteem in which the heir to the throne and his wife are held by the public. A gradual handover of responsibilities from the Queen to the Prince of Wales was the least controversial way in which to encourage improved acceptability. This process could almost be called a 'controlled abdication' – so elegantly described in the French media as 'une abdication en douceur' – a 'gentle' or 'soft' abdication[5]. Whatever it is called, the process raises a number of very serious concerns. Normally, the accession to the role of the head of state is a very definite and instant process. There can be no half-measures, no ambiguities. It is a sharply defined line in the constitutional sand. This time a kind of informal assumption of regal duties would seem to be taking place.

The family nature of an hereditary succession combined with an unwritten constitution could be said to encourage an almost 'informal' attitude in relation to matters which should properly be regulated by statute, not precedent or 'understandings'. The distinctions between the 'private' and the 'public' dimensions of the incumbents are blurred. The fact that Britain has been relatively free from major internal crises in the recent past tends to encourage a degree of complacency with regard to those powers. Firstly, the very possession of the office enables the incumbent to have a high degree of influence. As Edgar Wilson observed, the monarch is able to 'determine events indirectly through advice, force of personality, and the prestige attached to the office'⁶. To those who assert that the monarch would never use such powers but would defer to the government of the day, it should not be forgotten that the Prince of Wales has made clear that, had he been monarch, he would not have given Royal Assent to the legislation banning hunting with dogs. The fact that a constitutional crisis would have been provoked does not mean that he would simply back down. That, however, takes us into relatively uncharted constitutional territory, but it would be virtually 'suicidal' for the monarch, and possibly their dynasty.

DANGERS OF FUTURE CONFLICT

The traditional avoidance of intervention in the political arena, is only a convention, but failure to comply with it may lead to considerable problems. Edward VIII's abdication was as much occasioned by the then government's concern with his proven record of politically contentious statements and behaviour as with his choice of wife – divorced or not. Prince Charles has demonstrated a continuing propensity to intervene in sensitive areas and it might only be a matter of time before this resurfaces and creates such tension between Clarence House and the government that some kind of showdown occurs. Criticism of the Prince's opinions can provoke quite disproportionate 'outrage' from a minority. Yet in the deferential atmosphere that still exists, even a relatively insignificant comment challenging his pronouncements can provoke controversy.

In November, 2004, as a result of an employment tribunal hearing in which more of the Prince's personal views were revealed, inferring that people should 'know their place' the then Education Secretary Charles Clarke, took issue with the Prince's comments, arguing that the heir to the throne was hostile to the ambitions of ordinary people. His firm belief in a 'natural order' had been voiced before, notably by means of direct approach to a man at the heart of the Government's plans to introduce the Human Rights Act – Lord Irvine, the former Lord Chancellor. Prince Charles' criticism of the Act demonstrated a man uncomfortable with the notions of rights for the population as a whole, the legislation encouraging people, he felt, 'to take up causes which will make the pursuit of a sane, civilised and ordered existence ever more difficult'⁷.

Here was the heir to the throne in effect seeking to challenge legislation which would, he obviously felt, challenge his own particular notions of an 'ordered' world, one that better supported his selective views and which, conveniently, supported his own privileged position. Strangely, Charles' secretary Michael Peat, has claimed that the Prince 'is always careful to avoid party political and contentious issues'. That there may be instances where his views are more in line with popular opinion – the environment for example – should not be allowed to obscure the fact that his unique constitutional position should preclude the public articulation of such views.

VALUE FOR MONEY?
It is often asserted that one of the principal benefits of the monarchy – indeed frequently cited as one of the key justifications for its retention – is that the institution is 'good for tourism' and as such that it therefore 'pays its way'. Despite the virtual impossibility of such justification in quantifiable terms, the use of a quasi-commercial imperative has grown. An increased belief in the need for many public institutions to somehow justify themselves in market terms has developed. Many people, indeed, seem to forget that the monarch performs a legal, constitutional function as head of state, instead seeing it only as a decorative, 'heritage' institution, a mere offshoot of the tourist industry. The old argument, based upon the 'surrendering' of Crown Estates revenues in exchange for the Civil List payment (and from 2013 its Sovereign Grant replacement), that those revenues more than justify any royal expense, can be safely disregarded by now[8], but that does not stop it being wheeled out regularly to justify the claim that the institution somehow doesn't cost us anything.

The 'cost benefit' argument is a very recent one. In a political climate that has seem extensive 'marketisation' of the public realm and the commercial 'outsourcing' of many functions undertaken in the past by purely municipal and government institutions, then it is perhaps not so surprising that supporters of the monarchy have added this argument to their defensive arsenal. Margaret Thatcher instilled a sense of the price of every government function, though whether privatisation achieved the hoped-for improvements in formerly public services, from water to trains, is another matter. Public subsidy is still needed to keep them all on track, and to factor in a profit margin – and their directors' bonuses – and, if things go really pear-shaped, then the government would still have to step in to clear up the mess by writing out the cheques.

7 LOOKING TO THE FUTURE

The claim from the Palace and their supporters is clear. The tourists watching the 'Changing of the Guard' would never have bothered to come to the UK or its capital city if we didn't have a royal family. Somehow the French manage to pack out the Palace of Versailles all year round and they manage to run their country without a monarchy. It used to be said that the UK's 'Special Ambassador for Trade', the Duke of York, did so much for our export trade, but he became such an embarrassment that he had to step down. Will our trade figures now worsen without him? Germany operates a far healthier export economy than we do, and has done so for a very long time, without either the Duke of York, allegedly 'batting for Britain', or a royal yacht. And would no-one donate money to good causes without a royal 'patron' to front the operation. Are these royal icons really so indispensable and so good for exports?

One can quite easily change the Guard – as is usually the case – without a monarch. The Queen is seldom to be seen anyway, hardly ever in fact. The reality is far more prosaic: a favourable exchange rate and an appealing tourist culture as a whole are more likely to lure foreign visitors than an invisible monarch. Indeed, a report by national tourist body VisitBritain in October 2007 put low visitor numbers in the preceding summer down to just that, an unfavourable exchange rate – and poor weather.

As for international trade, a middle-aged former helicopter pilot with his mind on the next golf tournament could never have been seriously regarded as any match for competitive products and 'soft' loans. The real work of 'banging the drum' for the nation has in recent times been performed by the former head of the CBI, Sir Digby Jones, recruited by Prime Minister Gordon Brown because he felt the job of trade promotion needed to be performed by 'someone who knew about business'. The Duke of York's qualifications appeared to have been a fondness for international travel and, having retired very early, far too much time on his hands. Add to that an over-supply of self-importance and simply being a senior royal – not necessarily unrelated factors – and you have the classic ingredients for what was in effect an overblown, pretentious, self-appointed role of exceedingly dubious value[9].

Past research has even tended to suggest that a high-profile royal visit – rare as they are – to whatever destination has been chosen, may be followed by a drop in trade rather than the reverse[10]. If the Duke of York visited a Tesco food processing plant in Eastern Europe it was

243

more an official acknowledgement of the realities of economic life and a recognition of a trading 'fait accompli' that simply confirmed modern commercial practice and the impact of globalisation. The transnational corporation will not alter its trading policies whether a B-list royal 'celebrity' appears or not.

Recently, the blend of poor economic performance in the UK, blended with 'extra' Bank holidays to celebrate Royal weddings and Jubilees, have begun to be openly analysed in terms of their effect on the nation's economy itself. When an institution is able by its constitutional status to impose serious costs that impinge on economic growth and performance, then the estimated cost of the monarchy can rise enormously. Far from being around £170million a year, as we have seen earlier in Chapter Two, that cost can rise to nearer half a billion pounds a year. As the recession bites – and we have yet to feel the effects of ongoing problems in the Eurozone – such considerations could yet reverberate unfavourably on the monarchy.

Often lost in the argument is the simple fact that all one needs is a Head of State, and yet this elaborate institution has grown to the point where its enormous expense has to be justified on a whole array of other levels. Even monarchy advocate David Starkey has admitted that it is now 'too big'. Its function can, after all – and in a great many countries is – performed by one person for a really quite moderate cost. The justification of an unelected, hereditary position in an otherwise democratic nation is impossible to justify on rational grounds, and it is perhaps a reflection of increasingly market-orientated solutions in areas of public life that a commercial justification for the retention of such an institution is now often raised as a defence. Evidence is, by its nature, harder to quantify, and the matter really becomes emotive rather than empirical. Monarchists, at least in the first instance, appear to be prepared to pay almost anything to keep the royal family in the manner to which they have become accustomed. However, in times of stress, they can be far less forgiving. In 1992, the revelation that the Queen had paid virtually no tax in her entire reign caused widespread outrage.

A FUTURE MONARCH

In order for the monarchy to continue to be acceptable to the people of this country, it will be necessary for the institution to change. The fact that the heir to the throne has already begun to assume some of the duties of the ageing monarch raises a number of considerations which are of profound constitutional importance. In a democracy, this matter should be subject to a proper process of consultation, but it is surprising that even some Members of Parliament persist in regarding the monarchy as somehow 'different' and that it should be beyond normal scrutiny, even in terms of any proposed reform process. In response to a question for the first edition of this book, the then Conservative Spokesman for Constitutional Affairs, Oliver Heald, said that the Conservative Party had no plans to examine the powers and role of the monarchy, despite the currently low popularity of the heir to the throne and the Palace's own recognition that a new monarch would need to enjoy a high degree of public support to be viable: 'We have no proposals for reforms to the Monarchy, though even if we had you will be aware that it is accepted practice that these would never be made public prior to being agreed privately with the Monarch herself'[11].

The reference to 'accepted practice' refers to the vagaries of the unwritten British constitution in which fundamentally important changes to the role and conduct of the monarch can be 'arranged' without reference to our democratically elected representatives. The next time, and there will almost definitely be a next time, that the financial and tax arrangements for the monarch and the heir to the throne are questioned, will Parliament – and the public, be as prepared to be kept 'out of the loop' as they were in 1992 when the House of Commons was presented with no more than a *fait accompli*? Whilst the Sovereign Grant Act passed through Parliament relatively little noticed, it now sets arrangements for Parliamentary accountability firmly on a statutory level.

TOO MANY, TOO MUCH

Current arrangements tend to encourage a large 'extended' royal family. A large number of often very questionable appointments demands a large number of walk-on participants – a rather self-perpetuating situation really. There seems no logical justification for the retention of any other members of the royal family in any official capacity. The extended nature of the family means that the considerable multiplication of supposed roles and staffing leads to an unnecessarily large and costly institution. More appropriately scaled, it would require for practical purposes only the role of Head of State and that of an official deputy – the heir to the throne – with legally defined duties.

All 'minor' royals should cease to receive any Parliamentary allowances. These are now, with the exception of that payable to the Duke of Edinburgh – presently reimbursed by the Queen. A clear break with any official positions or duties – and expenses – for these individuals, should take place. Any specific housing benefits such as those relating to their present access to Crown Estate properties should cease. Their involvement with existing charities, for example, would be unaffected but a matter for private arrangement, possibly funded by the respective charities themselves. These bodies might also be required to pay a fee for the use of the royal titles borne by their patrons. They would thus be able to continue the valuable contribution for which they have become recognised in recent years.

PRINCE CHARLES: BUSIER AND BUSIER?
The Prince of Wales's high spending of about £6.5million on 'official' duties and 'charitable activities' in the financial year 2005-06 was excused by his private secretary – also key financial adviser and director of 'Duchy Originals' – Sir Michael Peat, saying there was 'not much that could be done to make savings…. We're in a difficult situation. We're always trying to make savings and be more efficient…', but then adding that '[t]he Prince gets busier and busier' as a justification for the large sum[12]. The fact that the heir to the throne is dashing around, consuming expensive resources, at an ever faster rate, does not of itself justify such behaviour. Indeed, one could argue that such frantic behaviour tends to imply a high degree of insecurity. Like someone performing an absurd plate-spinning act, the Prince probably feels that to do any less would provoke such levels of criticism that his present – and future – position might easily become unacceptable to the public.

Sir Michael's comment that Clarence House 'now employs 142 full and part-time staff', insisting that this was small compared with staffing levels at Buckingham Palace, demonstrates the wasteful and uncoordinated nature of the entire royal set-up. 'We have about a fifth of the staff', he continued, 'and we do more engagements and entertain the same number of people…. In terms of staff, we're actually very lean'. This would suggest that, firstly, the heir to the throne's over-elaborate and expensive lifestyle needs reform, but that also

Buckingham Palace is itself excessively grandiose and grossly inefficient. And don't forget those figures are from a few years ago – since then a further 16.9 'full-time equivalent' staff are needed to keep Prince Charles' show on the road.

The fact that an heir to the throne exists is itself a logical product of an hereditary system. This, however, does not automatically mean that such an heir should thereby become the recipient of public money, nor necessarily in the quantities deemed necessary in the present British system. All the more so in the absence of any statutorily defined role to accompany that status. An acceptance of the position of the heir as the official deputy to the monarch should impose on that person a clear contractual arrangement. It would be a recognition of the practical need for someone to share any such duties as head of state as and when the incumbent was unable to perform them – without resorting to the specific need to appoint a 'Regent'. It would also impose a clear contractual acceptance by the heir of their constitutional responsibilities which they could inherit at any time. The heir would undertake to pursue their duties with a commitment to political neutrality in the same way as that required of the monarch. Failure to comply with this requirement would entail resignation from the position.

WILL CHARLES BE ACCEPTABLE AS KING?

This is the ultimate question that must one day be answered. When the Prince of Wales' mother became Queen the succession was regarded as an inevitable process. This time, public acceptability for the Prince – recognised as being less than wholehearted at present – is crucial, and were it to remain at such a level it is more than possible that it would be difficult for the public to accept him as the next head of state. Half a century ago, public opinion polls were a rarity, but now they are numerous and persuasive in terms of measuring the views of the public on a wide range of matters. Today, the imminent prospect of a new monarch would be accompanied by the appearance of a wide range of internet polls, phone-in radio programmes and so on. From accredited polling organisations as well as the growing power of social media such as Twitter, opinion will be voiced in a manner scarcely envisaged a few years ago – let alone six decades. It may not have happened at the time of the last Coronation, but at the next one the prospect of a 'Do you want Charles as King?', or a 'William or Charles? – 'you decide' debate that could run for months in the media will be certain. This will change the very nature of the accession of the next head of state, previously merely a given, and will instead make popular consent a vital ingredient. Failure of the heir to the throne to obtain consistently high support ratings in such polls will be of vital significance.

Constitutional expert Robert Blackburn, writing on the likely future scenario for Charles as King, feels that his accession will also 'radically change the context for modernisation and reform of the monarchy'[13]. From his outspokenness on matters with a political dimension to his difficulties in fulfilling a credible role as Supreme Governor of the Church of England, Charles is far removed from his mother in the manner in which he is likely to behave, but, just as importantly, in the manner in which he is perceived by the British people. Whereas his mother acceded to the throne at a young age, newly married and in a nation anxious to celebrate a new post-war era, Charles will do so in front of a nation that has seen him, often in a far from flattering light, over a period of many decades, and through less credulous, more sceptical media-aware eyes.

Conservative Constitutional Affairs spokesman Oliver Heald, questioned for the first edition of this book in 2008, was confident that a change of role for the Prince, from heir to King, would bring about an overnight transformation:

> Once he accedes to the Throne, however, the Prince of Wales accepts that his role will change and that it would no longer be appropriate for him to express his views in public. He will of course continue to discuss the issues of the day in his audiences with the Prime Minister but within the strictly defined conventions of our constitution.

Heald believed that as long as he does not 'intervene in a way that demonstrates any kind of party political bias' then all will be well, again placing his reliance upon the fact that it 'has long been accepted within our constitution' – again an assumption that, within the confines, such as they are, of our unwritten constitution – everything will fine[14].

Others may be less easily convinced. Let us not forget that the last 'People's Prince' – the man who was, briefly, to become Edward VIII – was regarded as unacceptable by the establishment not so much for his wish to marry a divorcee than as a result of his frequent outspoken political statements which brought him into conflict with the government of the day, and a marked unwillingness to abide by 'accepted' practice. Whatever his or her personal beliefs, and no matter whether one agrees with them or not, the reality is that not only the role of monarch but also that of the heir to the throne should be one of clear political neutrality. Personal beliefs must be put aside entirely in favour of the public role. This may seem difficult to accept, but it is a fundamental condition of the job, and the very essence of the notion of public duty. The Prince has also displayed a disconcerting degree of inconsistency in his personal opinions. Whilst he has made no secret of his support for the Dalai Lama and the campaign for a free Tibet he has also supported far less desirable figures – such as King Mzwati III of Swaziland, an autocrat with a poor human rights record. Perhaps a case of royal blood being thicker than water. His attempt to intervene through royal connections in the Chelsea Barracks planning affair also highlights his propensity to interfere through less than democratic means.

In cases such as these, Prince Charles displays the very traits which make him so unsuitable to become the Head of State of a modern European democracy. Whilst his office has protested that such partiality will cease immediately he becomes King, this is rather hard to believe.

Indeed, does this mark the utter cynicism of someone who, whilst they presently flaunt their supposedly deeply-held principles, is prepared to immediately suppress them on succeeding to the throne? The dividing line between 'duty' and deceit then becomes very narrow and the suspicion of 'behind-the-scenes' partiality will always remain. All this points to a man who is unable to separate his private sentiments from his public duty – a fundamental requirement of a non-executive head of state. His unashamed self-promotion, pet causes and commercial projects run the risk of sitting awkwardly with his future role as the politically neutral head of state of a parliamentary democracy. The image he projects tends more to that of some selectively benign 'beneficent ruler'. Promoting himself as a 'charitable entrepreneur', his privileged position is enabled by his publicly funded status and virtually non-existent levels of proper scrutiny.

THE UNWRITTEN CONSTITUTION

It should be remembered that Britain has an unwritten constitution. Although large parts are set in statute law, fundamentally the system is a flexible forest of custom and precedent. When we come to the monarchy, this is augmented by a large element of quaint and pseudo-historical terminology and supposed royal 'protocol'. Much of this is periodically to be encountered at times of royal occasion or ceremony. Constitutional 'experts' – often of a keen monarchical persuasion, will intone in a peculiar tone which the British often adopt when talking to – or about – the royal family, that a particular bit of Palace protocol is 'how these things are done', when in fact there is little precedent or it is of far more recent historical provenance than might at first be inferred.

Such flexibility extends far beyond what colour of silk breeches to wear at a Coronation, or whatever. Constitutional expert Robert Blackburn has emphasised that, in practice, as this is dependent upon mere 'tradition', then making changes is easy. In his book 'King and Country', he notes that '...the weight of constitutional tradition today is of a far lighter nature' than when the present Queen 'ascended' the throne. A coronation is also not needed to legitimise the new monarch, and in his opinion it will in practice be the Prime Minister's Office which will ultimately decide upon matters of dispute as to royal lineage and a new monarch's accession. One might perhaps think that the new Supreme Court ought to adjudicate on such matters, but as with all things constitutional in the UK, it is very flexible and evolving territory.

CRACKS IN THE FACADE

The British are, at heart, a conservative nation, and no more so in their attachment to the concept of monarchy. However, the cracks are already clearly evident. The crucial fact is that, ahead of any succession, the public have been far from reluctant to express their doubts as to the suitability of the present heir to the throne. This is unprecedented, for whilst some monarchs in the past may have been unpopular, there was a general acceptance of their right to be the monarch. The electorate are used to the concept of democratic choice, as well the development in consumer choice. The old idea of a 'natural' order, in which one's place in society was largely pre-ordained, has gone, and the right to assert choice is everywhere. We may have even moved beyond 'traditional' meritocracy, as the rise of the 'celebrity' culture conveys the idea that ordinary individuals, regardless of actual skill, qualification or ability in any particular sphere, may attain fame and financial success simply for 'being' themselves. Many are actually

7 LOOKING TO THE FUTURE

famous for being flawed or even deeply dysfunctional. However, all face a high degree of public approval to maintain their position.

The idea that the next British head of state will be presented as a *fait accompli* does not now accord with people's experience in other areas, least of all the civic arena. Elizabeth II may have been accepted in 1952, but in the course of over sixty years we are now a world away from the Britain which celebrated her accession to the throne. In 1994 Buckingham Palace formed it's 'Way Ahead' Group, to plan and coordinate their response to growing demands for change. By this time the republican movement had emerged, free of the hitherto 'taboo' way in which the subject had been treated in the media, and had garnered considerable support and respectability as a valid and viable cause. While republican support in the country has remained in the minority, this has been in part due to the traditionally low level of constitutional awareness and education in the UK, and is still a area in which numerous misconceptions persist. Several years ago the 'Way Ahead' group suggested that there could be an 'affirmative vote' to register approval of the new monarch by the people. But what if they said 'No'? An election with one candidate is a curious concept. Besides what would happen if the turn-out was so low as to render the result so effectively discredited that it would lack validity? It would be the final acknowledgement that in the modern, democratic world, the concept of the traditional hereditary monarchy does not automatically guarantee a suitable successor. It is the ultimate admission that the genetic lottery does not provide an acceptable winner every time. Opinion polls – and increasingly social media – have become the modern barometer of public approval, and poor ratings around the time of a succession might condemn Charles to a reign of dubious legitimacy.

SKIPPING A GENERATION: WILLIAM V – THE 'BUDGET' KING?

By the end of April 2005 a 'Times/Populus poll' confirmed that the Royal family had further declined in the estimation of the British public. Usually, approval ratings climb in the aftermath of a Royal wedding, but following Charles and Camilla's nuptials, which had recently taken place, this was not the case, with a mere 24% approving of the decision to marry. Rather more, 27%, actually disapproved, but a whopping 62% just didn't care at all. One was reminded of Oscar Wilde's words, that 'if there is one thing worse than being talked about, it is not being talked about'. At this rate, if Charles were to become King, few might be tempted to make the effort to turn up at his Coronation at all. But within the figures there was worse news too for the monarchist camp. A solid 18% now believed that the monarchy should finish at the end of the present Queen's reign, a figure that had shown up in previous polling. In addition, royal support now continued to show, as in the past, a division between those 31% who want tradition to be maintained and Charles to become King, and 39% who want to skip a generation and see William on the throne.

William might also prove amenable to possible demands for a 'slimmed down' monarchy in a way that his father probably never would. With a demonstrably less lavish lifestyle than his father, and increasing popularity since his marriage, he could project a less elitist image of royalty. His wife Kate, now Duchess of Cambridge, certainly projects a down-to-earth image, and does not come from the customary aristocratic/royal background. However, it is interesting to note the degree to which opinion of Charles' sons has fluctuated. Whilst their military service may earn them approval points from the public, accusations of favouritism – notably William's 'fast-track' flight training, as well as the use of military helicopters for personal use, criticised no less by some members of the RAF have arisen. Beyond that military career, however, it may become harder to keep a low profile – and thus dodge the critics. Harry's 'night-clubbing' escapades have detracted somewhat, but his own active military service image has proved popular.

Both William and Harry have fallen back on that royal mainstay popularity booster – charity. This includes the endangered wildlife species charity 'Tusk', and Harry in particular has a greater involvement with charities involving the military disabled. Whether this will ensure consistent support, however, can never be guaranteed. Not even William can take a high level of public support entirely for granted, although he has appeared genuinely able to live a rather more modest lifestyle than his father, and the popularity of his wife – not to mention the inherited popularity of his late mother – has helped to boost him in the eyes of the public. His late mother's money has also given him a financial boost too. By June 2012 he was thought to be in line to receive around £10million from her estate as a result of having reached his 30th birthday.

The Windsors cannot take anything for granted – and most certainly not even their popularity. As a result, we may move to situation where the Palace may try to present two 'candidates' next time around, in order to seek to circumvent a potentially embarrassing slump in support with Charles taking the throne. In an uncertain world, being seen to benefit too well will not help their cause, and the different individuals project different qualities – or drawbacks – in PR terms. Even the form of the royal family's turn-out on the Buckingham Palace balcony at the closing stage of the Jubilee celebrations has been seen as a future indicator of the scale and form of the monarchy. Robert Hazel, of University College London, speaking on BBC Radio4's 'Today' programme on June 7th believed that the presence of just the Queen (the Duke of Edinburgh was still in hospital), the Prince of Wales and his wife, the Duchess of Cornwall, Prince William, his wife the Duchess of Cambridge, and Prince Harry, represented a newer, slimmed-down Windsor line-up. The Princess Royal, the Earl and Countess of Wessex, for example, and other 'fringe' royals were absent. So was this a coded indicator of a future 'budget' monarchy? If so, then the budget is still pretty large, and just because some of the players were absent did not mean that much in itself. The new Sovereign Grant Act arrangements change little, certainly in the next few years, for the amount of money available to run the monarchy will remain essentially the same as at present – although it would seem to increase handsomely in the next couple of years already. Besides that, the Queen and the heir to the throne will get their £31million plus combined income from the Duchies.

Ultimately, it will probably come down to money. A government forced to make further economies in difficult times may have to force the monarchy to accept a reduced deal. Then it will be a case of who is prepared to do the job for less. The next place on the throne could well go to the lowest bidder, and on present trends, William might well be prepared to undercut his rather less popular father.

GIVING UP?

It is possible that were matters brought to a head now or in the very near future, the Prince of Wales might consider that the game is not worth it after all. The 'down-sizing' of his income in the future might be enough to lead him to decide that the throne no longer resembles the luxury seat he had anticipated inheriting. Prince Charles has made it quite clear in the past that he would give up his right to the throne if there were 'undue pressure' or 'swingeing taxation'[15] insisting that he needed 'a degree of financial independence from the state'. So, is it a case of the selfless performance of public duty, or 'Give me lots of money or I'm not interested'?

Charles has succeeded, albeit with some difficulty much of the time, to be acceptable as King whilst he remains 'in waiting'. His charitable works help keep the critics at bay and promote a sense of royal 'business as usual'. Any interference in the political arena could precipitate a real constitutional crisis in which the very future of the monarchy would be at stake. Nevertheless, Charles epitomises an outdated image – of a Windsor dynasty that seems more at home in the mid-twentieth century than the twenty-first. Time will tell if he is able to resist the temptation to speak on matters which overlap with the political world. He has promised, as monarch, not to say anything contentious, whilst his private secretary has claimed that he has never said any such thing in the past. The prospect of Charles as monarch still remains a less than attractive product to sell to the British people.

THE UNCROWNED KING

A likely scenario: Charles will continue to be paraded as the future King. In this way the current line of succession is not affected, and it avoids introducing further uncertainty and opportunity for attempts at reform of the institution. Meanwhile, for as long as possible, the pretence that the Queen is still functioning as day-to-day monarch will continue to be promoted. Not difficult at present, but a few years on and this could be a very different matter. Monarchists have a habit of assuming that the object of their affections is all but immortal, but sooner or later, the grim reaper comes calling. This is where the twist in the tale takes place.

At some point in this 'phoney monarchy' period – the period between accession and coronation – Charles, the 'Pensioner Prince', by then enjoying poor opinion poll approval ratings, will make the announcement that, despite his whole life having been focused toward the moment of his Coronation as King, and his innate sense of duty to the people of the nation, he will, though with deep regret, step down in favour of his son, William. Ostensibly for the reason that he feels that a new era would be best served by a newer, younger monarch. Dressed up in all manner of personal angst and talk of 'sacrifice', Charles will thus abdicate within a year of becoming King.

7 LOOKING TO THE FUTURE

In doing so, it may well be because the Windsor family believes – as it has probably already done so for some considerable time already – that their long-term future will be more secure in the hands of a younger generation. Indeed, the Queen could require Charles' relinquishment of the throne as a precondition of his financial inheritance. William is more popular than his father, and were he to succeed sooner rather than much later, the monarchy could perceive itself secure for another half a century. Were Charles to remain as King, however, another succession could present itself within a couple of decades, and with all the associated risks that that might entail. It might even be the risk that even William decides that he simply doesn't want the job after all, or for other negative events to present themselves. The possibility of Scottish independence might mean the consequent need to reconfigure what remains of the United Kingdom, and the down-sized version might simply be more suited to a more modest royal couple like William and Kate. Prince Charles, looking like a pantomime potentate in fake medals with a wife who is far from comfortable with public appearances, represents an outdated version an 'old' imperial style Windsor brand which is now long past its sell-by date.

Money, always a most significant factor, could play a crucial part in Palace thinking. With the possibility of restrictions on royal finances, were economic conditions to worsen further, might mean that, as he has said in the past, Charles might simply no longer want the job. Also, for Charles to step down early could, if current tax treatment applies, be a smart move – with no tax on inheritance or 'transfers' still in force from the 1993 Memorandum of Understanding. The present monarch and heir could yet face a reduction in their Duchy incomes – or a more fundamental re-arrangement – and this might prompt Charles to re-evaluate his future. This scenario may explain why, despite having possibly had doubts about becoming King – and this has often been suggested, including by the late Princess of Wales – Prince Charles has not, and would not, dare risk saying so until after he actually becomes King. To do so any sooner would mean ceasing to become the heir to the throne, and would mean no longer receiving the multi-million pound income from the Duchy of Cornwall. Once King, under the remaining terms of the 1993 agreement, a big chunk of his mother's wealth could be bequeathed to him free of inheritance tax. His money safe, he could then abdicate. He would still go down in the history books as King, but the Windsor dynasty – bigger than any individual monarch – would have rendered its future safer than in the hands of someone who might have the propensity to challenge Parliament at some stage and risk a constitutional crisis, which could be disastrous for the monarchy's long-term future.

THE FINANCIAL CRUNCH

Pressure on the financial front could well arise – as it did in the early 1990s – at a time of economic uncertainty for the population as a whole. There are increasing concerns at the high levels of boardroom pay and the 'bonus' culture, with top British executives earning many millions annually, and with increasing differentials too; often a hundred times more than most of the staff they employ. Banks, bailed out by the taxpayer, have still handed out lavish bonuses, but the stripping of RBS chief Fred Goodwin's knighthood showed that patience was wearing thin, and the 2012 'Shareholder Spring' has further demonstrated the shift in the public mood. The Prince of Wales continued to prosper, for instance, in a year when house prices started to fall, the rate of house repossessions started to rise again and the customers of Northern Rock queued to take their money out. As happened twenty years ago, with an economy in recession, and wider threats to the Eurozone and the global financial system, sympathy for a royal family who still receive multi-million pound earnings from the state may well evaporate in more difficult economic times.

Governments have a habit of trying to defer decisions on royal finance. Not only is it an area which deference dictates is rather too 'unseemly' for general political discussion and less than compatible with ideas of the supposed 'dignity' of the institution, but it does also tend to bring out the critics. Ever-present, but increasingly outspoken, they no longer belong to what was once considered the eccentric fringe of the political landscape. Indeed, much criticism in the past has come from the more conservative – and Conservative – elements in Westminster. As a rule of thumb, it is usually the incumbent administration which wishes to avoid a fuss, and the opposition which seeks to capitalise upon it. Depending upon prevailing public opinion, the opposition would generally play the patriotic card, but might seek to take up a more reformist agenda in the face of a government with a poor popularity rating. The issue could have the potential to cause friction like no other, which means that solutions designed to push

7 LOOKING TO THE FUTURE

the problem into some point in the future when the current administration won't be around to deal with it, are generally preferred.

SOME REFORMS AT LAST?

Whilst money traditionally forms the focus for any reform of the monarchy, there are signs that the discussion of the monarchy's political powers are now no longer taboo. In February 2006, the new Conservative leader, David Cameron, announced that his party was considering fundamental changes by removing many of the royal prerogative powers[16]. In fact, his party's new 'democracy taskforce' was looking to 'consider the use by ministers of the power of the royal prerogative', and were not proposing to curb the specific powers exercised by the Queen which are actually necessary in order for her to act as head of state. However, the real problem is that this is very difficult territory if one is not also committed to the introduction of a written constitution.

If there are signs that the political class is openly stating their readiness to embrace change, what of the monarchy? For all the carefully 'leaked' mutterings of the royal 'Way Ahead Group', the reality is that the monarchy would rather that their life remain undisturbed and unchanged. Alastair Campbell's diaries revealed the state of mind of those behind the Palace walls. Speaking of the period following the death of Diana, Princess of Wales – a time when the government effectively saved the monarchy – he related that the then Prime Minister Tony Blair had said that 'the royals were very pleased with the help we had given, but whenever he tried to raise any suggestions of future change, the blinds came down. He said they are very different people in a very different age'.

Once in government, David Cameron has, like all his predecessors, been rather slow in implementing constitutional change. The House of Lords still awaits further reform, and while Cameron's Liberal Democrat Coalition partners have pressed for action, this is unlikely to be a priority for the government for the immediate forseeable future. The Sovereign Grant Act has instituted changes in the funding and parliamentary accountability of the monarchy, but the effects of this may not become apparent for some time yet.

AN ATTITUDE PROBLEM

It is worth remembering that in the run-up to the reforms brought in by the Sovereign Grant Act, there was still a high degree of deference shown to the monarchy by the elected government. When the draft of the Bill was sent to the Prince of Wales' office, it was noticeable by the wording of the accompanying letter that tugging of the forelock still appears to be a default mode: 'I should be grateful if you could lay this letter, with my humble duty, before the Prince of Wales and seek His consent so far as the interests of the Duke of Cornwall are concerned to place those interests at the disposal of Parliament for the purposes of this Bill'. A rather less childish attitude by those with a mandate from the electorate is called for. The Prince did not actually raise any objections, although it is not known if there was any negotiations prior to that consent being given[17]. ('Revealed: How Osborne's aide asked Charles's permission for law change that made the royal family millions' – *Daily Mail* – May 1st 2012). It is noticeable that the Sovereign Grant Act's yardstick used for calculation of the new Grant – a percentage of the Crown Estates annual profits reflected a diluted version of Prince Charles' previously voiced view that he as monarch ought to get the whole of the Crown Estates cash.

FUTURE THREATS

Other hazards to the future of the monarchy exist. The potential break-up of the United Kingdom should Scotland, as it increasingly appears, wish to 'go its own way' is now far more likely. Increased support for the Scottish Nationalist Party in the May 2007 elections pointed to a greater popular sentiment for independence for Scotland. The May 2012 announcement of a referendum on Scottish independence has moved the process up a gear. Should Scotland become independent, such a step would have profound implications for the UK's constituent nations, and also for the monarchy itself. Although SNP leader Alex Salmond has stated that the Queen could be retained as head of state, this could well change, especially with the enhanced confidence that a strong 'Yes' vote could bring. It is also a glib and rather naive presumption. The present monarch is the Head of State of the United Kingdom, and if one removes a part of that, bringing the Union to an end, then Britain would, as presently constituted, cease to exist. The present Queen, or her successor, might have to, in effect, re-apply for the position of monarch of a new region. Their demoted services might simply no longer be required in a changed landscape. Nor might they wish to 're-apply'. Would Charles, for instance, one day wish to become monarch of England, Wales and Northern Ireland – assuming that they wished to remain together in the same way as at present? And would this be an opportunity to downsize the funding along with the size of the kingdom?

Perhaps the future fate of Belgium – and its monarchy – with the possibility of a split between Dutch-speaking Flanders region, and French-speaking Wallonia, may soon provide an indicator for Britain. Further afield, the accession of a new UK monarch may well mark the point at which many members of the Commonwealth decide to assert their nationhood and appoint their own heads of state. Australia, New Zealand, and many others may find this a tactful opportunity to decline the offer of a new monarch. Jamaica has already stated this might be an opportunity to appoint its own head of state. Such events would reinforce the image of a smaller, more 'national' monarchy, and with it the sense that it should be less lavish – the House of 'Middleton-Windsor' might seem more appropriate at this juncture than the old 'Windsor Imperial' version. Perhaps all this would be too much for the dynasty, and they might step down – or public opinion might effectively force them out. If so, public opinion would insist on a level of input inappropriate for a new royal dynasty, and a republican solution might well by then become more generally acceptable.

Great Britain, it should be remembered, is in historic terms a relatively recent construct. The present Queen symbolises a Britain that has more in common with that past than the present, let alone the future, and it would be not altogether inappropriate if she were to be the last monarch to symbolise Great Britain. Any successor would have to reflect that changed reality.

THE REPUBLICAN ALTERNATIVE

As we have seen in Chapter 2, European republics are, on the whole, less expensive than monarchies. The exception to this in Europe is, of course, France, with its executive presidential system, which imposes an entirely different cost dynamic than a non-executive system. However, it is almost unthinkable that a similar system would be established in the UK were it to decide to elect its head of state. The best comparison with the UK is that of Germany. The UK played a key role in designing and establishing Germany's post-war constitution, which contains many elements similar to our own system. In many respects, it is a pity that when we drew up the German constitution, we didn't alter our own to match it. It differs in having a stronger regional – federal – element, a considerable improvement on the UK's highly centralised system.

The head of state is – like our own, non-executive in form, with no day to day political involvement, and possessing ceremonial and reserve constitutional powers Germany's presidency is famous – in an almost oxymoronic fashion – for being exceptionally low profile in nature. Few in the UK could name the present German president – at the time of writing, Joachim Glauck. Election is by a form of electoral college, perhaps not sufficiently involving of the electorate for UK tastes. However, there is no doubting the fact that Germany demonstrates that it is possible to run a large, politically and economically successful leading European nation without the need to resort to a grandiose imperial style monarchy in the manner of the UK. The British would probably wish for a presidency with a higher profile than the German model, but it is a powerful lesson that one does not need a large hereditary extended family at the top of the social, constitutional and cultural hierarchy. Ireland's non-executive presidency costs justs £1.8million a year, but that is an almost extreme example, and a presidency on that scale would almost certainly not be appropriate or achievable for a very much larger nation like Britain.

Even compared to fellow European monarchical systems, the UK system exhibits key differences. Firstly, UK the monarchy is not defined within the context of a written constitution, and this unwritten aspect encourages poor accountability and an ability to exploit the system. Elements of the monarchy are regulated by statute, but many aspects rely upon vague understanding and interpretation of custom and precedent. The differences between monarchical and presidential systems which have a huge impact – those relating to heredity, class and culture as a whole are largely beyond the scope of this book, but it is an inescapable fact that the UK monarchy represents a uniquely elaborate and expensive example of its type. For some strange reason, the British simply choose to pay an awful lot for their head of state. This is perhaps assisted by the fact that the true cost is consistemtly understated.

7 LOOKING TO THE FUTURE

A EUROPEAN COMPARISON: GERMANY

For a comparable major European nation, we could look to the example of Germany. The modern federal republic was set up in the aftermath of the Second World War and Britain was a key contributor in designing the new constitution, which contains elements not dissimilar to the UK system. It has a strong federal element, an improvement upon the UK's still distinctly centralised system. The position of the President of the Federal Republic is open to all Germans over the age of 40 who are entitled to vote in Bundestag elections. The candidate does not have to be a member of government or legislature, either at federal or state level. Election is by what is in effect an electoral college – the Federal Convention – consisting of all Bundestag members and Lander delegates (who need not necessarily be politicians) – comprises about 1,000 members in total.

Germany's presidential role is non-executive in nature, largely ceremonial but with reserve constitutional powers – not dissimilar, in fact, to those of the UK's present head of state. There the comparison ends, however, as the President receives a far more modest salary – €213,000 per annum (£171,465 at the time of writing), a sum which continues, in effect, as a pension following the incumbent leaving office. The President can serve a maximum of two five-year terms. The President's office is a modest, modern building in Berlin staffed by around 180 people close to the main official residence, the Schlosse Bellevue. There is a secondary official residence – the Villa Hammerschmidt – in Bonn.

The people of Germany do not support an extended family connected with their head of state. They do not have an hereditary dynasty who inherit wealth at public expense through a preferential tax system with advantageous exemptions. They do not have a royal family supported, not merely for life, but for generations who are overloaded with archaic and invented titles which place them at the head of a complex constitutional, social and cultural hierarchy. The entire German Presidency costs approximately £21million a year to operate. Britain pays well over £17million a year just to its heir to the throne, the Prince of Wales, as a personal income – plus around £2million a year to cover his official travel expenses and the cost of running Clarence House – and that is little more than a tenth of the overall cost of the UK monarchy. Germany does not have a special train for its head of state – nor a royal yacht to help its export industry. For that matter, it did not employ the Duke of York

> to travel the globe at great expense as a 'Special Trade Representative' – or merely as a 'stand-in' royal dressed in white tropical military 'colonial' style regalia – with a valet to carry his special ironing board. Germany's head of state cost Germany's taxpayers roughly one-seventh of that of the UK on an annual basis. Germany is Europe's strongest and most successful economy.

Employing a single person – the president – as non-executive head of state, and ensuring a low-profile role within the context of that office for any family they may have would by definition mean a institution very considerably less grandiose – and expensive – than our present monarchy. Britons might well regard a German-style presidency too low-key, but even allowing for an enhanced ceremonial role, there is no reason why a UK presidency need cost any more than £25million a year. A president would be elected for no more than two terms of office, and paid at a rate not dissimilar to the Prime Minister. Election costs could be considerably minimised by making the process contiguous with that of elections to the second chamber, something that will doubtless be instituted as the UK gradually brings its constitutional system into the twentieth century, albeit rather late in the day.

One – perhaps two – official residences would go with the job, the state would pay the expenses of running the presidential office. Gone would be the £31million plus paid to the monarch and heir to the throne, the £100million plus paid to maintain security for an extended family in myriad residences – many of them publicly owned but available to members of a single family by right of birth. Royal Palaces could be open to the public all year round, generating revenue and acting as a cultural asset – and containing the present Royal Collection – accessible to the entire nation. When a president leaves office – and it need not have been a former politician, incidentally – they would receive a modest pension. That is all. They would not, as is the case with the present royal family, be allowed to accumulate wealth and to retain it under especially favoured circumstances, for generation upon generation. Yes, a presidency would be far less expensive, it would be lower profile, and it would thus reflect a profoundly changed image of Britain on the world stage. That, in itself, would be no bad thing. It would help the nation to come to terms with the change in its economic position and world status. The retention of a grandiose monarchy has, without doubt, encouraged the nation to resist the acceptance of that changed reality.

However, it is ultimately for the people of this nation to make that choice. They may simply choose to demand a monarchy that is considerably reduced in scale, but it must be said that this would so fundamentally alter the institution itself that this option, whilst acceptable to the nation, might not be acceptable to the Windsor family itself. They essentially embody a Britain that no longer exists – especially were the Union to be dismantled in the aftermath of potential Scottish independence. It might perhaps be more appropriate if, as 'Great Britain' effectively disappears, they would do so too. A replacement hereditary dynasty would not be acceptable in today's society, the present family are accepted because they are already there. As so many monarchists concede, it is not a system that we would institute were we starting afresh.

TOO GOOD A DEAL?
The monarchy's financial arrangements are, on the basis of any comparison with their counterparts in other Western democracies, incredibly generous. Since their official expenses are met by government, no head of state actually needs to be rich in their own right – and certainly not as rich as at present. If it is felt that they should be, then that says something of our society which otherwise espouses equality of opportunity. When examining the royal family as a whole, their entitlement to state benefits accruing from their birth or marriage alone are increasingly difficult to justify.

The incomes produced by the Duchies of Cornwall and Lancaster are now so high as to compare with levels of executive pay that are now widely regarded as wholly excessive. Yet curiously the mode of presentation of royal remuneration is so opaque and 'different' that it is surprising that it fails to attract more widespread public criticism than is the case at present. Other benefits, such as favourable housing arrangements for other family members, fail to be seen for what they are. Cultural conditioning means that the public accept the right of the monarch and royal family to a publicly funded life of wealth and privilege as 'normal'. The evolving status of many members of the royal family as 'celebrities' in their own right with an increasing tendency to trade commercially on that status, encourages potential conflicts of interest.

Money remains an important element in the royal world, and increasing trends towards personal royal commercial intervention may tend towards the presentation of a self-interested individual at the broader expense of the institution itself. In a more market-orientated culture, 'royal' branding can now represent a significant financial benefit to these individuals. However, it would appear that the titles are not actually their own, but belong to the nation itself. Accusations of trading on their status can ultimately be avoided by a complete polarisation of roles. One should have either a title and perform a public role, or to lead a private career then any titles must be relinquished. The separation of the 'royal family' from the official duties of the head of state, and the re-evaluation of the presently vague role of the heir to the throne is long overdue Despite the defence that the royal family members really work so hard in return for this indulgence, there is no real sign that they are actually overworked. Indeed, one suspects that they are more than happy with the arrangement. If it were really that onerous, it is unlikely they would wish to do it.

The processes of accountability are, although recently somewhat improved, kept at arm's length and with a low profile. The Windsor family has, over generations, been indulged and over-rewarded for the role it has, and for the time being, continues to play. Whilst the present Queen has generally been able to deflect, or at least to pre-empt criticism, and to avoid conspicuous displays of wealth, her potential successor has been rather less successful. The heir to the throne would seem to want the best of both worlds. The British royal family enjoys a life of wealth and privilege funded by the taxpayer, and benefits to a degree unthinkable to heads of state in our neighbouring European countries. It embodies gross inequality at a time when the pernicious effects of such a situation are elsewhere regarded as a threat to social cohesion and the morality of a modern democracy. It is likely that the succession point for a new monarch – and that time is drawing closer – will reveal ever more distinctly the fault lines that run through this institution. Economic uncertainties both regionally and in the world as a whole now point towards a period in which the defence of the position of the financially privileged British monarchy will be progressively harder to maintain. Their wealth, and the lavish manner in which they are maintained by the British taxpayer could ultimately be the reason for their eventual demise.

Notes

CHAPTER 1
INTRODUCTION

1 'Verdict of Peace' – Corelli Barnett
2 'Royal Rich Report' – *The Mail on Sunday* – 2001
3 *The Neophiliacs* – Christopher Booker
4 *The Blair Years* – Alastair Campbell
5 *La Derniere Reine* – Marc Roche
6 Article: 'The Boardroom Bonanza' – *Guardian* – August 29th 2007

CHAPTER 2
MONEY AND THE MONARCHY

1 *The Neophiliacs* – Christopher Booker
2 *Royal Fortune: Tax, Money and the Monarchy* – Phillip Hall
3 Article: 'Queen to escape £28million inheritance tax' – Gethin Chamberlain – *The Scotsman* – May 7th 2002
4 *Financial Times*, March 8/9 2008
'Hard-up Queen Mother's secret deal revealed' – Ben Fenton
'Queen Mother's 1959 cash crisis' – Ben Fenton

5 Hansard – November 26th 1992
6 Report: Institute of Financial Studies 2005
7 Royal Rich Report 2001
8 *Daily Mail* – April 19th 2011
9 Royal Rich Report – 2001
10 Civil List 2004-5
11 Civil List 2004-5
12 *Who Owns Britain* – Kevin Cahill
13 Crown Estates Revenue Accounts 2007
14 Civil List 2004-5
15 Article: *Daily Mail*, June 28th 2006
16 Royal Rich Report 2001
17 Article: 'Horses, stamps, cars – and an invisible portfolio' – *The Guardian*, 30 May 2002
18 Royal Rich Report 2001
19 The Grant-in-aid for Royal Travel by Air and Rail – Annual Report 2007-8
20 'Head of RAF slates princes stag sorties' – Michael Smith and Brendan Montague – *Sunday Times*, April 20th 2008
21 House of Commons Public Accounts Committee – 'Royal Travel by Air and Rail – Sixtieth Report of Season 2001-2'
22 'Blairforce None' – *Aviation Week and Space Technology*, March 31st 2008
23 Maundy Money – 'Cost of manufacture commercially sensitive: not appropriate to disclose', under Exemption 13 of Code of Practice (20.11.02 – 81583 191W – Appendix 1: withheld answers to written parliamentary questions in session 2003-4).
24 Hansard, 20 Oct 2005: (Column 1196W) – Royal Family (Annual Accounts)
25 *The Unconventional Minister* – Geoffrey Robinson
26 ditto
27 ditto
28 ditto
29 'Royal Yacht Britannia – Details of proceeds from sale of yacht withheld under Exemption 13 of Code of Practice' (12.02.2003) 95776 738W – Appendix 1: Withheld answers to written parliamentary questions in session 2002–03
30 'Maintaining the Royal Palaces' – June 2000 National Audit Office
31 *Sunday Mail* – Royal Rich Report 2001

32 Article: 'Secret deals that obscure the royal finances' – Alan Travis – *The Guardian* – May 30th 2002
33 'Extraordinary details of the Queen's finances revealed' – Robert Verkaik, *The Independent* – March 31st 2010
34 Figures: Office of Manpower Economics
35 *Royal Throne: The Future of the Monarchy* – Elizabeth Longford
36 *Royal Fortune: Tax, Money and the Monarchy* – Phillip Hall
37 Hansard – June 7th 2000

CHAPTER 3
'NICE LITTLE EARNERS' – THE TWO DUCHIES

Note: The extracts in this chapter which were taken from the Minutes of the Public Accounts Committee (Monday, November 7th 2005) are subject to the following provisos: This is an uncorrected transcript of evidence taken in public and reported to the House. The transcript has been placed on the internet on the authority of the Committee, and copies have been made available by the Vote Office for the use of Members and others.

Any public use of, or reference to, the contents should make clear that neither witnesses nor Members have had the opportunity to correct the record. The transcript is not yet an approved formal record of these proceedings.

1 *Royal Fortune: Tax, Money and the Monarchy* – Phillip Hall
2 ditto
3 *My Queen and I* – Willie Hamilton
4 *Royal Fortune* – Phillip Hall, as above
5 Article: 'Secret deals that obscure the royal finances' – Alan Travis – *The Guardian* – May 30th 2002
6 Duchy of Cornwall Annual Report 2007
7 Royal Rich Report 2001 as above
8 Article: *The Times* – June 27th 2006
9 Article: 'Charles faces hostile deliveries before his Oval test' – *The Guardian* – August 16th 2006
10 *Royal Fortune* – Phillip Hall, as above
11 Article: 'Prince saves jewel in Scots crown' – *The Guardian* – June 28th 2007

12 Prince of Wales Annual Report 2007
13 'It came from nowhere – at one hell of a speed' – Christopher Leake and Alexandra Williams – *Mail on Sunday* May 18th 2008
14 Frank Prochaska – The Monarchy and Charity, Oxford DNB – online edition January 2006
15 The Peat Report 2003
16 www.duchyofcornwall.co.uk
17 Duchy of Cornwall Annual Report 2007
18 *Who Owns Britain* – Kevin Cahill
19 *Royal Fortune* – Phillip Hall, as above
20 ditto
21 ditto
22 Duchy of Cornwall Annual Accounts 2006
23 Duchy of Cornwall Annual Accounts 2005
24 Prince of Wales Annual Review 2007
25 Treasury Minutes on the Nineteenth and Twenty-seventh Reports from the Committee of Public Accounts 2004-2005: 19th Report – The Accounts of the Duchies of Cornwall and Lancaster
26 House of Commons Early Day Motion 1503 May 17th 2007
27 *Who Owns Britain* – Kevin Cahill
28 ditto

CHAPTER 4
WINDSORS' WORLD: LIFE AT THE TAXPAYERS' EXPENSE

1 *The Prefabricated Home* – Colin Davies
2 'Prince's village an ego-boost, says Blears' – *Daily Telegraph* – April 4th 2008
3 *The Prisoner* – Robert Fairclough
4 Article: 'Prince Charles was here' – Simon Garfield – *British Airways Highlife* magazine – July 2001
5 Public Accounts Committee hearing: Duchies of Cornwall and Lancaster – Question 20 – Nov 7th 2005
6 Article by Christopher Wilson – *Daily Mail* (19/8/2010)
7 'Why did 'rude' Andrew ever get trade role, asks ex-envoy' – *Daily Mail* – March 1st 2011
8 Andrew's grandmother, it should be remembered, had something of a track record of leaving properties in a bit of a state when she

vacated them. Clarence House, her grace and and favour London residence for half a century, cost her nothing in rent, yet required millions to make it habitable – or at least fit for Prince Charles – after her death. The £3.2million cost of the refurbishment was borne by the taxpayer. It is surprising that the Queen was not asked – or prepared to – pay for the work. She had, after all, avoided any inheritance tax liability – being, as monarch, exempt – on her mother's death, resulting in a saving estimated by some at around £28million.

9   'Prince's office confirms sale of house for £15m' – James Meikle – *The Guardian* – May 26th 2008. See also: 'Prince Andrew, the £15m house sale and an energy mogul from Kazakhstan' – Rebecca English and Olinka Koster – *Daily Mail* – May 26th 2008.
10 Report: 'The Crown Estate – Property Leases with the Royal Family' – Ian Davidson and Alan Williams – April 7th 2005
11 Hansard – June 19th 2003
12 Hansard – July 11th 2003
13 Estelle Morris June 26th 2003 Department of Culture Media and Sport
14 Hansard – Answer to Parliamentary question from Andrew Mackinlay – December 19th 2005, by Minister of State, Dept of Constitutional Affairs.
15 Website – www.royal.gov.uk/output/page3956.asp
16 Article: *The Scotsman* – April 11th 2006
17 'So why did a Russian oligarch give prince £320,000?' – *Daily Mail* – May 14th 2012

CHAPTER 5
CHARITY AND ROYAL 'BRAND' OWNERSHIP

1 Channel 4 *Dispatches* programme – March 12th 2007
2 'Meddling prince claims dismissed' – BBC online news: http://news.bbc.co.uk/1/hi/uk/6442109.stm
3 Article: 'All anyone wants to know is: how will Diana worshippers accept her successor?' – *The Guardian* – October 27th 2005
4 Article: 'Charles's charity chief's pay and perks hit £310,000' – *Daily Mail* – July 1st 2006
5 Website article: 'Palace defends Prince's Enron link' CNN February 4th 2002

6. Article: 'Uncharitable thoughts on millionaire generosity' – *Financial Times* – July 15th 2007
7. *On Royalty* – Jeremy Paxman
8. 'What the new Victorians did for us' – *The Guardian* – July 19th 2007
9. 'Rich donors' hefty cheques will never solve poverty' – *The Guardian* – July 19th 2007
10. 'Watchdog blows whistle on rugby charity's £2million bill for high living' – *The Guardian* – Robert Booth – October 29th 2007
11. Text of speech: IVCA Clarion Awards Portcullis House 15th July 2004 Companies House records: Trade Mark No. 2379665 – Registered December 4th 2004
12. Companies House records
13. Scottish Business in the Community (website press release).
14. Article: 'A night on the tiles' – *The Guardian* – August 23rd 2001
15. Public Accounts Committee hearing – Duchy of Cornwall and Lancaster November 7th 2005
16. Author – Meeting with Assistant Master of Household, Buckingham Palace. Present at a meeting – one of a number, with my them employer – already a Royal Warrant-Holder – in the early 1980s. The Palace were keen to purchase lamps and associated items, and at the outset it was emphasised that the Household were fully conversant with the 'never knowingly undersold' price list at a well known Sloane Square store. Notwithstanding the fact that items required were to be custom-made rather than their off-the-shelf equivalents available in such stores, and thus inevitably much more expensive to produce, such 'base' prices were insisted upon as the yardstick in negotiations. The atmosphere was one of quiet yet relentless pressure to yield, with the implicit understanding that both possession of the Warrant would be at risk and that there were others willing to supply instead, by definition at below cost.
17. Approaches are always made by the Palace, never the other way round – the system operates entirely on the Palace's terms and without any recourse to independent scrutiny.
18. 'Shopkeeper prince sets out stall' – Robert Booth – *The Guardian* – March 17th 2008
19. 'Prince to launch £1bn fund for eco-development' – Ben Marlow and Kate Walsh – *Sunday Times* Business Section – June 29th 2008

NOTES

CHAPTER 6
THE ROYAL COLLECTION: 'HELD' FOR THE NATION

1 Royal Rich Report 2001, as above
2 The Briefing on Royal Finances – Parliament – February 11th 1993
3 Responding to question by Norman Baker – Hansard – June 6th 2000
4 Royal Rich Report 2001, as above
5 In response to question to Royal Household by *Mail on Sunday* Royal Rich Report 2001
6 Hall defines the eight categories as: 1) Government Property; 2) Legally Inalienable Property; 3) Inalienable by Custom; 4) Lesser Properties; 5) The Duchy of Lancaster; 6) The Duchy of Cornwall; 7) The Queen's Private estates; 8) Private and Personal Wealth (*Royal Fortune: Tax, Money and the Monarchy*).
7 Hall, *Royal Fortune*
8 'Court ruling threatens secrecy of royal wills' – *Daily Telegraph* February 9th 2008. Subsequent to this article, the applicant, Robert Brown, was granted leave to appeal – it was however unsuccessful.
9 *The Sale of the Late King's Goods: Charles and his Art Collection* – Jerry Brotton
10 Royal Collection Annual Review 2005
11 Article: *The Times* – July 5th 2006
12 'War of the Windsors' – Lynn Picknett, Clive Prince, Stephen Prior
13 Article: 'Buried Treasure' – Charlotte Higgins – *The Guardian* – May 20th 2006
14 ditto
15 *The Sale of the Late King's Goods* – Jerry Brotton

CHAPTER 7
THE FUTURE

1 Based on poll data: Ipsos MORI 1993 to date
2 *Poverty and Inequality in the UK: 2008* – Institute of Fiscal Studies
3 *UK Wage Inequality: An industry and regional perspective* – Karl Taylor (Univesity of Leicester).
4 Article: 'Charles to rule as Regent while Queen takes back seat' – Susie Boniface – *Sunday Mirror* – 15 January 2006

5   Article: *Point de Vue* magazine – February 2006
6   *The Myth of the Monarchy* – Edgar Wilson
7   Article: quoting Prince Charles' letter to Lord Irvine – *Daily Telegraph* newspaper – November 26th 2002
8   *Royal Fortune* – Phillip Hall
9   Article: 'Evangelist Digby's passage to India' – *The Guardian* – September 27th 2007
10 *The Myth of the Monarchy* – Edgar Wilson
11 In response to questions by author
12 Press Association 2006
13 *King and Country: Monarchy and the Future King Charles III* – Robert Blackburn
14 In response to questions by author
15 *Royal Throne: the Future of the Monarchy* – Elizabeth Longford
16 Article: 'Queen's powers should be removed, says Cameron' – *The Guardian* – February 6th 2006
17 'Revealed: How Osborne's aide asked Charles's permission for law change that made the royal family millions' – *Daily Mail* – May 1st 2012

Bibliography and Sources

The Verdict of Peace – Corelli Barnett – Macmillan 2001

King and Country: Monarchy and the future King Charles III – Robert Blackburn – Politico's 2006

The Grand Delusion – Prof. Stephen Haseler – I B Tauris 2012

The Neophiliacs – Christopher Booker (Collins) 1969

The Sale of the Late King's Goods: Charles I and his art collection – Jerry Brotton – Macmillan 2006

A Royal Duty – Paul Burrell (Penguin/Michael Joseph 2003)

The Blair Years: Extracts from the Alastair Campbell diaries – Alastair Campbell – Random House 2007

Ornamentalism – David Cannadine – Allen Lane/Penguin 2001

The Prefabricated Home – Colin Davies (Reaktion Books) 2005

The Prisoner – Robert Fairclough – (Carlton 2002)

Global Village Idiot – John O'Farrell (Black Swan 2002)

The Third Way and its Critics – Anthony Giddens (Polity Press) 2000

Diana: The Last Days – Martyn Gregory (Virgin)2004

Royal Fortune: Tax, Money and the Monarchy – Phillip Hall (Bloomsbury) 1992

Modernising the Monarchy – Tim Hames and Marc Leonard (Demos)

My Queen and I – Willie Hamilton (Quartet) 1975

The Tarnished Crown – Anthony Holden (Bantam Press 1993)

The Control Freaks: How New Labour got its own way – Nicholas Jones (Politico's 2002)

The Powers Behind the Prime Minister – Dennis Kavanagh and Anthony Seldon (HarperCollins 2000)

The Royals – Kitty Kelley (Warner Books 1997)

Royal Throne: The Future of the Monarchy – Elizabeth Longford (Coronet 1993)

Brand New – Ed. Jane Pavitt (V&A Publications 2000)

On Royalty – Jeremy Paxman (Viking 2006)

War of the Windsors: A Century of Unconstitutional Monarchy – Lynn Picknett, Clive Prince and Stephen Prior (Random House 2002)

The Unconventional Minister – Geoffrey Robinson (Michael Joseph 2000)

Who Runs This Place?: The Anatomy of Britain in the 21st Century – Anthony Sampson – (John Murray) 2004

BIBLIOGRAPHY AND SOURCES

Servants of the People – Andrew Rawnsley (Penguin) 2001

The Prime Minister – Peter Hennessy (Penguin)

Pretty Straight Guys – Nick Cohen – (Faber & Faber) 2003

The Political Animal – Jeremy Paxman – (Michael Joseph) 2002

Monarchy – David Starkey – (Harper) 2006

Diana's Mourning: a people's history – James Thomas (University of Wales Press) 2002

Reforming Britain – New Labour, New Constitution? – John Morrison (Reuters) 2001

The Rape of the Constitution? – Ed. Keith Sutherland – Imprint Academic 2000

After Britain: New Labour and the return of Scotland – Tom Nairn (Granta 2000)

Living on Thin Air – The New Economy – Charles Leadbetter – Penguin 2000

Monarchies: What are Kings and Queens for? – Ed. Tom Bentley and James Wilsdon – (Demos) 2002

The Mail on Sunday Royal Rich Report – Secrets of the Queen's Billion Pound Fortune – (Associated Newspapers Ltd) 2001

The Control Freaks: How New Labour gets its own way – Nicholas Jones – Politico's 2002

Long to reign over us? – Paul Richards (Fabian Society 1996)

Elisabeth II: La derniere Reine – Marc Roche (Broche 2007)

The Myth of the British Monarchy – Edgar Wilson (Journeyman 1989)

OFFICIAL PUBLICATIONS

The Civil List Annual Reports 2004, 2005, 2006, 2007, 2008

Royal Public Finances – 2003-04, 2004-05, 2005-06, 2006-07, 2007-08

Maintaining the Royal Palaces – HC563 1999-2000 National Audit Office

The Crown Estates Annual Report 2006

The Crown Estate – Property Leases with the Royal Family – 07/04/05

The Grant in aid for the Maintenance of the Occupied Royal Palaces in England Annual Report 2004-05, 2005-06, 2006-07, 2007-08

The Grant in aid for Royal Travel by Air and Rail 2004-05, 2005-06, 2006-07, 2007-08

Royal Travel by Air and Rail – Report by Comptroller and Auditor-General – HC25 Session 2001-02

Royal Travel by Air and Rail – HC529 60th Report of Session 2001-02

Memorandum by Royal Historic Palaces 13/02/06

Treasury Minutes on the Nineteenth and Twenty-Seventh Reports from the Committee of Public Accounts 2004-05

Duchy of Cornwall Annual Report and Accounts 2005, 2006, 2007

Duchy of Lancaster Annual Reports 2005, 2006

Prince of Wales Annual Review 2005, 2006, 2007

Report to HRH Prince of Wales – Sir Michael Peat and Edmund Lawson QC

BIBLIOGRAPHY AND SOURCES

Duchy Originals Ltd – Directors Report and Financial Statements – 31/03/05

Duchy Originals Ltd – Annual Return 23/02/06

Duchy Originals Ltd – Current Appointments Report 13/09/06

Royal Collection Trust Annual Report 2005

Poverty and Inequality in the UK: 2008 – Institute of Fiscal Studies

APPENDIX 1
SOVEREIGN GRANT ACT

SOVEREIGN GRANT ACT: MAIN PROVISIONS

CLAUSE 1: THE SOVEREIGN GRANT (CLAUSE 1)
At present, funding for the monarch's official duties comes from three different sources:
- Civil List from the Exchequer;
- Grant-in-aid for royal travel by air and train from the Department for Transport; and
- Grants-in-aid for the maintenance of royal palaces and for communications and information from Department for Culture, Media and Sport.

In future, there will be a new system, the Sovereign Grant, which will combine all three sources of funding into one payment from the Treasury Estimate.

CLAUSE 2: ACCOUNTS OF THE ROYAL HOUSEHOLD
Currently, the Permanent Secretary to the Treasury audits the Civil list. The Comptroller & Auditor General (C&AG) has no access to Civil List expenditure, nor does he audit the grants-in-aid expenditure, though he can and has, carried out value for money studies on them. The C&AG has no access to the Civil List reserve.

Clause 2 provides that Sovereign Grant expenditure will be subject to audit by the Comptroller & Auditor General from 2012. The Treasury will set the form of the accounts and the C&AG will audit them. The Grant accounts will be laid before the House and will be open to full parliamentary scrutiny, including by the Committee of Public Accounts. The C&AG will, in addition be empowered to carry out value for money studies of Royal Household expenditure.

CLAUSE3: THE RESERVE FUND
Clause 3 sets up a Reserve Fund. It will contain Sovereign Grant not used for the year for which it is made. Similarly, in years when use of resources exceeds the amount of the grant, drawings from the reserve will supplement the Sovereign Grant.

CLAUSE 4: ACCOUNTS OF THE RESERVE FUND
Clause 4 provides that the Reserve Fund will also be subject to the same accountability arrangements as the Royal Household. Thus the Treasury will set the form of the Reserve Fund accounts and will be audited by the C&AG. The Reserve Fund will also be subject to value for money studies.

CLAUSE 5: ANNUAL REPORT AS TO THE AMOUNT OF SOVEREIGN GRANT
Clause 5 requires the Royal Trustees to prepare a report about the determination of the Sovereign Grant. They must calculate the amount of Sovereign Grant for the coming financial year and explain how it has been calculated. Because the report is published and laid in Parliament, the whole process will be transparent. The Royal Trustees are the Prime Minister, the Chancellor of the Exchequer and the Keeper of the Privy Purse.

CLAUSE 6: DETERMINATION OF THE SOVEREIGN GRANT
This clause set out how the Sovereign Grant is to be determined. Initially, the Sovereign Grant for a given year will be equal to 15% of the Crown Estate's net revenue in the financial year two years prior.

To ensure the Grant remains at an appropriate level, the clause provides that the amount will be subject to following safeguards:
- A capped reserve fund managed by the Royal Trustees. If the Grant proves greater than required in a given year, the surplus will be paid into a reserve fund, which may be drawn down in future years as required. The Trustees must set the sovereign grant to prevent the Reserve Fund remaining above 50%. If the Reserve is above this level, the Trustees may specify a lower grant amount than would otherwise have been implied by the formula;
- A cash terms floor. The grant amount is not normally allowed to fall in cash terms on the amount in the previous year. That is unless the Trustees have specified a lesser amount to manage the reserve in the way described above; and
- Regular reviews by the Royal Trustees. The Trustees will be bound to consider the suitability of the percentage at intervals of five years and to propose a new percentage where necessary. The Treasury would present an order to implement the change. Affirmative resolution would be required for an increase.

And so, the final level of the Sovereign Grant in a given year is either:

APPENDIX 1

- The greater of: 15% of Crown Estate profit in the year two years prior; and the amount of Grant in the previous year; or
- An amount lower than that, if deemed necessary by the Royal Trustees, in order to maintain the Reserve at a permissible level.

CLAUSE 7: REVIEWS BY ROYAL TRUSTEES OF SOVEREIGN GRANT
Clause 7 requires the Royal Trustees to consider every five years whether the percentage remains appropriate.

CLAUSE 8: POWER TO CHANGE LEVEL OF SOVEREIGN GRANT
Clause 8 applies if the Royal Trustees' review in clause 7 calls for a different percentage to be used in the formula in clause 6. It requires the Treasury to implement the conclusions of the review. The clause requires the Treasury to lay an order to amend the percentage in clause 6. An affirmative order is required if the percentage is to be increased. But there would only need a negative order for a decrease.

CLAUSE 9: DUCHY OF CORNWALL INCOME AND GRANT TO THE HEIR TO THE THRONE
Clause 9 ensures that equivalent financial provision is made for heirs to the throne, whether Duke of Cornwall or not.

It provides that, if the heir is not the Duke of Cornwall and is over 18, the heir is given a grant equal to the Duchy revenues, unless Duchy revenues are more than the Sovereign Grant. The monarch would receive the Duchy revenues, and the Sovereign Grant would be reduced by an equal amount. In effect, the heir would receive the Duchy income.

If the Duke of Cornwall is a minor, 90% of the revenues of the Duchy would go to the monarch and the Sovereign Grant would be reduced by an equivalent amount.

CLAUSE 10: REPEAL OF CERTAIN FINANCIAL PROVISIONS
Clause 10 repeals certain financial provisions in the Civil List Acts of 1952, 1972 and 1975.

CLAUSE 11: MAINTENANCE OF ROYAL PALACES AND RELATED LAND
This clause removes the responsibility of the Secretary of State for the Department of Culture, Media and Sport to maintain the Royal Palaces and related land that are in future to be maintained by Her Majesty out of the Sovereign Grant.

CLAUSE 12: MEANING OF 'THE AUDITED NET RELEVANT RESOURCES', 'THE VALUE OF THE RESERVE FUND' AND 'THE INCOME ACCOUNT NET SURPLUS OF THE CROWN ESTATE'
This clause explains the meaning of certain terms in the Bill.

CLAUSE 16: DURATION OF SOVEREIGN GRANT PROVISIONS
Powers in previous civil list legislation have been set to expire six months after end of a monarch's reign. In this time Parliament must enact primary legislation for the successor sovereign. Clause 16 allows future incoming monarchs to extend the new grant provisions for their reign by Order in Council, and thereby signify their willingness to put their hereditary revenues at Parliament's disposal.

MISCELLANEOUS PROVISIONS: ANNUITIES
Provisions in Clause 10 and Schedule 1 repeal a number of annuities that are payable to other members of the Royal Family to relieve expenditure incurred in connection with official duties. They are currently repaid by the Queen from Her Privy Purse. Her Majesty has indicated that She will continue to provide equivalent financial support.

There is no change to the annuity paid to the Duke of Edinburgh. The Parliamentary Annuity for HRH Prince Philip (£359,000 p.a.) will continue to be payable from the Consolidated Fund on a calendar year basis.

APPENDIX 2

APPENDIX 2
ROYAL WEDDING SECURITY COSTS

From: Deputy Chief of Defence Staff Personnel and Training (Secretariat)
Zone D, Sixth Floor,
MINISTRY OF DEFENCE
Main Building, London, SW1A 2HB.

Tony Flury
[request-69903-e3b3e15c@whatdotheyknow.com]

Our Reference:

FOI – 03-05-2011-112622-004

Date: 22 July 2011

Dear Mr Flury,

1. Thank you for your e-mail of 29 April 2011 that has been considered to be a request for information in accordance with the Freedom of Information Act 2000. I am sorry for the delay in providing a response. You requested:

"Can you please provide a breakdown of the total cost to the MOD of their contribution to the Royal Wedding – not only on the day in terms of the troops taking part, but any other security requirements prior to the event. Can you also confirm if extra funds were made available to cover these extra costs."

2. The marginal costs to the Ministry of Defence in support of the Royal Wedding consisted of the following:

Transportation	£21,080
Subsistence	£ 1,700
Flypast	£55,038
	£77,818

The majority of the Service personnel on parade on 29 April 2011 were drawn from London District and from those employed on Ceremonial Duties, as well as other London based units in order to minimise travel and subsistence expenditure.

3. Security for the Royal Wedding was the responsibility of the Home Office and military personnel were not employed on security duties. Accordingly, costs in terms of security both prior to, and during, the Royal Wedding are not held by the Ministry of Defence.

Yours sincerely

Deputy Chief of the Defence Staff – Personnel and Training

If you are not satisfied with this response or you wish to complain about any aspect of the handling of your request, then you should contact me in the first instance. If informal resolution is not possible and you are still dissatisfied then you may apply for an independent internal review by contacting the Head of Corporate Information, 1st Floor, Zone N, MOD Main Building, Whitehall, SW1A 2HB (e-mail CIO-FOI-IR@mod.uk). Please note that any request for an internal review must be made within 40 working days of the date on which the attempt to reach informal resolution has come to an end.

If you remain dissatisfied following an internal review, you may take your complaint to the Information Commissioner under the provisions of Section 50 of the Freedom of Information Act. Please note that the Information Commissioner will not investigate your case until the MOD internal review process has been completed. Further details of the role and powers of the Information Commissioner can be found on the Commissioner's website, http://www.ico.gov.uk.

APPENDIX 3

APPENDIX 3
BANK OF ENGLAND NOMINEES LTD

BANK OF ENGLAND
London EC2R 8AH

Ben Norman
Deputy Secretary of the Bank
Tel: 020-7601 4748
Fax: 020-7601 5460
E-mail: ben.norman@bankofengland.co.uk

5 March 2010

Mr E Danielyan
Via email to: request-28738-5d32ba2c@whatdotheyknow.com

Dear Mr Danielyan

Thank you for your email of 10 February requesting certain information under the Freedom of Information Act 2000 ('FoI Act') regarding Bank of England Nominees Ltd ('BOEN').

It might be helpful if I were to clarify at the outset the status of BOEN and the Bank of England (the Bank) under the FoI Act, in relation to any information which may be held by BOEN or the Bank concerning the questions you have raised. BOEN is not a 'public authority' within the meaning of the FoI Act and accordingly is not subject to the Act. As regards the Bank, Parts I to V of the FoI Act (including the general right of access under section 1) do not apply to information which it holds for the purposes *'of its functions with respect to...(c) the provision of private banking services and related services'* (see section 7 and Schedule 1, Part VI of the FoI Act). Information which the Bank holds in relation to any banking services it provides to BOEN is covered by this provision.

Subject to this, I can provide the following information in response to your questions. BOEN acts as a nominee company to hold securities on behalf of certain customers. It is a private limited company, incorporated in England and Wales in 1977, and is a wholly-owned subsidiary of the Bank. The shareholders are the Bank and John Footman, who holds his share as nominee on behalf of the Bank. The directors are John Footman and Andrew Bailey. The Secretary of State has granted BOEN an exemption under section 796 Companies Act 2006, which means that BOEN is not subject to the notification provisions in section 793 Companies Act 2006. The exemption has been granted to a subsidiary of the Bank because it is intended to apply only to BOEN and persons on whose behalf securities are held by BOEN, rather than the Bank itself.

Yours sincerely

Ben Norman

Ben Norman
Deputy Secretary of the Bank

Index

Act of Settlement 1701 126
Albert, Prince 14, 116, 130
Allan, Richard, MP 132
Alexandra, Princess 177
Andrew, Prince, see York, Duke of
'Annus Horribilis' (1992) 6, 77
Austria, cost of presidency 80

Bacon, Richard, MP 129-130
Bagshot Park 175-176
Baker, Norman, MP 67, 95, 161, 180, 184, 196
Balmoral estate, acquisition 14
Bank of England Nominees Ltd. 23, 54
Belgium, cost of monarchy 79
Berezovsky, Boris 183
'Black Wednesday' (1992) 6
Blackburn, Robert 238, 248, 250
Blears, Hazel 164
Blair, Tony, Rt. Hon. 8, 28, 71, 148, 257
Bona Vacantia 132-135
Britannia, (Royal Yacht) 4, **67-76**, 158

Brooke, Sir Peter 76
Brown, Gordon, Rt. Hon. 62, 72, 95, 243
Buckingham Palace 76
Butler, R.A. ('RAB') 18, 53
Butler, Sir Robin (Cabinet Secretary) 72

Cahill, Kevin, author 121, 127, 143, 145
Cambridge, Duke and Duchess of 167-168, 231, 233, 252, 253
Cameron, David, Rt. Hon. 257
Campbell, Alastair 8
Candy Brothers 162
Charles I 220, 228
Charles II 226
Charles, Prince see Prince of Wales
Charter88 7
Chough's Nominees Ltd. 205
Churchill, Winston, Sir 18, 53
Civil List 17, 20 origin 102, presentation 50-51, savings from 47-48
Civil List Act 1972 17
Civil List Reserve 33, 46-47
Civil War, English 13
Clarence House 25, 113, 178-179
Clarke, Charles, Rt. Hon. 241
Clarke, Paul 129-130, 136
Cobbold, Lord (Lord Chamberlain) 83
'Commissioners of the Crown', 1971 proposal 83
Cornwall, Duchess of (Camilla Parker-Bowles) 37
Credit Suisse 211
Crown and monarchy, terminology 142-143
Crown Estates, income 'surrender' **49-50**
Crown Jewels 19
Crown Lands Act 1702 123, 145
Crown Private Estates Act 1800 26, 95, 124, 128

Dalai Lama 161, 249
Daly, Janet 76
Davidson, Ian, MP 112, 137-139, 177, 208
Denmark, cost of monarchy 79
Diana, Princess of Wales 7, marriage 110, death 8, 74, 231, divorce 8

INDEX

Duchy of Cornwall, 11, 45, **99-153**, assets 109, 'brand' 119-120, and charity 116, history 104, income produced for heir to the throne 23, **114** ownership: 'peculiar title' of heir to the throne 110, 123, 149, promotional vehicle for Prince 115

Duchy of Lancaster, 11, **99-153**, history 103, income produced for monarch 22, 43-44, **147**, regional influence 125, 126, ownership 144-145, reform 149, role of Chancellor 146

Duchy Collections, see Duchy Originals

Duchy Originals Ltd 105-106, 111, 193 company 'brand' trade mark 120, 123, 200-205

Edinburgh, Duke of, official income 22, 64, wealth 52-53, 157-158
Edward, Prince, see Wessex, Earl of
Edward VIII, King 103, 241, 248
Eire, see Ireland
Elizabeth II: Coronation 3, estimates of wealth 16-17, 22, tax exemption 18, official income 20, 22, Privy Purse 22, secret 1952 tax deal 18, 53
Enron Corporation 195
Ernst, Prof. Edzard 192-193
European heads of state, comparative costs: monarchies **79**, presidencies **80**

Falklands campaign 68
Fawcett, Michael 208
Fellowes, Sir Robin 74
Finland, cost of presidency 80
Flynn, Paul MP 86
France, cost of presidency 80

Gaunt, John of 103
George I, King 101
George III, King 10, 124
George V, King 48
George VI, King, 4, 127, 133, 220
Germany, cost of presidency 80, 261-262
Gershon, Sir Michael 62
Glauck, Joachim (German President) 260
Gloucester, Duke and Duchess of 65

289

Glover, Stephen 51-52
Gosling, Sir Donald 72, 73, 75
Gove, Michael 75
Government Art Collection 228
Grants-in-aid, purpose 17, property **35**, travel by air and rail **35**
Grigg, John 16

Hall, Phillip, author 17, 24, 26, 53, 54, 100, 133
Hamilton, Willie, MP 70, 102, 187
Harman, Rt. Hon. Harriet 182
Harverson, Paddy 107
Haseler, Professor Stephen 9
Haskins, Lord 193
Heald, Oliver, MP 245, 248
Heir to the Throne, income **23**
Higgins, Charlotte 225
Highgrove House 111, 113, 166
Historic Royal Palaces Trust 223
Hong Kong, handover ceremony 69, 75
Honours system 9
Hosking, Patrick 108
Houghton, Lord 83
House of Lords 2, 28, 148
Human Rights Act 2, 143

Iddon, Brian, MP 140
Inequality 94-95
Ireland, cost of presidency 80

James II, King 101
Jenkins, Brian, MP 131
Jones, Sir Digby 243

Kellaway, Lucy, journalist 197
Kelley, Kitty, author 194
Kensington Palace 182-183
Kent, Duke and Duchess of 64
Kent, Prince and Princess Michael 182-183
Kulibayev, Timur 171

Lancaster, Chancellor of the Duchy of Lancaster 146-147
Laurence, Mrs. Anne, see Princess Royal
Leigh, Edward MP 99, 120
Linley, Viscount 223
Lloyd-George, Rt. Hon. David 110
Luxembourg, cost of monarchy 79

Macmillan, Harold, Rt. Hon 26
MacShane, Dennis, MP 86
Major, John, Rt. Hon. 24
Mandelson, Peter 29
Marshall Aid 4, 67
Margaret, Princess 69, 70
Maundy Money 66
Memorandum of Understanding (1993) 7, 11, 18, 24, 110
Middleton family, business 211
Monarchy, British, constitutional position 3, 19th century 're-invention' 14-15, terminology 11, finances **13-97,** future **229-264**, official government expenditure on **31-33**, public opinion 236-238, 251-252, 'real cost' **39-42**, 233-234, security costs 36-38, tax 7, 18, wealth 4
Mountbatten, Lord Louis 224
Mowlam, Mo 180
Muggeridge, Malcolm 187
'Mutton Renaissance Campaign' 161

National Gallery 228
Netherlands, cost of monarchy 79
North Sea oil 5
Norway, cost of monarchy 79

Opinion polls 236-238, 251-252

Parker-Bowles, Camilla 30, 181
Paxman, Jeremy 198
Peat Report (2003) 116
Peat, Michael, Sir 116, 168, 207, 242, 246
Philip, Prince, see Edinburgh, Duke of
Phillips, Zara 55, 172

Porcelanosa 206-207
Portillo, Michael, Rt. Hon. 71-72
Poundbury 163-165
Prince Harry (aka 'Harry Wales') 173, 188, 252
Prince and Princess Michael of Kent 182-183
Princess Royal, (Mrs. Anne Laurence) 74, 172, 199, 210
Prince of Wales, (Charles, Prince of) 7, 11, 12, acceptability as King 7, cars 112-113, campaigning 9, 192-193, charity 188-211, income from Duchy of Cornwall 44, 112, interference in Chelsea Barracks planning process 162, lifestyle 6, 159-168, medals 191, personal beliefs 9, tax 106-108, wealth 111-112, 114
Prince of Wales Foundation (USA) 194
Princess of Wales, Diana, see Diana, Princess of Wales
Prince's Council (Duchy of Cornwall ruling body) 122
Prince's Trust 189 et seq.
'Privy Purse' **22**
Prochaska, Frank 116
Public Accounts Committee, House of Commons 106, recommendations on Duchies 99, 109, 112, 120, 121, 125, 131, 140-142
'Punch' magazine 14

Queen Elizabeth II, see Elizabeth II, Queen
'Queen Mother' **25**, 25-26
Queen Victoria, see Victoria, Queen

Rausing, Dr Hans (Snr) 196
Redwood, John, MP 71
Rees-Mogg MP, Jacob 87
Reid, Sir Alan, 'Keeper of the Privy Purse' 89
Republic (UK campaign group) 40, 140, 171
Robinson, Geoffrey, Rt. Hon. 71-74
Roche, Marc, 'Le Monde' London correspondent 9
Ross, Bertie 121, 122, 131, 136-139
Royal Archives 223-224
Royal 'branding' 200-201, 209-211
Royal Collection 17, 19, 27, **213-228**, ownership 77, 216-220, contents 214-215, 221
Royal family: members 5, **155-185**, and charity **188-211**, potential conflicts of interest 174-175, housing 155-185, Parliamentary

INDEX

Allowances to members 22, 64-66, security 36-38, 'working' royals 182
Royal Finance, general arrangements **20**, **13-97**, future reform 78-79, 96-97
Royal flights **61-63**
Royal Palaces 35-36
Royal Rich Report 2001 (Mail on Sunday) 54, 111
Royal Train **59-61**
Royal travel **55-64**
Royal Warrant-Holders 208-209
Royal wills, 'tradition' of secrecy 25

Sandringham, estate, acquisition 14
Saxe-Coburg-Gotha, dynasty 14
Scotland, moves towards independence 258
Scottish Business in the Community 205
Security, see Royal family, security
Shaoul, Prof. Jean 198
Simon, Robin 77, 224
Simon, Sion, MP 131
Smith, John, Leader of Opposition (1992) 27
SNP (Scottish Nationalist Party) 258-259
Soames, Rt. Hon., Nicholas 70
Sophia, Electress of Hanover 126
Sovereign Grant Act 2012 9, 11, 17, 19, **21-22**, 35-36, 44, 47, 65, 127, 180, 235-235, 257-258, audit of Royal Household accounts 67, 104
Sovereign Support Grant, 235
Spain, cost of monarchy 79
Starkey, David 244
Sterling, Jeffery (P&O Chairman) 72
Strathclyde, Lord 146
Straw, Jack, Rt. Hon. 196
Suez Crisis (1956) 4, 68
Supreme Court (UK) 250
Sweden, cost of monarchy 79

Thatcher, Margaret, Rt. Hon. 242
Toynbee, Polly 198
Travel, royal: see Royal travel; Royal flights; Royal train

United States of America (President) official income 150,
    tax return 150
Uzam, Czem 195

Victoria, Queen 48, 146, 229
VisitBritain, UK tourist organisation 243
Waitrose Plc 106, 201, 210

Wales, Prince of, see Prince of Wales
Wales, Princess of, see Diana, Princess of Wales
'Way Ahead' Group 251, 257
Wessex, Sophie, Countess of   public relations business 55, 175-176
Wessex, Earl of, housing 175-176
William of Orange (William III, King) 101
William, Prince (aka 'William Wales') 38, 59,167, 168, 207, 231, 233,
    237-9, 251-2, 254-255
Williams, Alan, MP 70, 166, 177, 184
Wilson, Dr. Edgar 240
Windsor Castle, fire 27-8, **76-77**
'Wooden Spoon' charity 199
World Health Organisation 192-193

York, Prince Andrew, Duke of 63, 66, **168-172**, 243,
    daughters: Princesses Beatrice and Eugenie 37, 83,173

Lightning Source UK Ltd.
Milton Keynes UK
UKHW040407080620
364501UK00003B/402